W. H. Cologan

The Church Of Old England. Being A Collection Of Papers Bearing On The Continuity Of The Church In England, And On Attempts To Justify The Anglican Position

W. H. Cologan

The Church Of Old England. Being A Collection Of Papers Bearing On The Continuity Of The Church In England, And On Attempts To Justify The Anglican Position

ISBN/EAN: 9783744653497

Printed in Europe, USA, Canada, Australia, Japan

Cover: Foto ©Thomas Meinert / pixelio.de

More available books at **www.hansebooks.com**

The Church of Old England:

*A Collection of Papers bearing on the Continuity of the
Church in England, and on the attempts to justify
the Anglican position.*

VOL. IV.

LONDON:

OFFICE: 18 WEST SQUARE, SOUTHWARK, S.E.

DEPÔTS: 21 WESTMINSTER BRIDGE ROAD, S.E.; 245 BROMPTON
ROAD, S.W.; 22 PATERNOSTER ROW, E.C.

1894.

CONTENTS.

THE ENGLISH PEOPLE

AND

BLESSED PETER.

BY

THE BISHOP OF SALFORD.

LONDON:

21 WESTMINSTER BRIDGE ROAD, S.E. ; 245 BROMPTON ROAD,
S.W. ; 23 KING EDWARD STREET, E.C.

Price One Penny.

One Penny each.

Church Defence—First Series. *This comprises the following Leaflets, which may be also had separately :—*
Plain Truths in answer to Transparent Falsehoods. 1s. 100.
Was the British Church Roman Catholic? 1s. 100.
The English Church always Roman Catholic. 2s. 100.
How Henry VIII. robbed England of the Faith. 2s. 100.

Church Defence—Second Series. *Comprising:—*
Popery in the First Century. 2s. 100.
The Four Doctors. 2s. 100.
The Reformation under Queen Elizabeth. 1s. 100.
Church Endowments—Whose are they? 1s. 100.

Church Defence—Third Series. *Comprising:—*
Are they Priests? 3s. 6d. 100.
"Catholic not Roman Catholic." 1s. 100.
Henry VIII. and the Royal Supremacy. 2s. 100.

Questions and Answers—*Comprising:*
Friendly Advice. 1s. 100.
Why am I a Roman Catholic? 1s. 100.
Why are you a Protestant? 1s. 100.
What does the Bible say? 1s. 100.
How can I find God's true Church? 1s. 100.
What do Catholics believe? 1s. 100.
Questions for one whom it concerns. 6d. 100.

The Conversion of England. By the Bishop of Salford.

The Old Religion in England. By Rev. P. Lynch.

Before and After Gunpowder Plot. By E. Healy Thompson.

The Catholic Church and the Bible.

Before and After the Reformation.

A Voice from the Dead; Being a letter to an Anglican Friend, by the Count de Montalembert.

The Continuity of the English Church. By Very Rev. Canon Croft.

The Popes and the English Church. By the Rev. W. Waterworth, S.J.

Was Barlow a Bishop? By the late Sergeant Bellasis.

189: or, the Church of old England protests. By the Rev. J. D. Breen, O.S.B.

The Faith of the Ancient English Church concerning the Holy Eucharist. By the Very Rev. Provost Northcote.

The Faith of the Ancient English Church concerning the Blessed Virgin. By the same.

CATHOLIC TRUTH SOCIETY, 18 WEST SQUARE, LONDON, S.E.

Blessed Peter and the English Church and People.*

BY

THE BISHOP OF SALFORD.

I.—Purport of this Paper.

No Saint ever entered more deeply into the life of a nation than St. Peter into the life of our English forefathers from the sixth century onward. His singular prerogatives, his touching character, his watchful love for his children were seen by our ancestors to be as so many living realities, which took their place in moulding and elevating the thoughts, the desires, the life of the nation.

No one can say that the devotion of our forefathers to St. Peter was the outcome of mediæval ignorance, or a parasitical overgrowth of latter times upon the English Church, which it was the business of the Reformation to destroy. On the contrary, it sprang up in the first fervour of the conversion of England, and was strongest and most conspicuous in the earliest, or what some would call the purest, period of the English Church.

Any one, then, who professes to be in harmony with the English Church during the first centuries of her existence, or who boasts, as all who belong to the Province of Westminster may do, that his religious life is not merely in direct continuity, but is *identical* with that of the ancient Church in England, must find himself personally bound up with St. Peter as with no other Saint, and must profess himself a loyal subject of St. Peter's See.

* A Paper read at the Catholic Conference, 1891.

My purpose is to call attention to the extraordinary devotion of the ancient English Church to St. Peter; and this, not to gratify a taste for antiquarian lore, but because this devotion furnishes a test of genuine continuity in doctrine, while it offers a standard of piety for all who, in the midst of an age of material progress, aspire after the faith and noble ideals of the olden time.

II.—THREE UNIVERSAL SAINTS.

Three persons stood to Christ in an exceptional position of nearness and love. Mary and Joseph, His parents; and Peter, whom He identified with Himself as the Rock and the Shepherd, in the constitution and government of His Church.

We, His brethren by adoption, and the members of His Church, have also contracted relationships with these three persons, which are both exclusive and unique in kind and character.

Our forefathers, as you know, gloried in being Mary's children, and called England "Our Lady's Dowry." But they understood full well that it was, not to Mary, but to Peter, that the government of the Church was confided. They realised that while the Lord committed us to the tenderest love of His own sweet Mother, He reserved to Himself our teaching and guidance, when He chose out Peter from among all men to be, not His successor, but His Vicar, to teach and confirm us in His Name.*

III.—SOLEMNITY OF THE RITE CREATING PETER'S SUPREMACY.

Before entering upon the subject of the devotional relations which grew up between Blessed Peter and

---

* For England's devotion to the Blessed Virgin all should read Father Bridgett's incomparable book, *Our Lady's Dowry.* The right of England to this touching title may be traced back to the year 694, when King Withred, his Nobles, Bishops, Abbots, and Abbesses, in solemn assembly in Kent, formally declared all Church property in the kingdom to be from that day consecrated and given over to God, and to the Blessed Virgin Mary, and the Apostles.

England, let me by way of general introduction call attention to the wonderful ceremonial which our Lord was pleased to adopt in raising Peter to the high position of a fellowship with Himself in the supreme government of the Church. In vain will you look through the Old or New Testament for a parallel to the solemnity of the rite taken as a whole, whether you consider the number of steps and interstices by which it proceeded, or the significant fact that it covered the whole length of our Lord's public ministry.

Christ did not raise Peter to the great height of the Supremacy by a sudden or by a single act of His Divine authority. The creation of the Supremacy bore a due proportion to the creation of the Body, over which Peter was to become the Ruler. The two creations went on, so to speak, *pari passu*, from the commencement of the Public Ministry to the eve of the Ascension.

Let us sketch an outline of the Divine ceremonial. It began in the first days of the first year of the Public Ministry. Peter came into the presence of Christ, and "Jesus *looking upon* him said: Thou art Simon, the son of Jona: *thou shalt be called Cephas*, which is interpreted *Peter.*" (St. John i. 42.) This is the whole, brief but pregnant, record of that first meeting. The act of "Jesus *looking* upon him," was sacramental, as when He afterwards *"breathed"* upon His Apostles. Here is the formal and public announcement of a promise that, at the proper time, Christ will change the name of this man, whom He had chosen to be the head of the New Dispensation, as at the beginning of the Old He had chosen Abram, and had changed his name to a name signifiying the office he was to bear.

The year following, about the Feast of Pentecost, our Lord solemnly fulfilled the recorded promise. It was at Cæsarea Philippi, upon the occasion of the Apostle's confession of His Divinity: "And I say to thee that *thou art* Peter;" and then He went on, as with a sacred rite, to publish a further promise: "And upon this Rock I *will build* My Church, and the gates of hell shall not prevail against it. And *I will give to thee* the keys of the kingdom of heaven, &c." (St. Matt. xvi.)

Another interstice followed, and then our Lord, choosing the sacred moment which intervened between the Last Supper and the Passion, once more in the presence of the Apostles resumed the solemn rite whereby he was preparing for His own departure, by creating a Prince, a King, a Vicar to take His place. Turning to the body of the Apostles He said: "Satan hath desired to have you that he might sift you as wheat," and then, turning to Peter, He went on : "But I have prayed for *thee* that *thy faith* fail not, and thou being once converted, confirm thy brethren." (St. Luke xxii. 31, 32.)

And now there remained but the last act of the solemn rite which was to complete the creation of the Papal Supremacy. It was to take place after the Passion and Resurrection, almost on the eve of the Ascension. It was to take place near the spot where it had commenced, on the coast of the sea of Galilee.

The Lord had prepared for this final ceremony, by something of unwonted care to secure the presence of His Apostles and witnesses. They had been told repeatedly to meet Him in Galilee.

And now behold them assembled in Galilee. The Shepherd-King is about publicly to commit the care of His entire flock to that one man whom He had *looked upon* and chosen three years before in preparation for this solemn event.

The history of this last event stands out with exceptional prominence in the Sacred Text. St. John had written his Gospel to prove that Christ was God, and he completed the proof in twenty chapters, with the confession of his Master's Divinity by the Apostle Thomas : "My Lord and my God !" The task was done. He sums up his Gospel in two verses more, and it is over.— But no, he has yet another Gospel to write—the Gospel of Peter's Jurisdiction, the Gospel of the Papal Supremacy. He had proved that Christ was God ; he must now show that he had left behind Him, not a successor, but a Vicar, a Representative, a Visible Head over the whole flock, over the whole Church which He had created in His Blood. Read this 21st chapter and examine it well. You will note:—

1. The similarity in order of procedure, of preparation and of charitable condescension to the minds of men, which marks the Sixth Chapter where the Lord treats of that other mystery, the Blessed Eucharist. The creation of the two Institutions, that of the Real Presence and that of the Supremacy, seemed to require a greater care, as they were to make a greater demand upon the mind and heart of man.

2. That the Divine Commission, the authority and jurisdiction given to Peter over the whole flock, is bound up with most tender appeals to love and devotedness. God founded the Church in love, Christ loved the Church as His own flesh. He had prayed before His Passion for its unity, and He now makes formal provision for that unity, until the end of time. He places the whole under one. To him He commits the care and the feeding of the sheep and the lambs. "Feed My lambs, feed My sheep." Thus the great work was finally completed, completed in power and in love, completed amid the tears and perhaps broken-hearted sobs of Peter, completed in the sight of witnesses—Apostles and Disciples—in Galilee.

3. The Remainder of the Chapter is all personal to Peter.

IV.—ITS ACCEPTANCE BY THE CHURCH.

The Church at once recognised the Headship constituted by its Divine Founder. Without burdening this introduction with long quotations, let me cite three witnesses.

St. Cyprian, A.D. 284: "There is but one Church founded by Christ *on Peter.*" (*Ep.* 70.)

St. Ambrose, A.D. 385: "Where *Peter* is there is the Church and eternal life." (in *Ps.* 40.)

St. Leo, A.D. 440: "Out of the whole world *Peter alone* is chosen, and is set over the vocation of all nations and over all the Apostles and all the Fathers of the

Church. Peter in his own person rules all whom Christ rules as Head. A great and marvellous fellowship in its power has God conferred upon this man." *

The Church has ever considered St. Peter as continuing through all time to preside over the entire Church. As St. Boniface wrote in the fifth century: "The Blessed Apostle Peter looks on you with his own eyes, nor can he who received charge of all fail to be near to all." Peter, then, is ever living in his see, and his voice is heard to-day through Leo, as yesterday through Pius, and the day before through Gregory, up the long pathway of the Christian era.

V.—DOCTRINE HELD BY THE EARLY ENGLISH CHURCH.

The faith received by the English people in the sixth and seventh centuries was identical with the Catholic and Roman faith that had been taught throughout the world.

Let our two earliest English writers, St. Aldhelm and St. Bede, briefly bear their authentic witness to the doctrine of the English Church before I enter on the main subject of this paper.

And first, St. Aldhelm winds up an address thus:

"To conclude all in one short sentence: foolishly and vainly does he boast of holding the Catholic faith, if he follow not the teaching (dogma) and the ruling of St. Peter. For the foundation of the Church and the solidity of the faith, reposing first on Christ then on Peter, cannot be shaken by the most violent storms and tempests; so the Apostle declares (1 Cor. iii. 2), *for other foundation no man can lay, but that which is laid, which is Christ Jesus.* But in Peter, the truth irrevocably established the prerogative of the Church in these words: 'Thou art Peter and upon this rock I will build My Church.'" (St. Matt. xvi.)†

---

* *Serm.* iv. cap. 2, in anni ejusd. Assumpt.

† Letter to Geraint, King of the Welsh or Britons of Devon and Cornwall by St. Aldhelm or Eadhelm, Abbot of Malmesbury 675–705 ; first Bishop of Sherborn, 705–709.

The other early English witness to the supreme authority of Peter is Bede. Commenting on the 16th chapter of St. Matthew, which speaks of the power and authority of Blessed Peter, Bede premisses his remarks by warning his readers that what follows should be the more attentively considered and borne in more constant remembrance because it sets forth the great perfection of divine faith, and furnishes most important strength to overcome temptations against this great virtue.

"Wherefore," he writes, "Blessed Peter, who confessed Christ with true faith and followed Him with true love, received in a special way the keys of the kingdom of heaven and the *sovereignty* of judicial power in the Church; to the end that *all the faithful* throughout the world might know that, whosoever shall separate himself from *the unity of Peter's faith* and from *Peter's fellowship,* can neither obtain absolution from the bonds of sin, nor admission through the gates of the heavenly kingdom. Hence it is necessary to learn with great care the sacred *doctrines of the faith which Peter taught* and to show forth good works corresponding to that faith."*

VI.—ENGLISH DEVOTION TO PETER BASED ON DOCTRINE.

It was not therefore upon mere sentiment or accident or personal attraction, but upon the solid basis of revealed Catholic doctrine, upon the undisputed fact that Christ had chosen Peter to be His Vicar and *alter ego,* that our forefathers built up the national devotion to St. Peter—a devotion for which they became conspicuous among the nations of Europe. To England belongs this honorable pre-eminence in the Church, that as she was most singularly devout to St. Peter during her religious prosperity, so did she prove herself in the time of adversity to be more fruitful than any other nation in the number and heroism of her martyrs for Peter's Supremacy. At the Reformation it was the authority of St.

* *Bede's Works.* Hom. 27, Giles' ed.

Peter that formed the main object of attack. The attack was met by a multitude of Englishmen and women of every rank and degree, who poured out their life's blood in defence of the Supremacy: and the cause of no less than 315 of these martyrs is now before the Holy See for canonization.

VII.—Proofs of the close connection between England and St. Peter.

1.—*Dedication of Churches to Blesssd Peter.*

The first great Abbatial Church of Canterbury was dedicated to St. Peter. To him are dedicated England's two most famous Minsters, Westminster, where the Sovereigns of England are crowned, and the Metropolitan Church of York. For a considerable period all the churches in Northumbria were dedicated to St. Peter. After a time England became, as it were, girdled by stately fanes bearing Peter's name. Begin with Bamborough in the North, and travel round England, and you pass great cathedrals, noble abbatial or conventual churches reared to St. Peter's honour, in Lindisfarne, Wearmouth, Whitby, Ripon, and York; in Bardney, Peterborough, and Ely; then come Westminster, Canterbury, Selsey and Chichester, Winchester, Exeter, Bath, Coventry, Worcester, Gloucester and Llandaff. No less than 13 Cathedrals and Abbatial churches, dedicated to St. Peter, sent Lords to Parliament.

Nineteen of our old English Collegiate Churches and 61 Abbatial and Conventual Establishments were dedicated in honour of St. Peter.

Sometimes it seemed impossible to satisfy devotion by dedicating one church in a town to St. Peter, but several must bear his name. Thus we have *seven* Peter churches in the city of Lincoln alone: St. Peter at Arches; St. Peter Eastgate; St. Peter at Gowts; St. Peter by the Pump; St. Peter Fishmarket; St. Peter beyond the Bar; St. Peter Broadgate.

By the 16th century the number of St. Peter's churches

very considerably exceeded a thousand. We know of
1,105 that were dedicated to him; the number may have
been much larger, for there are many chapels, over 30 for
instance in Lancashire, whose dedications have been
lost.

Of course, some of the churches dedicated to St. Peter
were also dedicated to his companion St. Paul or to
some local saint, such as to St. Hilda, who for local
reasons outshone him at Whitby, as St. Etheldreda did
at Ely, St. Aldhelm at Malmesbury, St. Swithin at
Winchester.

2.—*Grants and Bequests to Blessed Peter.*

Deeds of gift and bequests used frequently to recite
that the lands or property were devised "*to St. Peter,*"
"*in honour of St. Peter,*" or "*to God and St. Peter,*"
or "*to Christ and St. Peter.*"

Thus Æthelbert King of Kent, "grants to God in
honour of St Peter a certain portion of land in my own
right," &c.

King Æthelred's reputed Charter of Peterborough in
680 reads thus : "These lands will I give *to St. Peter* as
freely as I possess them myself." Peterborough was
for many centuries the most famous shrine of St. Peter
in England. Bulls were issued by the Holy See granting to it particular honour and privileges, so that Peterborough was called "a second Rome."

> "Hither I will that we seek St. Peter,
> We that to Rome cannot go."

Extracts of this kind might be given indefinitely; but
these are sufficiently illustrative for the present purpose.

3.—*Pilgrimages to St. Peter's Shrine.*

Another evidence of the faith and devotion of the
English people to St. Peter is to be found in their con-
tinual pilgrimages to the tomb of this Apostle and to the
sacred person of his successor in Rome.

Bede and the *Anglo-Saxon Chronicle* furnish us with

the earliest records of this devotion, which has never died out among us.

Bede tells us that Oswy, King of Northumbria,—after he had settled at Whitby in 664 the disciplinary differences which divided the Scots and the English by an appeal to the authority of St. Peter,—"bore so great an affection for the Roman and Apostolic See that he determined, in the 58th year of his age, to go to Rome and there to end his days, close to the Holy Places."*

In the year 688, Ceadwalla, King of Wessex, received the faith from St. Wilfrid; but such was his devotion to the Prince of the Apostles that he determined to receive baptism, not from his friend Wilfrid, but from the hand of the successor of St. Peter, and he journeyed to Rome for that purpose, and was baptized by the Pope with the name of Peter.

But the most remarkable for its splendour of all Royal pilgrimages to Rome, recorded by the ancient chroniclers, was that undertaken, in 1030, by the famous warrior and conqueror, King Cnut or Canute.   It attracted the attention of the whole of Europe.   It was undertaken entirely out of devotion to St. Peter, and in belief in the power of that Apostle, as will appear from the following passage of the Royal letter, which Canute sent to England during the year he spent at the shrine of the Apostles.

"Canute, King of Denmark, England, and Norway, and of part of Sweden, to Egelnoth the Metropolitan, to Archbishop Ælfric, to all the Bishops and Chiefs, and to all the nation of the English, both Nobles and Commoners, greeting: I write to inform you that I have lately been in Rome to pray for the remission of my sins, and for the safety of my kingdom, and for the nations that are subject to my sceptre.   It is long since I bound myself by vow to make this pilgrimage; but I had hitherto been prevented by affairs of State and other impediments.   Now, however, I return humble thanks to the Almighty God that He has allowed me to visit the tombs of the Blessed Apostles, Peter and Paul, and to honour and venerate them in person.   And *this I have*

---

* *Bede's Hist.*, b. iv. c. 5.

done because I have learned from my teachers that the Apostle St. Peter received from the Lord the great power of binding and loosing, with the keys of the kingdom of heaven. *On this account I thought it highly useful to solicit his patronage with God,"* &c.

The history of St. Edward the Confessor's vow is well known. It was to make pilgrimage, as he himself writes, "to the tombs of the glorious Apostles St. Peter and St. Paul, and there return thanks for the mercies I have received, and implore God to grant perpetual peace and prosperity to me and to my successors. . . . "

If during this important period of the making of England the Royal Houses were seen in pilgrimage to the tomb of the Apostle on some fourteen or fifteen different occasions, it may be said of the bishops, clergy, and people that they were continually crossing the Alps, to and fro, between England and Rome. . . .

4.—*The Angle-School in Rome.*

Another proof that England was in religion essentially Roman Catholic, from the earliest period, may be seen in the foundation of the Angle-school, or the school of the Anglo-Saxons in Rome.

Matthew Paris, in his *Chronicles*, points out a distinct object, apart from hospitality to pilgrims, for which provision was made. He says: "The Anglo-Saxon school was founded in Rome in order that the Kings of England and their race, as well as the English Bishops and priests and students might resort there to be instructed in the doctrines of the Catholic faith, lest anything faulty or contrary to the Catholic faith might grow up in the English Church, so that confirmed and strengthened in a lasting faith they might return to their own country." How curiously illustrative this is of the dependence of the old English Church for the purity of the faith upon the See of Peter! The English College in Rome of to-day is heir to the spirit and intention which established and animated the Anglo-Saxon school in the Borgo a thousand years ago.

5.—*Statute Law on Peter-pence.*

But perhaps nothing shows more strikingly the national faith and love for Blessed Peter than the institution, of purely English origin, called at different times, smoke-penny, hearth-penny, fire-penny, Rom-feoh, Romescot, or Peter-penny. It grew from a seed, sown by Ina or Offa, until it spread over the whole land. In the 16th century it was spoken of as a venerable national institution, that had been in existence for 800 years.

The payment of Peter-pence soon became part of the Statute law of England. It was the subject of legislation by Eadward and Guthrum (about 900), by Eadgar (about 959), by Æthelred (about 998), by Cnut 1017, by St. Edward the Confessor 1043, and it formed part of the laws of the Conqueror and of Henry I.

" Every one who has a house with chattels worth 30 pence, shall give the penny of St. Peter. He shall be summoned to pay on the Feast of SS. Peter and Paul, and the money shall be paid by the Feast of St. Peter's Chains. If he withhold it, the claim shall be brought before the King's Judge, and the King's Judge shall compel him to pay the penny and forfeiture to the King and to the Bishop. If a man have many houses he shall pay the penny for the house he is living in at the Feast of St. Peter and St. Paul."—(*Laws of King Edward the Confessor.* Thorpe I., 446.)

The amount of Peter-pence sent annually to Rome was, after a time, compounded with the Holy See for an annual sum of £200 or 300 marks, which at one period had the purchasing value of from £8,000 to £9,000 of our present money. Peter-pence continued to be levied annually by law (with the exception of a brief period towards the close of the reign of Edward III.) till the Henrician Schism. A Papal collector lived in England and received the amount from the various dioceses and forwarded it, along with other Apostolic dues, to Rome. And it is interesting to hear Pope Paul III., in an Allocution delivered in public consistory in 1555, stating that "he had himself been for three years Collector of Peter-pence in England, and that he had been much struck and edified by seeing the forwardness of the people to contribute, especially those of the poorer and working classes."

The worldly-minded may pretend not to see a national movement in the dedication of Churches to St. Peter and in pilgrimages to Rome. But they cannot deny that a tax such as Peter-pence, imposed by Statute and maintained by an English Parliament during the long course of centuries, is a distinct and unequivocal national demonstration of a national homage to Blessed Peter and to the Apostolic See. What English Parliament ever imposed taxes unless urged by an adequate sense of duty or necessity? Could a national tax have been levied for centuries in England but in obedience to a national sense of duty?

6.—*St. Peter and the Gilds.*

The presence of Peter may be discerned in numberless phases of English history. When the gilds sprang up for the protection of the weak and the promotion of our industrial liberties, there was Blessed Peter in their midst. The first gild of which we have minute records was St. Peter's Gild, founded at Abbotsbury. By its statutes the members protected the helpless against the strong, avenged injuries offered to the innocent, nursed the sick, buried the dead, and prayed for the repose of their souls. On the eve of St. Peter's Feast, alms were doled out to the needy, and on the Feast itself there was a great religious function, with High Mass, in the Church, followed in the afternoon by popular amusements and good cheer. The following is taken from Orky's foundation-Charter of the Abbotsbury Gild :—

"Here is made known, in this writing, that Orky has given the Gildhall and the Stead at Abbotsbury to the praise of God *and St. Peter*, and for the Gildship to possess now and henceforth, of him and his consort in long remembrance. Whoso shall avert this, let him account

with God at the great doom. Now these are the covenants
which Orky and the gild-brothers at Abbotsbury have
chosen, to the praise of God, and honour of *St. Peter*, and
for their souls' need."

And it concludes with this exhortation:—" Let us
pray fervently to God Almighty, with inward heart, that
He have mercy on us; and also to His holy Apostle *St.
Peter*, that he intercede for us and make clear our way
to everlasting rest; because *for love of him* we have
gathered this Gild. He has the power in heaven that
he may let into heaven whom he will, and refuse whom
he will not; as Christ Himself said to him in this Gospel :
' *Peter*, I deliver to thee the key of heaven's Kingdom,
and whatsoever thou wilt have bound on earth, that shall
be bound in heaven, and whatsoever thou wilt have
unbound on earth, that shall be unbound in heaven.' Let
us have trust and hope in him, that he will soon have
care of us here in the world, and after our departure
hence, be a help to our souls.   May he bring us to everlasting rest.   Amen. "*

7.—*English Devotions and Prayers to St. Peter.*

Not only in the churches dedicated to St. Peter, but in
all others, the Feasts of St. Peter were celebrated with
great joy and solemnity in England. His principal Feast
was a day of rest, a holiday of obligation, and the annual
collection of Peter-pence, which began on that day, used
to be completed by the Feast of St. Peter's Chains.

The city of Exeter was the scene of great festivity
every year in honour of St. Peter. The records of the
Cathedral still bear witness, by details of the expenses
incurred, to the splendid cavalcade procession which
used to sally forth on the eve of his annual festival.
Over 200 of the clergy and their attendants, mounted on
horseback, bearing shields with the keys of St. Peter
emblazoned on them, and the sword of St. Paul, used to
march round the city; and in the evening the great

* Thorpe's Diplomatarium, as above, pp. 605–8. Also Kemble's
Saxons in England, vol. I., p. 511.

"Peter-tide bonfire" used to light up the dusk and blaze away, till it ushered in the coming day.

The relics of St. Peter, which were brought over from Rome to many of the greater churches, were treated with the greatest devotion, lights burned before them, and they were carried in procession. Many of the old extant records describe them, and the nature and value of the costly reliquaries in which they were enshrined.

Golden crosses and keys from the shrine of *St. Peter*, or containing particles of filings from the Jerusalem or Mamertine chains, which are still preserved in Rome, were sent over to England by different Pontiffs.

There was a great devotion to St. Peter's high Altar in the York Minster. It was here that William I. of Scotland did homage to Henry II. when, in token of subjection, he deposited on the Altar of St. Peter his breast-plate, spear and saddle, in 1171. By an immemorial tradition, all the faithful of the diocese of York were obliged to visit St. Peter's altar annually, and to deposit thereon the sum of one penny; and the tradition used to be enforced from time to time in documents which have come down to our time.

St. Peter's image in York, which was most richly and expensively gilt and decorated, as can be seen by the bills which are extant, was a famous object of devotion. By a Statute of the Minster, it was decreed that a wax candle be kept burning before St. Peter's image during the whole of the Octave of his Feast. The burning of candles before statues of St. Peter was a very common practice of devotion, in different parts of England.

The image of St. Peter used sometimes to be dressed with the insignia of the Popes. At Peterborough there was a statue of St. Peter robed as the Pope, wearing a Mitre and holding the Keys.

Some of the images of St. Peter were of great value. The archives of the old parish church of Manchester tell us that among its treasures was a silver statue of St. Peter, weighing nearly three pounds, to which the people were very devout, and that it was carried away to Louvain when the Royal Supremacy was set up instead of the Papal. And Piazza, whom I have already quoted, mentions that a life size silver statue of St. Peter was presented by one of the English sovereigns to the Vatican Basilica.

Indeed our forefathers, who visited Rome from the seventh century downwards, must all have venerated the great bronze seated statue of St. Peter, made by order of Leo the Great, and now kept in St. Peter's. It had been an object of devotion to the Christian world long before St. Augustine had set foot in England. It is the same statue which every Catholic pilgrim to Rome venerates and kisses, down to the present day.

Prayers, of course, indicate the tone and temper of devotion to a Saint. Here is a prayer composed in Latin metre by Alcuin (725-804) for the dedication of St. Peter's Church.

"May Peter, Prince of the Apostles and faithful shepherd, glory of the flock above as of the Church below, key-bearer for all time of the Eternal Kingdom, able by voice alone to loose and to bind, in whose sacred honour this church is dedicated—may he, the shepherd, protect and guide his flock, and may he vouchsafe, we pray, in his perpetual office, to open the gates of heaven unto his sheep."

I might add much more by way of illustrating the devotions of our English forefathers to St. Peter; but I must defer this to another occasion, so as not to exceed the limits allowed in this publication.

8.—*Apparitions and Miracles of St. Peter in England.*

I have not been able to make anything approaching a complete collection of the apparitions and miracles of St. Peter in England, as recorded by different writers and chroniclers. It will suffice for the present purpose to say that they were of not unfrequent occurrence, and to give a few instances which may be added to on another occasion. I am not here concerned with the truth of each reputed vision or miracle, my object is to show what was the state of mind, the belief of Catholics, in those days as to the power, the goodness, and the love of St. Peter towards his English children. As to the occurrence of miracles, Catholics have never for a moment doubted ; the only question can be as to the authenticity of this or that particular instance and the weight of the evidence that can be alleged in support of it.

Bede tells us that Blessed Peter appeared to Lawrence, second Archbishop of Canterbury, when his heart failed him and he had determined to fly the country upon the relapse of the Kentish Kingdom into idolatry, after the death of King St. Ethelbert. The night before his intended departure the Apostle appeared to him in the church at Canterbury, and "having scourged him with Apostolic severity," upbraided him with his want of generosity, saying, "you have forgotten my example who underwent all manner of suffering for the sake of the little ones confided to me by Christ, &c." Lawrence determined to remain at his post, and next day, having gone to King Eadbald and shown him his bleeding shoulders, he pleaded effectually with the Pagan, and the work begun by St. Augustine was persevered in.

The appearances of St. Peter on the Thames, between Lambeth and Westminster, his having been said to have silently consecrated the Abbey of Westminster during the night, his apparition to and conversation with St. Edward the Confessor, are well-known traditions and need no remark. Other instances must be omitted.

All the above mentioned things, taken together, might well encourage the belief that Blessed Peter had a special love for the English people, and that the English people were justified in their devotion.

9.—*St. Peter in Profane and Common Life.*

Profane customs and the popular love of a name often testify to popular devotions. And so the name of Peter became of common use as an expletive or as a mild form of swearing. *By St. Peter of Rome* was not an uncommon oath, and the name of *Peter!* in the same sense was constantly made use of. · This may be seen in Langland and Chaucer, the great witnesses in their time

to the life and morals of the people, who put the name
of "Peter" into the mouth of both priest and layman.

> "'*Peter !*' quod a plowman and put forth his hed,
> 'I knowe him as kyndely as clerke doth his bokes.'"
> (Piers the Plowman, Passus, v. 544.)
> "Quoth Perkin the plouman, '*bi seynt Peter of Rome*,
> I have an half acre to eyre'. . . .—(*Passus* vi. 3.)
> '*Peter !*' quod the prest, 'tho' I can no pardon fynde,'
> (Passus vii. 112.)
> "'What !' quod the prest to Perkin, '*Peter !* as me
>   thinketh.
> Thow art lettred a litel.'"—(130.)
> "'*Peter !*' quod he, 'God yeve it harde grace.'"
> (Canterbury Tales, Group G. 665.)
> "*Peter !* lyke the beating of the see,
> Quod I, against the roches below."—(*House of Fame*,
>   ii. 526.)

But it is interesting to note how the thought of St.
Peter penetrated every day life, and how many common
things became associated with his name and as it were
consecrated to him.

Thus a series of notes on Holy Wells have been
appearing of late in *The Antiquary*, and among them
there are several dedicated to St. Peter, for instance in
Derby, Doncaster, Barnby in the Marsh, Yorks, Leeds,
and Shrewsbury* "Peterspool," is a chalybeate spring
in Lincolnshire,† which like other springs seems to
derive its name from Peter's healing and strength-giving
power.

St. Peter is also connected with our popular plant
names: Samphire is a corruption of *St. Pierre*, christened
after St. Peter either on account of St. Peter's early
calling or because of its growing upon rocks by the sea.

Then we have *St. Peter's wort*, or *Peter*, a name
which formerly was popularly given to the Cowslip,
because of the likeness of its clustering flowers to a bunch

---

* See *The Antiquary*, xx. 98 : xx. 40 and 253, xxiv. 27.
† *Quarterly Review*, July 1891, p. 113.

of keys. From a similar likeness the fruit of the Ash was
called *Peter-Keys*. The Great Mullein was *Peter's* Staff;
and a species of *Hypericum (H. tetrapterum)* flowering
about St. Peter's Day, was called St. Peter's wort, probably to distinguish it from the St. John's wort *(H. per-
foratum).*

"Peter-corn" was the annual levy of corn, throughout
the diocese of York, ordered by king Atherstone, to be
distributed among the poor, in thanksgiving *to God and
St. Peter*, for his victory over the Scots at Dunbar.

In the animal kingdom we have the haddock called
from its marks, like those made by fingers, St. Peter's fish;
and the Petrel, a sea bird, deriving its name from the
Apostle on account of its appearing to walk on the sea.

"The Cross Keys" is a well-known signboard,
evidently taken from St. Peter's keys, and "St. Peter's
Finger" is another, but of less certain signification.

"Peter-tide bonfires" were common on St. Peter's eve,
especially in West Cornwall and on Mount's Bay, a
traditional practice surviving, I believe, to the present
day. A "Peter-man" is a familiar term on the Thames to
this day for a boat man, and a "Peter-boat" is the name
given to a build of boat which is sharp or pointed at
each end. "Peter-men" on land were members of a
gild who prayed for the founders and benefactors of a
Peter Church, such as existed at Gloucester.

Even the children of our forefathers used to be brought
up with a salutary respect for St. Peter's authority, for
"to go through St. Peter's needle" was an expression
signifying due subjection to discipline or authority, "I'll
put you through St. Peter's needle."

VIII.—St. Peter, the ancient Patron of England.

Have I not already brought forward abundant evidence
to prove that an extraordinary national devotion existed
to St. Peter, and that immense confidence was felt in his
patronage? Popular desires and aspirations are constantly made known by the captains of the people.

* See Britten and Holland's *Dictionary of English Plant-names.*

Take as witnesses, King Offa ascribing his victories to his *Patron, St. Peter;* Ceadwalla changing his name for that of his *Patron, St. Peter;* the Royal Charter of the foundation of the great Church and monastery of Exeter speaking of St. Peter as the Patron of the King, "quem rex sibi *in Patronum* elegerat," King Edgar quite naturally describing *St. Peter* in one of his Charters as "our special Patron and Protector."

King Canute is quoted by de Macedo,* I know not on what authority, as speaking of St. Peter as "*the Patron and Protector of the English.*"

St. Aelred, in his Life of Edward the Confessor, says that while in exile in Normandy, the future King of England prayed thus: "Thou wilt always be to me, O Lord, a God, and *Blessed Peter*, the Apostle, will be *my Patron*," &c. And later, in one of the Charters of Westminster Abbey, the King describes St. Peter as "*Our special Patron.*"

One of the greatest and most imposing national religious ceremonies is that of the coronation of the Sovereign. In the Anglo-Saxon rite, used down to the time of Henry I., who ordered it to be shortened, there was a special invocation of the Patrons and Protectors of England, and among these was of course *St. Peter.* This may be seen in the Leofric Missal.†

And now if we turn from the Sovereigns to the Roman Pontiffs, we find them bearing the same kind of testimony.

Boniface IV., writing in the beginning of the seventh century to an English king, says: "I have sent you the blessing of *your Patron, the Blessed Peter*, Prince of the Apostles." Nicholas II., in an Apostolic Letter to the king of England, uses these remarkable words: "May Blessed Peter ever be your guardian and helper in all trials. For it is clear that the kings of England have flourished with glory and honour on account of the reverence and devotion which they paid to Blessed Peter, and that they have obtained great victories under his patronage."

* Macedo's *Divi titulares Orbis Christiani*, p. 457.
† See also the Cottonian MS. Claudius, A. III.

And Alexander II., writing to William the Conqueror, reminds him that "from the time of the spread of the Christian religion in England, the kingdom of the English has always been under the care and guardianship of the Prince of the Apostles."

Pope Innocent III., addressing King Stephen, incidentally bears witness to the close relationship ever subsisting between England and St. Peter. "Knowing," he says, "that you vowed obedience and reverence *to St. Peter*, on the day of your consecration. We receive you with fatherly affection as a *favoured Son of St. Peter and the Holy Roman Church*."

The historic English evidence exhibiting the special devotion of England to St. Peter and his Roman See may be summed up by two separate testimonies, borne independently by the State and by the Church.

We may take the State as represented by Edward the Confessor. This King, in a formal document, declares that down to his time, "*The English people had ever borne a supreme devotion towards St. Peter and his Vicar*" (summam devotionem quam habuit semper gens Anglorum erga eum [Petrum] et Vicarios ejus."*

The English Church was fully represented by the Primate, Bishops and Clergy of England assembled in the Synod of Westminster in 1246. In this Synod it was declared that, "*the English nation has always been specially devoted to the Holy Roman Church*," and, a little further on, that, "*the English Church*, which was renowned for many glories, *has always been a Special Member of the Holy Church of Rome*."

The historical evidence, which can be gathered from foreign authorities as to the devotion of England for the great Apostle St. Peter, is quite as remarkable; and it has the further advantage of being free from any suspicion of partiality or of vain-glorious boasting. Baronius, Piazza, Macedo, Alford and Mesmana might all be quoted at considerable length : but it is necessary to be brief.

Baronius says that the English Kings used to be

* H. Wilkins's *Concilia*, vol. I., p. 319.

crowned as the eldest sons of the Church, "tanquam primogeniti ecclesiæ filii:" such was their devotion to St. Peter and his successors. Alford tells us that "the English people dedicated to St. Peter, after Christ, altars, Churches and towns, and that *their kings placed the whole island under St. Peter.*"

Piazza, in his *Efemeride Vaticane,* published some two centuries ago, declares that "the English were *more devout than any other nation* to the glorious Apostles Peter and Paul, so that they consequently used to experience their help and protection in all their necessities."

From all that has been said, one would be naturally led to suppose that St. Peter must have been the Patron Saint of England before the Reformation. But have we any warrant for asserting that he was in fact the Patron of England, in any sense,—for instance, as St. George was? Few people would say that we have, so completely has the tradition died out. It was only the other day that, in turning over the pages of the *Archæologia,* I came upon a buried reminiscence, which set forth the fact that the Blessed Virgin Mary and St. Peter had always been considered the Patrons of England, while St. George had been held to be her Military Protector.

But more important and more authoritative than the *Archæologia* is the testimony of Antonio de Macedo, a learned Jesuit writer, in the folio volume which he published on the Patron Saints of the different countries in Christendom.*

In the part wherein he treats of England, he says that " England had especially three Patron Saints while it professed the true and pure faith, namely, the most Blessed Virgin Mary, *St. Peter, the Prince of the Apostles,* and St. George the Martyr," p. 451. The Blessed Virgin, he says, became the Patron of England from the very earliest time, and " England was formerly known and spoken of most deservedly *(jure optimo)* as the Dowry of the Virgin Mary." St. George, on the

---

* Divi titulares Orbis Christiani : opus singulare, in quo de Sanctis Regnorum, Provinciarum, Urbium maximorum Patronis agitur. Lisbon. 1687.

other hand, he points out, was considered only as the military Patron or Protector of England.   The national devotion to this Saint commenced not earlier than during the reign of Edward III., whereas devotion to St. Peter, as the Patron of England, took its rise with the first establishment of the Church in this country.   "*St. Peter,*" —these are Macedo's words—"holds a primary place amongst the Patrons of the English."—" Primarium inter Patronos Anglorum locum tenet Sanctus Petrus, Apostolorum princeps"   But how is it possible that, if St. Peter was the Patron of England, the record of the fact should have fallen so completely out of mind? Macedo himself supplies the answer.   He points out that the reformers did their best to blot out of the memory of the people all thought and recollection of their Patron Saints.   They set themselves especially to destroy veneration and love for the Blessed Virgin and St. Peter,—the one "the destroyer of all heresies," and the other the touchstone of the faith.   As to St. George, they passed a law declaring that his Order should no longer be called by his name, but should be known simply as the Order of the Garter and that its Feast should no longer be kept on the 23rd of April, but on Whitsunday.   So well did they succeed in wiping out all memory of our great Patron Saints, that Fr. Bridgett's discovery a few years ago, that England had been extraordinarily devout to Mary and had been known as "Our Lady's Dowry," came upon the public with the force of a surprise and as an historical revelation.   It is the same with St. Peter.   So thoroughly had the reformers done their work, that the thought of Mary and Peter, as the great Patrons of England, though they had been recognised by Church and State as "universæ Anglorum genti Patroni," entirely passed away and was hidden for three centuries, from the recollection of men.   Surely the present discovery is a happy one, and not without significance?   It has been a long, tempestuous, dark night ; but when at last the clouds break and the moon and the polar star both stand out again clear in the sky, a new hope of salvation springs up in the heart of the wayfarer.

Some will at once ask, Can nothing be done to restore
to England, by some formal act, the Patrons that have
been so long forgotten? The matter rests almost entirely.
in the hands of the Catholic public. If it be the mind
of the people and their priests to petition the Bishops for
a declaration that Mary and Peter are still the Patrons
of England, the Bishops no doubt will forward their
petition to Rome. The result could hardly be doubtful.
Peter would then probably declare, through his See,
that the Mother and the Vicar of Christ are still the
Patrons of England, and to be regarded as such by all
Catholics.

IX. Some Results of Peter's Influence.

1.—*English Liberties.*

I began this paper by affirming that no man ever
impressed himself more deeply upon the life and
character of a nation than Blessed Peter upon the
English people. In one respect this is not surprising.
For, given a race of sincere, strong, and religious
character—a race whose intellect had not been perverted
by pride, whose will had not been debauched by luxury,.
one might legitimately expect that, on such a race, the.
man chosen out by God Himself to be the guide and
teacher of mankind would exercise a marked and lasting
influence. Now if this English race was enthusiastically
devoted to Peter and his See, it is because England was
enthusiastically and essentially Christian. "A thousand
years ago," writes Mr. Thomas Hughes, in his *Life of
Alfred the Great,* (p. 27.) "England was not only in name
a Christian nation, but a living faith in Christ was
practically the deepest and strongest force in the national
life."
This devotion and obedience of the English people
and of their Sovereigns to Blessed Peter fostered and,
secured to the nation not only her religious unity, but.
those liberties, which we prize so highly. No Metropolitan

or Primate, no mere local clergy, abandoned to themselves and to their surrounding influences, could ever
have accomplished in England the work which was
achieved under the guidance of St. Peter alone. Attempts at Cæsarism and State tyranny were overmatched
by Peter. The religious strength and unity imparted to
the nation, as it cleaved to Peter, brought liberty to all,
and peace and plenty to the door of the poor. A clear
demarcation was hacked out by Peter between the
domains of the spiritual and the civil Powers. The
authority of the Sovereign was asserted; the freedom of
the subject secured, while full play was afforded to noble
ideals of life, and to splendid aspirations after Christian
perfection. Lecky and Hallam both recognize that our
national liberties and our noblest characteristics were all
derived from the days when Blessed Peter's influence
was moulding the life of the English people. Our actual
liberties are due, says Mr. Hallam, "to the old Saxon
principles, that survived the Conquest of William and
infused themselves into our common law." And it is
well known that in England, up to the very eve of the
Reformation, the See of Peter was constantly described
and appealed to by Englishmen as being "the refuge
of the oppressed."

In those days, says Montalembert, when England
was ruled by "emissaries of Rome," they not only
made her "a nation of Christians more fervent than
any other contemporary nation," but formed "the boldness and independence of their character." "Self-
government, that is to say, the proud independence of
the freeman among his fellows in the general common-
wealth," and "the essential elements of Parliamentary
Government" grew up during the period in which love
and devotion to Blessed Peter were paramount among
the English people.

Free Education.

Look carefully into English history and you will smile
to find how frequently Blessed Peter and his See have
anticipated in a Christian sense our modern movements.

To-day the *freeing of the schools* is heralded as a modern
doctrine proving the progress of the times.   It may be
convenient for some people to forget that many of their
measures in behalf of the industrial classes were long
since anticipated by Blessed Peter.   It was by the action
of the Holy See that the Catholic Church offered free
education centuries ago through the length and breadth
of England—and this without taxing the population.
And it was only after the Royal Supremacy had been
substituted for the Papal, and the teachers banished,
their goods confiscated, and their books thrown into the
flames, that a money price was set upon knowledge, and
the children of the people were compelled either to pay
for learning or to grow up in ignorance.   The See of
Peter has ever, in Rome, in England, and elsewhere,
promoted free education.   If the Catholics of England
have not been forward in the present movement, it is
not because they believe that *free Christian education*
weakens parental authority (an argument exploded by
the Church long before the birth of Protestantism), but
because they have been duly warned by an aggressive
political party that the ultimate end in view is the
forfeiture by the people to the State of their parental
right and duty to determine the Christian education
of their children.   "Local control" of Christian education by the majority of a creedless population is a
distinct form of popular Cæsarism.   And Cæsarism
means the loss of at least some of those personal and
parental liberties which Peter has always defended, and
is defending this day by the voice of Leo.

X.—Blessed Peter's Present Relation to the
E nglish People.

Having briefly passed in review the devotion of our
forefathers to St. Peter and some of the fruits of this
devotion, I conclude this paper by asking :

1. What is the relation of Blessed Peter to the English
people at the present day?   And,

2. How can we Catholics of England best justify and

hand down the old national boast that "the English
people has ever had a *supreme devotion* towards St.
Peter," and that "the English Church has always been
a *special member* of the Holy Church of Rome?"

To the first I reply that, we may be certain that Blessed
Peter bears to the English people the compassionate
tenderness proper to one who had himself been led to
deny His Master. He knows that the English people
were unwittingly drawn away from their allegiance by
the profligate Herods and the Pilates of that day. They
sinned by weakness. We may be sure, therefore, that
he bears them mercifully in mind, while through his See
he labours for their return to the faith.

As to his authority, it remains intact over every baptized soul. For whoever is rightly baptized, no matter
where or by whom, is baptized into the Church of Peter,
the one Church of Christ. Though a soul may be
induced to renounce allegiance after baptism, the solici-
tude of that good shepherd for his wandering sheep is
not thereby quenched, his paternal right over his prodigal
son is never parted with.

Who can count the multitude in England to-day, who
are subject to the jurisdiction of Peter, though they know
it not? Peter prays and toils for their conversion. The
eyes of many have been opened as were the eyes of
Peter after his fall. Thousands upon thousands of
sincere and candid souls have come trooping back to
Peter's fold.

Look at that ever growing crowd that has for years
been throwing off one by one, the heresies and errors of
the Reformation. There is now scarcely a Catholic
doctrine which they do not hold, however imperfectly,
scarcely one for which they would not suffer. Still,
while out of communion with Peter and rebellious
against the authority of Christ's Vicar, they are, like the
Donatists, out of the Church, out of the ark of salvation.
But think not unkindly of these men; think tenderly,
lovingly of them. They teach us many a lesson.

Consider the Bishop of Lincoln and his followers.
Here is a man of singularly blameless life, devoted to

God and loving souls according to his light; using his persuasive and attractive gifts in behalf of religion. Despite the prejudice of education and the Thirty-nine Articles, which hang about him like broken chains, by the study of history he has mastered many of the doctrines of the Church.   See him now rejecting the Royal Supremacy as a usurpation, and declining even to appear before its tribunal, ready to suffer all things rather than sacrifice the liberty and independence of that which, for the present, he accounts the Church of God.

Yes, these men have looked into the history of the English Church to good account; but their enquiry is not yet complete.

They have renounced the Protestant Reformation; to call them Protestants is to insult them.   They claim continuity with the old Church of St. Augustine, St. Edward, St. Anselm, and St. Thomas of Canterbury. God grant that they may continue their studies.   There is one devotion, one fundamental doctrine against which they still rebel, no doubt unknowingly.   It is not a modern doctrine, but one that runs like a string through every generation. and century up to the time of St. Augustine,—one that preserved unity, peace, and harmony, and imparted invincible strength and certainty to the humblest as to the noblest in the land.   Need I say that it is devotion to Blessed Peter and belief in his supremacy?

O that he who claims to fill the see of St. Hugh of Lincoln, and of Bishop Grossetête, would seriously ask himself, by what spirit it was that in olden times the diocese of Lincoln reared two hundred and seventy-one churches to St. Peter; and that, while the purest and fairest of cathedrals sat as a crown of beauty upon the head of Lincoln, seven churches consecrated to St. Peter enwrapped the whole city as in a mantle of veneration and love for the Prince of Apostles.

O that they who, in the midst of trial and opposition, have abandoned so much of the Protestant tradition, would open their eyes and see that, after all, Peter is the keystone of the arch, and that " *Ubi Petrus, ibi ecclesia et vita aeterna.*"

For ourselves, we should ever remember that Faith is a supernatural gift of God. Though the *intellectus cogitabundus est principium omnis boni*, humble persevering prayer is the heavenly ladder whereby men must ascend to bring down the gifts of faith. Our mission to bring back England to the love and obedience of Blessed Peter will be discharged by prayer and charity, and by appeals to faith and reason.

XI.—How to Increase Devotion to St. Peter.

The answer to my second question is very simple. To lift our love of Peter and of his See into its proper sphere, we must use our intellect, and ponder Peter's claim to love and devotion. We must prove our love by works.

We should think of Peter as the solid Rock on which our feet are placed, the Doorkeeper of the ark of refuge from the flood, the Shepherd of the Flock, the Fisherman of the Universe, the Teacher of the habitable world, pointing out their duty to sovereigns, states, and peoples. He is the Christ-like keybearer of the Heavenly Kingdom.

But it will greatly help our heart if, while contemplating the powerful majesty of his Office, we seek access to the loving personal character of Peter's human nature.

Personal Traits in the Petrine Character.

The Prince of the Apostles was a real man, both in the weakness and in the generosity of his nature. While he was a child in discipline, his love for his Master was continually outstripping his strength. In his eager desire to embrace his Lord, he would throw himself upon the waves, and then, trusting to himself, would begin to sink through fear. He would openly confess the Divinity of Christ, and then would dissuade his Lord from His mission. He was ready to go with Him to prison and to death, yet could not give to Him one hour of prayer. He could gird the sword and wield it, and then, trembling at the voice of a maid, would deny that he had even known his Master. Yet strange to say, he fell into so grievous a sin because, as St. John Chrysostom points out, his love exceeded that of those who fled, and urged him to venture beyond his depth rather than forsake his Lord. Poor, frail human heart, how little to be trusted by thyself! But presently humility and grace came hand in hand, and raised and perfected his fallen nature. He became a model of compassion for poor sinners and quick to help them. The same warm, eager, loving heart, beat within his bosom; but now strong and invincible. Think how the words, "Peter, lovest thou Me more than these?" bring tears of love and sorrow to his eyes. See how that old weather-beaten face, after long years of toil and trials without number, is furrowed more by weeping than even by the lines of time.

Read the Gospel written by his disciple Mark, and note how full it is of minute and touching details which none but the most loving eye-witness could have stored up, while such was now his humility that "he perhaps entreated St. Mark (as Chrysostom affirms) not to mention the great things that redounded to his honour, but to pass them in silence and to dwell rather upon his fall."

St. Ambrose sees in Peter a continuation of Christ's love for us, and calls this Apostle "the Vicar of His love." One would, therefore, expect to find in his heart an overflowing fountain of affection. And so it was. An early writer records a tradition illustrating this. He says that while Peter was walking one evening outside the walls of Rome, near to what is now known as the Porta San Pancrazio, he was seen by his companions to be suddenly overcome by emotion and to burst into tears. They inquired the cause. "See what the poor mother has just done," he said; "she has drawn off her own cloak to cover up her child who is asleep upon the bank. It was thus the Master treated us. While He prayed on the mountain side, we slept and He often would come and cast His own cloak about a disciple as he slept, to protect him from the cold of the night."

Finally, if in fear and hatred the Roman Emperor took the life of Peter, in love Peter triumphed over the

Roman Empire; and in love, the triumphant love of Christ, he never ceases to carry on his mission of good will and of salvation to the world.

XII.—Six Works of Devotion to St. Peter.

The works we can perform are these:—

1. To honour him publicly as an act of propitiation and impetration. This might be done by raising an altar to him, or, at least, a statue, in all our churches. Measures are being taken to supply to any church, at moderate cost, a half-size facsimile of the bronze statue of St. Peter, venerated in Rome since the 5th century.*

2. To address public and private prayers to him with great confidence in his power.

3. To spread, as widely as possible, knowledge of the life and writings of St. Peter, especially of the devotion of the English Church to him. The English people are drawn to the truth when it is presented to them in the concrete far more powerfully than when set before them by dry, lifeless, abstract reasoning.

4. To contribute Peter Pence after the manner of our forefathers during Peter-tide, that is, between the Feasts of St. Peter and of St. Peter's Chains. We may note as a happy omen and as another link with the past, that whereas our Anglo-Saxon ancestors were the first to introduce into the Church the devotion of Peter Pence, we their children were the first to revive it as an institution in 1859.†

* Application may be made to the Secretary, *Christian Art and Craft School*, Dover St., Manchester, for details as to price, &c., also for altar pieces representing the Patrons of England, including St. Peter, painted in the best style of Catholic art.

† The cry for the revival of Peter Pence sprang up in England exactly three centuries to the year after its suppression by Elizabeth. "Let the Peter penny be re-introduced," were the words in the appeal published in November, 1859, by *The Tablet*, "not as a momentary help merely, but as a regular and lasting contribution. . . . We cannot doubt that this glorious and practical example [set by Great Britain and Ireland] will be followed by every part of the world."

It was Cardinal Wiseman who suggested the formation of the Confraternity of St. Peter.

5. To pray and to work for the independence of the See of Peter—that is, for the restoration of the Temporal Power; never to listen to timid and worldly counsels acquiescing in the spoliation of the Pope; never to despair, never to fall short of the demand made by Christ's Vicar; to organize ourselves and to unite with the nations of Christendom in demanding and insisting upon the triumph of justice; in a word, to use all lawful means to restore to Peter the independent position of Sovereignty which his office and dignity, as Vicar of God and Head of Christendom, demand.

Sixthly, and lastly, loyally to accept and zealously to propagate the teaching and the counsels of the See of Peter. Society is sick and out of joint, in England as elsewhere. But Peter has spoken through the mouth of Leo. He reprimands the encroaching power of the State and the tyranny of wealth. Once more he earns the title, which the English people used to give him, " *The Refuge of the oppressed.*" He teaches the labourer his duties and protects his liberties, while he safeguards legitimate authority and private property. It is thus that Peter has been guiding society through all centuries.

It rests with us, the Catholics of England, to wean our countrymen from their prejudices against him, by an example of worthy conduct, and by translating his Instructions into practice. This at least we can do,—and it should become the special business of the Catholic Truth Society,—namely, disseminate broadcast throughout England, among all classes, in public reading rooms and libraries, in clubs and private houses, the last Encyclical of Leo XIII., *On the Conditions of Labour.* Through the careful perusal of this document, the English people may learn that now, as of old, they have no better friend to their rights and liberties than Peter and the successors in his See.

Price One Shilling, cloth.

PAPERS READ

AT THE

CATHOLIC TRUTH SOCIETY'S

ANNUAL CONFERENCE

AT BIRMINGHAM,

June 30th, July 1st and 2nd, 1890.

Christianity and the Masses. By the Rev. W. Barry, D.D.

How to reach the Rural Population. By the Rev. P. Sweeny, D.D.

The Salvation Army. By the Rev. J. Lawless.

The Public Press. By the Rev. A. Richardson.

Latitudinarianism. By the Rev. W. D. Strappini, S.J.

Art and Education. By the Rev. A. L. Chattaway.

Catholics and Art. By J. B. Hardman, Esq.

Christian Art. By C. T. Gatty, F.S.A.

Church Music and Schools. By the Rev. J. Connelly.

The Temperance Movement. By the Very Rev. Canon Murnane, V.G.

Thrift. By the Rev. E. Nolan.

England's Conversion by the Power of Prayer. By the Bishop of Salford,

The Controversy of the Future. By the Rev. H. I. D. Ryder.

———

CATHOLIC TRUTH SOCIETY, 18 WEST SQUARE, LONDON, S.E.

CONFERENCE PAPERS 1891:

BEING THE PAPERS READ AT THE

CATHOLIC TRUTH SOCIETY'S
LONDON CONFERENCE.

Sanitary Associations. By LORD CLIFFORD.
Protection of Young Servants. By the HON. MRS. FRASER.
Prevention of Cruelty to Children. By the HON. MRS. PEREIRA.
*Penny Banks. By MISS AGNES LAMBERT.
*The Drink Traffic. By the REV. W. H. COLOGAN.
*The Reform of the Poor Law. By B. F. C. COSTELLOE, ESQ., L.C.C.
*Mixed Marriages. By the REV. C. W. WOOD.
Lay Work. By the VERY REV. CANON MCGRATH.
The Sunday School. By the VERY REV. DEAN RICHARDSON.
*Catholic Clubs. By JAMES BRITTEN, ESQ.
*Catholic Benefit Societies. By the REV. E. NOLAN.
The Salvation Army. By the REV. R. F. CLARKE, S.J.
*The English People and Blessed Peter. By the BISHOP OF SALFORD.
The Missionary Work of the Church at home:—
    (i) in the Work of the Centre. By the HON. SECRETARIES.
    (ii) in the Work of the Branches. By T. G. KING, ESQ.
*The Missionary Work of the Church abroad. By the REV. L. C. CASARTELLI.

* The papers marked * can be had separately at One Penny each.

CATHOLIC TRUTH SOCIETY, 18 WEST SQUARE, LONDON, S.E.

Printed at the Catholic Reformatory School, Market Weighton.

Ibow "tbe Cburcb of England wasbed ber face."

BY THE REV. SYDNEY F. SMITH, S.J.

WHEN the continuity of Anglicanism with the Church of England is questioned, and the serious nature of the Reformation changes is insisted upon, the Church Defence lecturer has his ready reply in a comparison which is considered to settle the controversy without need of further examination. What the Reformation did was to sweep away certain Popish abuses, which had sprung up in the middle ages, and tarnished the primitive purity of doctrine. The Church of England "washed her face," an operation which did not involve then, any more than it does elsewhere, a dissolution of personal identity.

In the mouth of a Protestant who glories in that designation, the similitude is in some sense intelligible. Whether continuity was broken or not, there was certainly a transition of English belief from a doctrinal system which Protestants regard as filthy to one which they regard as pure. But Dean Hook, who first used the phrase, believed, when he spoke of the Church "washing her face," that the spirit actuating the Reformation changes was Catholic in the sense in which High Churchmen understand the term. And the Dean has managed to read this idea into his history of the period so completely, that, as a writer in the *Guardian* of September 17, 1890, has observed, "any one might read his Lives of Parker and Grindal without discovering that they were distinctly Zwinglian, and would find the Calvinism of Whitgift almost concealed." In this strange perversion of history he has been followed by modern advocates of continuity, who probably rely largely for their facts on a convenient work like the Dean's *Archbishops of Canterbury*. There are other High Churchmen, however, who have given heed to the new publications of original documents, and the more exhaustive studies of recent years, and they have come to a very different conclusion as to the character and effect of the Tudor measures. For them the scrubbing-brush was dipped in very muddy water indeed. Not till the days of Laud, nearly a century later, did any operation which could be called washing take place, and then the dirt removed was just that which the Tudor changes had laid on :

There is no history of the Church of England which gives any adequate idea of the degradation into which religious observances had fallen at the end of the sixteenth and beginning of the seventeenth centuries, and the consequence is that few people understand the immense debt of gratitude which they owe to Archbishop Laud for the recovery from that condition—a recovery almost wholly due to his indefatigable endeavours to restore a more Catholic tone to doctrine and practice. We propose, therefore, in this and two following articles to supply this defect as far as may be possible. (*Guardian*, Nov. 9.)

These are the words of Mr. Pocock, words with which he begins his three recent articles in the *Guardian*[1] on the "Church of England in the Times

---

[1] See *Guardian*, Nov. 9, Nov. 23, Nov. 30, 1892.

of the Tudors and Stuarts." Mr. Pocock's authority on the Reformation period is well known, and he is a leader among those who have pointed out that till the time of Laud hardly a vestige of modern High Church views can be discovered. It is to be hoped that he will republish his three valuable articles. Meanwhile, as their interest is so great, we propose to set before our readers a summary of their contents.

Mr. Pocock's purpose is to show that the Elizabethan Church passed through an original Zwinglianism to more and more pronounced Calvinism, and that the passage was attended by a parallel downward progress in the religious spirit and morality of the country.

Elizabeth's religious policy, though worked out under different conditions, was in principle identical with that of her father. She probably felt very little attraction for Protestantism in itself, and was certainly averse to its harsher manifestations. She placed herself at its head, because circumstances indicated this position as her best chance of maintaining and enlarging her sovereignty. The two ideas in reference to ecclesiastical affairs which she had most at heart, were that the Bishops were nothing but her delegates, and that Church property was an excellent quarry for replenishing her finances. Her well-known answer to the Bishop of Ely illustrates the first of these points:

Proud Prelate, I understand you are backward in complying with your agreement, but I would have you know that I who made you what you are can unmake you, and if you do not forthwith fulfil your engagement by God I will immediately unfrock you.

And, says Mr. Pocock :

Cecil regarded them as mere officers of the State. . . .
Among his memoranda occurs the following : "It is expedient that the Queen shall be well informed of the sufficiency of the Bishops, with a view to the removal or reform
of such as are out of credit with the people under their
charge for their manifest insufficiency or covetousness."
. . . Neither can any other view of the office of a Bishop
be found in any utterance till near the time when Bancroft
preached his celebrated sermon in 1588.

Of the Queen's inroads on the Church lands he
gives the following account :

By an Act passed in the first year of the reign of
Elizabeth, the Queen was empowered to exchange the
lands of any vacant bishopric for impropriate tithes which
had belonged to the monasteries in the diocese. The Act
provided that the exchange should be on equal terms.
But during the vacancy of the see there was no one to
raise objections, and the exchange effected was simply
robbery, the newly appointed Bishop being generally some
insignificant person who was glad enough to accept the
preferment, however impoverished and clogged with uncom-
fortable conditions. . . . Grindal, it seems, had scruples
whether he ought to accept a bishopric fettered with such
conditions, and applied by letter to his friend Peter Martyr
for advice. But before he received any answer he had
decided the question on his own responsibility, and
consented to the spoliation, without which he would never
have succeeded to the see of London, rendered vacant by
the deprivation of the celebrated Edmund Bonner. The
value of the lands taken from Canterbury alone was
£1,300, which is equivalent to several thousand pounds
of the present day. And it appears from a letter written
by the Queen herself, which has never been printed, that
the long delay which took place before the confirmation
of the elects of Canterbury, London, and Ely, was owing
chiefly to the fact that the exchange between these sees

and the Crown of certain temporalities had not yet been effected. The same account has to be given of the long intervals that took place between the death or translation of a Bishop and the appointment of his successor. The sees had been in some cases stripped too much to admit of any further spoliation, but it was easy to appropriate the revenues of the bishopric during the vacancy of the see, and this is the only reason to be assigned for the average interval of two to three years during which each bishopric was from time to time kept vacant; as well as for the fact that Bristol and Ely were each without a Bishop for thirty years of the reign. Oxford enjoyed episcopal superintendence for exactly three years and six months during the forty-four years of the reign of Elizabeth, the revenue of the see going to Sir Francis Walsingham, who was accused when he founded a divinity lecture in the University of hiding sacrilege under the pretence of propagating truth. This system of spoliation was continued all through the reign at each successive avoidance of a see; so that when Day succeeded Wickham at Winchester in 1596 he demurred to surrendering a rent charge of £400 a year, on the ground that the see which had been estimated at £3,000 a year would then be reduced to £500. He was thereupon suspended by the Queen till he had made a compromise, much, it was said, to the prejudice of his successors in the bishopric, but as he himself expressed it, as much as his conscience would allow.

Nor was it the Sovereign only who saw in the Church property mainly an opportunity for plunder:

We have said that the Bishops were for the most part insignificant persons. Many of them were also men of indifferent character, and few of them are altogether free from the imputation of nepotism, covetousness, truckling to the civil authorities, impoverishing their sees by letting out the lands on long leases, and in more than one or two cases, one an Archbishop, purloining the lead from the cathedrals.

And again, in the second article :

I suppose I should not be far from the truth if I were to describe the Episcopate of Elizabeth's reign as having scarcely any other history than that of entering upon their bishoprics under simoniacal contracts made with the Queen or her favourites, of spoiling their dioceses to the prejudice of their successors during their occupancy of the see, of engaging in suits for dilapidations upon a death or translation between the newly appointed Bishop and the outgoing prelate or his heirs.

Mr. Pocock tells us, "it is no subject for wonder that the Bishops are such as we have described them. The choice for the Queen and her sagacious Minister was very limited," and all the bishoprics save one had to be filled up. Perhaps the Queen and her Minister had independent reasons for not desiring men of much character. Better men, even if they were to be found among the Protestants, would have been less pliant instruments in the royal hands. Still, as Mr. Pocock reminds us, her choice was limited to a certain class, the men of Protestant leanings, who on her sister's accession had fled into Germany and Switzerland :

Of the clergy who had been imprisoned or banished during the reign of her sister Mary, there were two classes who may be roughly designated as Zwinglians and Calvinists. Those who had been imprisoned had such violent altercations that one party refused to communicate with the others, whom they designated as free-willers, because they would not commit themselves to all the horrors of an unmitigated Calvinism. They were also at issue about certain minor matters, such as the lawfulness of playing at bowls. Quarrels of a similar kind had originated amongst the exiles, who had been refused admission at all places where Lutheranism prevailed, being designated by the Lutherans as the devil's martyrs, because of their supposed

adoption of the tenets of Zwingli or Calvin. They had
settled in various towns of Switzerland and in considerable
numbers at Frankfort. Here violent altercations arose, the
moderate party being content to abide by the Zwinglian
form of doctrine which as they thought pervaded the
Second Prayer-book of the reign of Edward VI., whilst the
more fanatical considered the book as too Papistical, and
were for a further reformation of it, such as had been con-
templated at the time of the premature death of the King.
These latter retired in a body to Geneva and Basel.
Speaking generally these were Calvinists and the others
Zwinglians. The two systems may be sufficiently, though,
perhaps, roughly described as the one consisting mainly
in the disparagement or denial of sacramental grace, the
sacraments being regarded as symbols and not instruments
of grace; the other, pronouncing the sacraments as in some
way efficacious, but only to the elect, by increasing the grace
they previously possessed and from which it was impossible
for them entirely and finally to fall away. Zwinglianism
had been, however, somewhat on the wane since the
Consensus Tigurinus of 1549, when rationalism seemed
for a time to have bowed before the piety and the genius
of Calvin. Such were the parties from which Bishops had
to be chosen, and for the most part the preference was
given to the Frankfort and Zurich exiles who adopted the
more moderate position, and were likely to give less trouble
to the civil power.

We can thus perceive what was the doctrinal position of the Elizabethan Hierarchy, how far removed
they were from the thoughts of modern High Churchmen. Cheney, the former tutor of Campion, who
became Bishop of Gloucester, was the only one
among them who was so much as a Lutheran in his
views, and his Lutheranism brought him into trouble.
That such people had no conception of anything
Divine or sacramental in their office goes without
saying :

As to the belief in an Apostolical succession in the Episcopate, it is not to be found in any of the writings of the Elizabethan Bishops. Unmistakable evidence of this as regards Bishop Jewel of Salisbury exists in his correspondence with Archbishop Parker with regard to the interference of Lancaster, Archbishop-elect of Armagh, in ordaining priests in his diocese. It seems that Lancaster had taken upon himself to admit divers persons into holy orders, and amongst them one whom Jewel had for eight years, for what appeared to himself good reasons, refused to ordain. He makes no complaint of the illegality, much less of the invalidity of the act, but only of the indiscretion of the Archbishop-elect. Now, this letter is dated April 26th, 1568, and June 13th in the same year Lancaster was consecrated by the Archbishop of Dublin and the Bishops of Meath and Kildare. If he is the same person who had held the see of Kildare 1550–4, he must either have acted as Bishop without being consecrated, or else he underwent a second consecration in 1568. There is nothing more wonderful in the whole history of the Church in England at a time when probably not a single Bishop was to be found who believed in his own Divine commission or in the efficacy of the sacraments, when almost without exception they were indifferent to any other considerations than that of promotion and the providing for their own families.

Mr. Pocock does not discuss the bearing of this general disbelief in the sacramental character of Holy Orders on the validity of the Orders conferred. Personally he would evidently say that it had none ; that by God's singular providence a sufficient rite had been administered by prelates sufficiently qualified and that validity was therefore happily secured. The *Guardian* (Nov. 9th) also takes this line, in a leader on Mr. Gilbert Child's article in the November *Contemporary*. It is there maintained that the intention of the minister being acknowledged even by (Roman) Catholics to be merely the intention to do whatever our Lord may have intended by the ceremony, no argument against the Elizabethan Orders can be raised on this ground. It would be beside our purpose to enter adequately into this question, but we would remark by the way that an equivocation lurks in this representation of the Catholic doctrine. When the form employed is free of ambiguity, and has its own certain sense attached to it by the Church which sanctions it, the intention above stated is enough, and there may consequently be valid administration even when there are heretical views as to the meaning of the form in the mind of the officiating minister. But when the form employed is ambiguous, still more when the ambiguity is determined in an heretical sense by the authorities who draw it up, an heretical acceptation of its meaning in the mind of the officiating minister can render his act invalid. This is only according to the ordinary laws of speech. When words are plain we go by their plain meaning ; when they are ambiguous, we look to the mind of the speaker to determine which of the possible senses comprised within the ambiguity is intended. Now the form of ordination used under Elizabeth was at the least ambiguous. When compared with the Catholic ordinals in previous use, we see that it had been altered in such a way as to lend itself to the Zwinglian doctrine, according to which the essence of ordination lies in appointment by public authority to minister in the congregation, and the religious rite is merely a ceremonious mode of conferring the appointment.[1] Such a rite in the hands of men with views like

---

[1] Cf. Art. xxiii., which contains a similar studied ambiguity.

these Elizabethan clergy is held by us to be clearly invalid.[1]

To return from this digression. Other sacraments fared as ill as Orders. Extreme Unction disappeared for ever : and Confirmation was lightly regarded.

As regards the rite of confirmation, there seems every reason to believe that it was seldom administered even in the early days of Elizabeth. We know for certain that it was much neglected towards the end of the sixteenth century. The early age at which it had been usual to administer it probably formed an excuse for its gradual disuse, for it is not likely that any Bishop in the reign of Elizabeth believed in it as anything else but a ratification of the baptismal promises on the part of the recipient of the rite.

Such is Mr. Pocock's account of the Bishops. Of the inferior clergy he has as unpleasant a tale to tell. The Church Defence doctrine is that the Elizabethan changes were generally felt to be both necessary and becoming, even by the Catholics, who accordingly found little difficulty in conforming : that the number of the clergy who stood out and started the " Roman schism" in the country fell short of two hundred. Catholic writers have often shown the untenability of this view. But in vain : it is still preached up and down the country, and even Archbishops have not refused to smile upon it. Will they now abandon this unhistorical contention, in view of Mr. Pocock's testimony against it ?

What is commonly affirmed that all the clergy conformed to the new order with the exception of about 200 cannot possibly be true. That number nearly represents the number of Bishops, Deans, Archdeacons, Canons of

[1] Cf. Estcourt, *Anglican Orders*, cc. iv. v.

Cathedrals, Heads of Houses, and Fellows of Colleges at Oxford and Cambridge who are known to have refused to adopt the new service of the Prayer-book, which, it must not be forgotten, was materially different from that which is in use now. And the great number of ordinations which took place in the early years of Elizabeth's reign, and the number of priests and deacons ordained from time to time, prove that there must have been a large number of vacancies in the parsonages of the country. It is impossible that the number should have been so small as 192, as thirty-four years later, in the year 1602, the number of Roman priests who were living peaceably and giving no trouble to the authorities is spoken of as being considerable. The survivors of persons who were priests in 1558 could have been counted on the fingers in 1602 if there had been, as has been alleged, only 192 at the earlier date. Moreover, we know that in many dioceses a large proportion of the parishes were not served at all. Again, in the first year of Grindal's episcopate many of the clergy had obtained licence to live beyond seas, upon what was called misliking of religion, and their places were partially filled by thirty different ordinations which he held, at which he admitted 160 deacons and nearly as many priests to holy orders, a much larger number than can be accounted for by the deaths of incumbents or curates. . . . Archbishop Parker, too, held five ordinations at Lambeth in less than three months after his consecration, at the last of which alone there were 155 priests and deacons ordered. The same conclusion comes out from the information given, January 24, 1561, by the Bishop of Ely—viz., that of the 152 churches in his diocese only 52 were properly served, there being 34 that had neither rectors nor vicars. It appears also that in the diocese of Norwich about half of the eight or nine hundred parishes had no rector or vicar, though the want was in some places supplied by a curate. And in the year 1565, so great was the destitution that the returns from about half the dioceses show that nearly a thousand parishes were wholly without spiritual superintendence. In the diocese of Lincoln there were about 100 vacant cures, whereas in two Welsh dioceses

there were none.   Is it conceivable that here and in the
Isle of Man, where there could scarcely have been services
in the vernacular, there being no translations of either Bible
or Prayer-book, the older clergy should have continued
their ministrations for a time after the old fashion?   About
the same time Parkhurst, Bishop of Norwich, says of his
1,200 churches 430 were vacant.   If this is not sufficient
to prove that the clergy did not all conform, what is the
meaning of Jewel's observation in his letter to Peter Martyr,
August 1, 1559? "Now that religion is everywhere changed
the Mass priests absent themselves altogether from public
worship, as if it were the greatest impiety to have anything
in common with the people of God." (*Zurich Letters*, i. p. 39.)

If the clergy were so largely Catholic, we can
assume that the laity were similarly disposed towards
the old faith : and we should anticipate the same
distinction among them of a smaller number remaining
true to their faith at all costs, and a large majority
yielding outward conformity out of deference to the
times, while they preserved their Catholicism in secret·
And so it was.   We have Mr. Brewer's well-known
testimony that not till late in her reign would it have
been safe for Elizabeth to take a religious census
of the nation.   Mr. Pocock cites a passage from an
interesting account of the diocese of Chichester in
1569, which tells in the same direction.

In many churches they have no sermons, not one in
seven years, and some not one in twelve years.   Few
churches have their quarter sermons according to the
Queen's injunctions.   In Boxgrave there is a very fair
church and therein is neither parson, vicar, nor curate, but
a sorry reader.   In the deanery of Medhurst there are some
beneficed men which did preach in Queen Mary's days and
now they do not, nor will not, and yet keep their livings.
Others are fostered in gentlemen's houses, and some betwixt
Surrey and Hampshire, and are hindrances of true religion,

and do not minister. Others come not at their parish church, nor receive the Holy Communion at Easter: but at that time get them out of the country until that feast be passed. In the church of Arundel certain altars do stand yet to the offence of the godly. They have yet in many places images hidden and other Popish ornaments ready to set up the Mass again within twenty-four hours' warning. In the town of Battle when a preacher doth speak anything against the Pope's doctrine, they will not abide, but get them out of the church. In many places the people cannot yet say their Commandments, and in some not the articles of their belief. In the Cathedral Church of Chichester there be very few preachers resident; of thirty-one Prebendaries scarcely four or five. Few of the aldermen of Chichester be of a good religion, but are vehemently suspected to favour the Pope's doctrine, and yet they be Justices of the Peace.

The number of those who conformed was very considerable, and we should be far from denying it. Martyrs are seldom other than a small minority, and that was an age of which fortitude was far from being a characteristic. Still Mr. Pocock is with us in judging that their conformity was outward only.

The apparent acquiescence of many was, perhaps, less due to an approval of the changes than to the hope they entertained that either they might be only temporary or that they might perhaps eventually be sanctioned by the Pope. Many gradually dropped off as such hopes began to appear illusory, and this in part accounts for the gradual increase of the Roman party all over the country.

This widespread refusal to conform and still more general dislike of the new doctrines caused great difficulty to the Crown and the Bishops. What had happened two centuries previously repeated itself, though without the same excuse. Then the Black

Death had almost denuded the country of its clergy, and necessitated the recruiting of their ranks by persons of no proper education or preparation. The Reformation itself was but the distant consequence of the evil. Now a still direr pestilence had passed over the country, and left the flock without shepherds to feed it. And those who had done the deed must needs have recourse again to the ranks of the un-educated and unprepared to supply their own con-ception of the shepherd's office. Grindal's experience at London, in the first ordination he held, is mentioned by Mr. Pocock as a typical case. " Few of his candi-dates had a University or any other education, most of these being tradesmen or mechanics of mature age, many being over forty, one of fifty, and another of sixty." And, again, we read :

In February, 1585, at an interview between the Queen in Council and some of the Bishops, Burleigh accused them of making many rude and unlearned ministers, instancing particularly Overton, Bishop of Coventry and Lichfield, who made seventy ministers in one day, some shoemakers and other craftsmen, to which the reply of the Bishop of Rochester was that if they would have none but learned ministers admitted, and he had himself never ordained more than three at once, better livings must be provided for them, and the Archbishop of Canterbury added that it was impossible for the realm to provide learned preachers enough for the thirteen thousand parishes. To this the Queen rejoined with an oath that what she wanted was not learned men, who were not to be found, but honest, sober, and wise men, and such as can read the Scriptures and homilies unto the people.

And yet after all " many churches were served by laymen : " for " the Bishops were at their wits' ends to find men to fill the vacant ones."

These clergy of the second order outran their superiors in their Protestant proclivities. The Bishops were Zwinglian. The clergy were Calvinistic.

Calvinism, which subsequently overran the whole Church, was the dominant creed even at the very beginning of the reign of Elizabeth. For though Elizabeth's first appointed Bishops were of the Zwinglian rather than of the Calvinistic school, the laity, as well as the majority of the clergy who had fallen in with the new learning, were for the most part Calvinists, the tenets of the French Reformer having already been extensively adopted, though their great development in the country belongs to a later date.

Calvinism was firmly enthroned at the Universities. Thus the Cambridge authorities in 1581, returning thanks to Beza, who had presented them the famous Codex D of the Bible, say: "We assure you that, saving the unique position which we recognize in Holy Scripture, there are no writers of any age whose works we esteem of higher value than those of that remarkable man, John Calvin, or your own." And at Oxford, in 1579, a statute was passed: "That the younger members of the University should be instructed either in Calvin's or in the Heidelberg Catechism, and that they should afterwards read the works of the Swiss divine, Bullinger, who had succeeded Zwingli as a teacher at Zurich, and the Institutes of Calvin." Another cause and witness of the prevalence of Calvinism was the popularity of the Geneva Bible—the *Breeches* Bible, as it is usually called. This was a translation made at Geneva by the English Calvinists "fortified with marginal notes, short and terse and much to the point, intermixed with a good deal of Calvinistic misinterpretation;"

and "the form of belief fostered by these notes can scarcely be said to have expired till the present century, if indeed it does not still survive here and there among members of the Church of England." This version was hateful to the Queen, and also to Parker and the Bishops, who with an exception or two were Zwinglians. These tried to suppress it, but in vain. It was the version most used in churches, and one hundred and forty editions of it were printed before it was effectually suppressed a century later on by Laud. When Grindal, who had Calvinistic tendencies, succeeded Parker in the Primacy, this Genevan Bible began to be printed in England, and a Calvinistic Catechism of a pronounced character was inserted between the two Testaments.

We naturally inquire in what manner these new ministers, so uncultivated and fanatical, discharged their official duties, and what was the general effect on the religious worship of the country. · Mr. Pocock meets our desires with several passages.

Pilkington, Bishop of Durham, had attributed the burning of St. Paul's Cathedral to a judgment of God on the "walkings, talkings, chidings, fightings which had been going on in the church, and that especially in time of Divine Service." And the same Bishop, not in the impassioned language of a sermon, but in a sober piece of writing, says :

"Come into a church the Sabbath day, and ye shall see but few, though there be a sermon, but the ale-house is ever full. Woe worth the Papist therefore, in this kingdom, for they be earnest, zealous, and painful in their doings. . . . A Popish summoner, spy, or promoter will drive more to a church with a word, to hear a Latin Mass, than seven preachers will bring in a week's preaching to hear a godly sermon. O what a condemnation shall this be, to see the wicked so diligent and earnest in their doings to set up anti-Christ, and Christian rulers and officers of all sorts having the whip of correction in their hands by God's law, and the Princes have so coldly behaved themselves in setting up the kingdom of Christ, that neither they give good examples themselves in diligent praying, and resorting to the church, nor, by the whip of discipline, drive others thitherward."

This was in the earlier part of Elizabeth's reign. Later on we have a report sent to the Council by the Ecclesiastical Commissioners regarding the condition of the counties of Cheshire and Lancashire. They say that:

Small reformation has been made as may appear by the emptiness of the churches on Sundays and festivals, and the multitude of bastards and drunkards. Preachers are few; most parsons unlearned, and those that are learned non-resident, divers unlearned persons being daily admitted by the Bishops to rich benefices. Many, even Justices and coroners, have never communicated for more than thirty years. The people so swarm in the streets and ale-houses during service-time that in many churches there is only the curate and the clerk, and open markets are kept during service-time. Cock-fights and other unlawful games are tolerated on Sunday during Divine Service, and Justices of the Peace and Ecclesiastical Commissioners are often present.

And a century later Mr. Pocock thus presents us with the picture of the state of affairs which Laud was endeavouring to remedy.

The account of the state of things which the Archbishop [Laud] set himself to remedy would simply be incredible were it not attested by hundreds of contemporary documents, which Protestant historians have found it convenient to pass over in silence, but which can no longer be ignored since they have been analyzed and their contents calendared in the volumes of State Papers issued under the authority of the Master of the Rolls.

From these documents it appears that the ordinary matins and evensong, the only service used on Sunday in the churches, was said by the minister, who, in most cases, wore no surplice and curtailed the prayers in various ways, to make room for the sermon, if indeed he did not omit them altogether. The congregation sat, the men wearing their hats or not, as it suited their convenience, the Communion-table, standing in the body of the church, being made the receptacle for such hats and clothes as were not worn, and frequently used as a seat by any one who was not accommodated with a pew. Sometimes a clergyman will defend his practice by alleging that he has not worn a surplice for thirty years; and it is plain that its disuse had been gradually increasing as the Puritan ministers succeeded to the places of such priests as had conformed at the beginning of the reign of Elizabeth. During the time that Laud had held the bishopric of London he had exerted all his influence to put down these irregularities, but he was sadly hampered by the class of Bishops with whom he had to deal, so great was their ignorance and worldliness. Wright, Bishop of Bristol, we must suppose was one of the better sort, for in 1632 Laud got him promoted to Lichfield and Coventry. Yet even he allowed the singing men of his Cathedral to act as if they were priests in laying hands on the clergy ordained by him, and he apologized to Archbishop Harsnet of York and Laud of London for having allowed this of very necessity, the Dean and Chapter not being available for the purpose.

And there were worse things even than these.

The Vicar-General of Lincoln says, in his Visitation of the diocese, September 19, 1634, that many Prebendaries had never seen the church, that ale-houses, hounds, and swine were kept in the churchyard very offensively : that at Louth the clergy and laity were much given to drunkenness, the goodly church of Boston much decayed, whilst at Huntingdon the vicar of Odell never used the surplice or the sign of the Cross at Baptism, and at Alesbury the clergy performed clandestine marriages with gloves and masks on. Neither are these at all exceptional cases. Even as late as October, 1637, we find the churchwardens of the parish of Knotting, in Bedfordshire, charged before the Official Commissary of the Archdeacon with having allowed for the last three years cock-fighting to go on in the chancel of the church, the minister of the church, with his sons, being present and enjoying the sport.

When we read of all this we are prone to ask if Norwich did not deserve congratulations rather than condolences, when, as its new Bishop reported in 1635, "in all the thirty-two churches in the city of Norwich there was not one in which there was any morning service or sermon."

Religious decadence like this could hardly fail to bring moral decadence along with it, and this is the description which Mr. Pocock gives of the reign of Elizabeth :

And now the question may fairly be asked, What was the effect of this kind of teaching upon the nation at large, or at least, whether directly consequent or not upon the religious teaching in the churches, what was the general standard of religion and morality in the country? This question can be approximately answered by reference to contemporary sermons and diaries and the State Papers of the period. The account given by Bristowe in his *Motives to the Catholic Faith*, published in 1575, must of course be looked on with some suspicion. After enumerating the results of Calvinistic teaching of the last sixteen years, he says he need not refer to the testimonies of Luther and Erasmus, because the deterioration of morals was most evident in our own country :

"Never was less humility and charity, never more whoredom and perjury, so that nothing is to be looked for but universal destruction and utter desolation."

He concludes his account as follows :

"And of all most ill, most wicked, and therefore everywhere most despised, most scorned, the superintendents and ministers themselves, that if a book should be made of their several behaviours, as it would presently be confessed, so would it of posterity be scarcely believed."

Some deduction has also to be made from the impassioned invectives of Protestant preachers such as the French convert John Veron, who says that he laments that many who were a match if they go to plain Scripture with any doctor of the Papist part, lived so abominably :

"Whoredom, drunkenness, and gluttony unto them is but sport and pastime. They backbite, they slander, they chide, and strive. Among them there is no modesty, no soberness, no temperancy. All deceit, all craft, all subtlety, and falsehood reigneth among them. Whereas if ye hear them dispute and reason of the Scriptures and Word of God, ye will think that they be very angels that be come down from Heaven. So godly they talk. So godly they speak."

Such is the uniform testimony of the Reformers even in the reign of Edward VI. The witness given by Bradford, perhaps the most earnest and sincere of all the prominent members of the Protestant party, is too well known to need repetition here ; and the character of the man renders it entirely trustworthy. The State Papers of the reign of Elizabeth bear the same testimony. On February 18, 1560, Horne, Dean of Durham, complains of the licentious manners of the people. In 1561 Scory, Bishop of Hereford, writing to Cecil, says that his Cathedral is a very nursery of blasphemy, whoredom, pride, superstition, and ignorance. The scandal had reached the Archbishop's ears, for in the following year he and the Bishop of London petitioned Cecil to get the Queen to authorize the Bishop to hold a Visitation of the Cathedral from time to time, "Whereby that church shall be purged of many enormities and God's glory greatly advanced." The Visitations, however, produced but little fruit, for twenty years later in a letter addressed to the Bishop the writer complains of the contrast between the listlessness of the service and the disregard of the truth of the Gospel in his day, and the fervour of the frequent services and the zeal and devotion which he could himself remember in the dark days of Queen Mary.

In the same year Bishop Best of Carlisle reports the priests of his diocese to be wicked imps of anti-Christ, false and subtle; and three years later Bishop Pilkington of Durham gives a most lamentable account, of the northern counties, the wickedness of which he attributes to the neglect of their dioceses by the Bishops of Chester and Man.

We have confined ourselves almost exclusively in this article to citations from Mr. Pocock. It would have been possible to confirm and supplement what he tells us from other sources, but, considering his high authority, it has seemed better to leave his statement as it stands, rather than to mix it up with facts, which, however true in themselves, might seem doubtful to an Anglican reader as coming from a suspected source.

Perhaps it may be pleaded in reply to this formidable indictment that the responsibility for the condition of things ought not to be laid exclusively on the backs of the Elizabethan clergy; that the same dissolution of morals and irreligious spirit had existed in the years immediately antecedent to the Reformation, and that such an Augean stable necessarily took a long time to cleanse.

We are far from denying that there was much demoralization to the earlier period referred to. On the contrary, we would trace to its existence the very possibility of the Reformation. Dom Gasquet, when commenting on the unsatisfactory condition of the clergy at the time when Henry VIII. began his evil course, quotes very appropriately a passage from Bellarmine :

I declare that false teaching, heresy, the falling away of so many peoples and kingdoms from the true faith, in fine all the calamities, wars, tumults, and seditions of these distressing times, take their source from no other cause than because pastors, and the other priests of the Lord sought Christ, not for Christ's sake, but that they might eat His bread. For some years before the Lutheran and Calvinistic heresy, as those testify who were then living, there was in ecclesiastical judgments hardly any severity, in morals no discipline, in sacred learning no teaching, towards holy things no reverence. The renowned glory of the clergy and sacred orders had perished ; priests were despised, laughed at by the people, and lay under grave and constant infamy.[1]

But the Anglicanism of Elizabeth and her successors, instead of effecting any amelioration in the country, made things much worse than before. Mr. Pocock, in a passage quoted above, has referred in illustration of this to a letter written about 1583 or 1584, to Scory, from his cathedral city of Hereford, by one whose sympathies were all on the Protestant side. Dom Gasquet has introduced this letter into the first chapter of his book on Edward VI. and the Book of Common Prayer, and it is worth extracting :

Right honourable and reverend Father, my bounden duty always remembered. May it please your lordship to be advised or put in memory that in the dark days of Queen Mary the Dean then and clergy of your Cathedral Church of Hereford, did orderly observe their superstitious orders and were present thereat continually, except certain days of license which are called days of jubilee, and did preach their superstitious dregs not only but also did in their outward living keep great hospitality, for every night

---

[1] *Concio de Dom.* Lætare.   Ap. Gasquet, *Monasteries*, i. p. 20.

at midnight they with the whole vicars choral would rise to
Matins, and especially the domydary for the week being,
would be first there at five o'clock in the morning, at
St. Nicholas Mass, then at other Masses at certain altars,
then at eight of the clock our Lady's Mass was solemnly
said, then at nine the Prime and None, then the High
Mass was in saying until it was eleven of the clock, besides
every man must have said his own private Mass at some
one altar or other daily. Then after dinner to evensong
until five o'clock, in which time of service a number of
tapers were burning every day and there was great incensing
at the high altar daily to their idols and there was a lamp
burning day and night continually before their gods, and
every Sabbath-day and festival-days St. Thomas' bell should
ring to procession, and then the Dean would send his
somner to warn the mayor of the procession, and then
upon the somner's warning the mayor would send the
serjeants to the parish churches, every man in his ward to
the aldermen, then the aldermen would cause the parish
priest to command all the free men to attend on the mayor
to the procession and sermon, or lecture (if) for want of a
sermon there should be a lecture in the chapter-house every
Sabbath and holy day notwithstanding they were at High
Mass in the choir. So zealous and diligent were the
temporality then in observing those dregs of the clergy.
Then the Dean and clergy would come so orderly to
church with such a godly show of humbleness and in
keeping such hospitality that it did allure the people to
what order they would request them. This is true for I
did see and know it, but then did I as a child and knew
not the truth and then such heavy burdens were but light,
but now in these joyful days of light how heavy is it
amongst a number of us to come two hours in the day to
serve the true God, the everlasting King of all glory, but
too lamentable to think on it, and much more grievous to
him that did see the blind zeal in darkness so observed, and
now in the true light and pathway to salvation neglected.
Then were these tapers and lamps greatly plentiful with
incensing to idols most costly even in the clearest day of
summer, and now not scarce one little candle is allowed

or maintained to read a chapter in the dark evening in the choir. And as for resorting to hear the truth of the Gospel it is little regarded. I will not nor dare say in those that reap the fruits thereof, although I speak the truth, notwithstanding the visitation.

Had the change been from error to truth, it should have been attended with a marked improvement in religious fervour and morals: just as has invariably been the result when any Catholic reformers, like St. Francis and St. Dominic, or like St. Ignatius, have risen up and warred against the sinfulness of their age. Since the transition was from bad to much worse, and we have a direct causal connection between the increased evil and the "new learning," we can only apply the principle, " By their fruits you shall know them."

It would be unjust in itself and contrary to our own wishes not to notice the other side of Mr. Pocock's picture. The purpose of his articles is not merely to show up the state of religion under Elizabeth and James as quite unworthy of our sympathy, but to bring into prominence the work of Laud in effecting an improvement. It was then that High Church ideas were first originated, and it was natural that the attempt should be made to graft these on the organization which these strivers after better things found in existence among them. It was over this that Laud laboured during the thirty years of his episcopate, with success which Mr. Pocock judges considerable, and though the Rebellion cut short his life and interrupted his work, since Juxon and Sheldon, Gunning, Wren, and others who took it up again after the Restoration, were men of his formation, he may justly be credited with the paternity of their labours and results. In some sense also Mr. Pocock seems to be right in attributing to them "the late development (of the recovery at the Restoration) of which, after two hundred and thirty years of a wonderfully chequered history, we are in the present enjoyment of." That is to say, although the Anglican Church relapsed into its earlier condition of religious apathy and neglect, and had its fits of Puritan revivalism, till close on our own times, and although, on the other hand, the ideas now in favour with the High Church party go far beyond any that can be found in the works of the Caroline divines, still the ideas generated under Laud and his more immediate successors have persisted, and have been among the true causes of the modern movement.

We have said that we have no wish to ignore this Laudian reformation, but rather every wish to view it sympathetically. It was a movement towards, not away from, Catholic truth as we understand it ; and it has always seemed to us a matter for great regret that High Churchmen should regard us, rather than the Puritan party, as the objects of their special doctrinal antipathy ; and matter for still greater regret that Catholics should have reacted on this hostility of certain Anglicans towards them by employing bitter language and indulging at times (at times only) in harsh feelings. There is no doubt that men like Dr. Littledale in the past, and a few others who might be named in the present, by their gross unfairness and manifest insincerity are responsible for a great deal of this irritation among us. But why must we take these men as typical of the entire party?   Cannot we remember other names besides theirs, and do we not often meet in private life with Anglicans who are equally conspicuous for their fairness and friendliness?   If there is a *Church Times* with a gallery that it can play to, is there not also a *Guardian*, which is always fair and courteous?   And if we thus admonish ourselves, may we not appeal also to all truth-loving Anglicans to meet us in the same spirit?   It is at all events in this spirit that we invite attention to Mr. Pocock's picture of the religious collapse under Elizabeth and James ; that is to say, not in the way of exultation over the discomfiture of an Anglican illusion, but rather in the way of hope that a better understanding between us may be promoted.   Modern High Churchmen, unless they go out of their way for the purpose, are not committed to the defence of all this revolting lawlessness which Mr. Pocock describes.   They are quite entitled to detest it all as a deplorable calamity, and to attach themselves in preference to the real amelioration dating from Laud.   But then it follows that the movement to which they belong represents not a departure from the Catholic ideal, as it is understood by all others save themselves, but an approximation towards it.   And if it is such, is it not becoming that, like many of the older Tractarians, they should regard us not as their special foes, but rather as persons with whose religious position they can have more sympathy than with any other?

They complain, we know, of our exclusiveness as being so uncharitable, and ask how it is possible to sympathize with a position which meets you only with uncharitableness. There is something plausible in this way of stating the case, and perhaps it is not surprising that minds should be captivated by it. But we would ask any Anglican reader of these pages to reflect whether after all to be exclusive in the matter of religious belief is necessarily to be uncharitable. The Anglican conception of the Catholic Church considerably enlarges its borders, but are not Anglicans quite as exclusive as ourselves in their attitude towards those who lie outside the Church as they conceive it? And yet, do they feel themselves to be uncharitable in this exclusiveness, and not rather to be showing the truest charity when they exhort Dissenters to give a candid hearing to their arguments, and hope to gather them into their communion? Now, this is just our position towards all others, Anglicans included. We have confidence in the truth of our position, which involves that momentous benefits to the human race are to be found only in communion with the Holy See: and we accordingly are impelled to lay the grounds of our conviction before our brethren without and beseech them to give a candid hearing. It is charity which impels us, not any wretched party feeling: the desire that friends should share the good things of truth along with us, not that we should score a triumph over adversaries. Is there anything unsympathetic in an attitude like this?

And if there is nothing in our personal bearing to repel friendliness, may we not recur to our former point and suggest that the moral of such a lesson as Mr. Pocock has to teach us is to attract a candid and sympathetic attention to the claims of our position?

The High Church movement, from its commencement under Laud, has been a progressive abandonment of the Protestant creed and return to that of the Catholic Church. Then why such hostility to the articles of that creed which still remain ungrasped, and towards the communion in which they find their fullest realization? Would it not at least be desirable to give them a fair study, and to seek help in understanding them from those who are able to give it, rather than from those who have a direct interest in misrepresentation.

The Faith of the Ancient English Church concerning the Blessed Virgin Mary.

We are indebted for the following tract to the Rev. T. E. Bridgett, C.SS.R., who has kindly allowed us to compile it from his work, entitled "Our Lady's Dowry."

"THE contemplation of the great mystery of the Incarnation," wrote Thomas Arundel, Archbishop of Canterbury, in 1399, "has drawn all Christian nations to venerate her from whom came the first beginnings of our Redemption. But we English, being the servants of her special inheritance and her own Dowry, as we are commonly called, ought to surpass others in the fervour of our praises and devotions."

Some have thought that this title arose from an act of donation or consecration, made by King Richard II., but, be this as it may, it is clear from the testimony of the highest ecclesiastical authority in England, making public appeal to well-known fact, that in the 14th century England was commonly called, throughout Europe, Our Lady's Dowry.

There are some who think that this title is one of England's greatest glories. There are others who reckon it to her disgrace. It is not my intention in the following pages to be the apologist of our forefathers, but rather to be the historian, simply putting on record evidence of their faith and devotion to our Blessed Lady. Yet I feel that I can hardly enter upon the subject with any profit to Protestant readers without giving, by way of preface, some few words of explanation and defence.

The veneration paid by Catholics to our Blessed Lady is technically called *hyperdulia*, as being greater in degree than the honour given to other saints or to angels (*dulia*), and is distinguished from the worship given exclusively to God *(latria)*. Many Protestants seem to suspect that these are distinctions *invented* by Catholics in self-defence: and especially that *hyperdulia* must be, even in the Catholic view, a veneration but one step removed from divine. It is, of course, the highest veneration after that of God. And yet, so far is it from encroaching on divine worship, that I may truly say that though all the honours paid to the saints tend to God's glory, yet *hyperdulia* gives to God incomparably more glory than simple *dulia*, for the reason that it exalts the Majesty of God in a more striking manner. I will try to explain this by examining its nature.

The Blessed Virgin Mary is venerated from a double point of view—in her relation as a saint to the God Who is her beginning and her end, and in her special relation to the Incarnation, and through the Incarnation to each of the Three Divine Persons. I may say she is venerated as the Queen of the Saints, and as Mother of God. It is as Queen of Saints I will now consider her, and the honour we pay to her. Let us first get an accurate notion of sanctity, and then we shall comprehend what is meant by *dulia* and by *hyperdulia*.

There are many attributes of God which we are bound to imitate: "Be ye imitators of God, as most dear children." There are some which we are forbidden to copy: "Revenge not yourselves, for it is written, 'Vengeance is Mine.'" Now that which is above all—inimitable and incommunicable—is the independence of God. God is His own beginning, His own end, His own rule. Yet this is the very attribute of God which we are tempted to imitate; and sin is nothing else but this imitation—man taking himself and his inclinations for his rule, and making himself his end. "You shall be as gods, knowing good and evil."

On the other hand, the renunciation of this spurious imitating of God, the refusal to live for self, the constant taking of the mind and will of God for the rule of thought, and will, and act, the living for God only,—this is sanctity.

What, then, is the divine excellence which is the object

of supreme worship? .It is an infinite excellence, which is independent and exists for itself.

What is the excellence called sanctity, which is the object of inferior worship? It is especially dependence, submission.

Though the saint is like God, yet the distinctive character of his sanctity is unlikeness to God in that of which God is jealous; and the more perfect he is in sanctity, the more perfect is this opposition, as I have just explained.

What then is *hyperdulia?* It is the recognition that the Blessed Virgin, just because she copied God most perfectly, usurped nothing of His incommunicable prerogative of independence; that she is highest because lowliest; that she is deserving of the highest honour after what is Divine, because she was most perfectly what a creature should be.

There is no paradox in all this. When a servant is praised in his quality of servant, it is for virtues the very opposite to those praised in the master in his quality of master. There may be many points of likeness between them as men, but the ideas of master or servant exclude each other.

But in the saints this opposition which I have pointed out, this quality of dependence opposed to God's independence, does not merely affect some part of their lives—it enters into every act. It is the very character of Christian virtue, that it is done for God. Humility is not merely one virtue among many, it is of the essence of every virtue. If we praise the faith of a saint, we indicate the humility of his mind, captivating every thought into submission to the revealed mind of God. If we praise his hope, we mean that his heart was lowly, not trusting in itself, but in the strength of Him in Whom it could do all things. His love is the humility of His will, subject in all things to the will of God, and making the infinite perfections of God all its good. And so with other virtues.

The theory of *dulia* and *hyperdulia* and *latria* may be somewhat subtle, but so is the theory of walking, while the practice is most simple.

Listen to a simple English woman writing five

hundred years ago. Mother Juliana was an Anchorite of Norwich who lived in the reign of Edward III. She has left a book of revelations in one of which she writes: "Wisdom and Truth made our Lady Mary to behold her God so great, so high, so mighty, and so good: This greatness and this nobility of her beholding of God fulfilled her of reverend dread, and with this she saw herself so little, and so low, so simple and so poor in regard of her God, that this reverend dread fulfilled her of meekness. And thus by this ground she was fulfilled of grace and all manner of virtues and *passeth all creatures.*"

With Protestants then, who know nothing practically of the Invocation of Saints, and who approach the subject with their minds warped by false representations, or at least with the vague idea of finding something like what is familiar to them in heathen worship as the greater and the lesser gods, it is a natural error to suppose that the abolition of prayer to the saints would throw into sharper prominence the prayers addressed to God. In their minds the saints are like so many hills which rear their heads around the mountain of God. To exalt the hill is to make a rival to the mountain and to obscure the view of it. But with Catholics, if God in His infinite, uncreated, independent excellence is a mountain, the saints are valleys at' its foot; and the deepest of these valleys, and that which by its very depth exalts the height of the mountain is the Blessed Virgin Mary.

St. John saw in his vision "a throne set in heaven, and upon the throne One sitting." (Apoc. 4) But also round about the throne were four and twenty seats, and upon the seats four and twenty ancients sitting, clothed in white garments and on their heads were crowns of gold. Now, according to the Protestant plan, it would have brought the throne of the Eternal into sharper prominence if the seats of the ancients had been removed and the golden crowns hidden away. But God had a far different plan of bringing His own throne into prominence. "The four and twenty ancients fell down before Him that sitteth on the throne and adored Him that liveth for ever and ever, and cast their crowns before the throne, saying: Thou art worthy, O Lord our God, to receive glory and honour and power, because Thou hast created all things and for Thy will they were and have been created."

So acts the Catholic Church in her Litany which gives so much offence to Protestants. Her saints are crowned indeed, and sit on thrones around the throne of God; but the Church, after imploring mercy (*miserere nobis*) from each of the Persons of the ever Blessed Trinity, turns to the saints, and with her *Ora pro nobis* begs them to fall before the throne of God, and, casting their crowns at His feet, help her to obtain mercy from Him Who liveth for ever and ever.

Catholics, however, it is said sometimes, do much more than this. The language in which they address our Lady is often very similar, if not actually identical in certain expressions with that which is used in praying to her Divine Son. They ask our Blessed Lady and the saints, not only to pray for them, but also to give them this or that temporal or spiritual blessing, to help or defend them,—in a word, to interfere actively in their behalf as though they were themselves possessed of power and could bestow gifts and blessings according to their own will independently of Almighty God. Such is the inference which a Protestant draws from the language of Catholic devotion; and he refuses to believe us when we tell him that the true meaning of that language is, that we beg the saints to move Almighty God to give us the things we ask for. Yet Holy Scripture, if he would but study it with more attention, would supply him with instances of the same use of language. Thus we read in IV. Kings ii., 9, 10, that Elias said to Eliseus, "*Ask what thou wilt have me to do for thee*, before I be taken away from thee: and Eliseus said: I beseech thee that in me may be thy double spirit. And he answered, Thou hast asked a hard thing, nevertheless, if thou see me when I am taken from thee thou shalt have what thou hast asked. But if thou see me not, thou shalt not have it." Eliseus here asked what Elias could not possibly give him of his own power, yet the latter promises that he shall have it on the fulfilment of a certain condition. Eliseus asked a petition of Elias which none but God could grant: so we too in like manner often call upon the saints to do what belongs only to the power of God. If the words of Eliseus do not attribute omnipotence to Elias, no more do our prayers ascribe omnipotence to the saints. Again, St. Paul exhorts St. Timothy to behave in a certain manner and gives him a solemn promise that "in doing this he shall both save himself and them that hear him." (1. Tim. iv. 16.) Yet nobody surely could ever misunderstand the Apostle's meaning, or accuse him of holding that Timothy could save both himself and his people without the help of God's grace. We are continually using the same kind of language in the ordinary affairs of life; for instance, we do not scruple to say to a physician who has been called in to advise in some desperate illness of a friend or relative: "You are our only hope." Or again, we hear it said of some eminent politician that in very difficult times he was the only hope of his country: yet in neither of these cases does any one dream of accusing the speaker of an intention to exclude the idea of Divine Providence over-ruling all, without whom the best human aid would be utterly useless. Such an expression therefore as "Thou art our only hope," addressed to our Blessed Lady in the devotions of a Catholic, means simply this, "Thou art our only hope of obtaining this from Almighty God. We have no confidence in ourselves, or our own worthiness or power, to obtain it without thy help."

And so in like manner, when the name of our Blessed Lady or any other saint is joined with the name of God in the same sentence, as for instance, "We put our trust in God and the saints," the word common to both is not necessarily applied to both in the same sense, and Catholics may fairly claim to be believed when they assert that they do not use it in the same sense. For here again we may refer our accusers to the language of Holy Scripture. Among the chief duties we owe to God are to believe in Him, to worship Him, to fear Him and to put our trust in Him. We cannot render these duties to another in the same way and with the same intention as we render them to God, without committing the heinous sin of idolatry. Nevertheless, it is written in the Book of Exodus (14. 31) that "the people believed the Lord and His servant Moses." And in another place (1 Paralip. xxix. 20) "All the congregation bowed down their heads and worshipped the Lord and the King;" and again (Judges vii. 20) "they cried, the sword of the Lord and of Gedeon." And (I. Kings xii. 18) "All the people greatly feared the Lord and Samuel."

In all these instances the same word is used in reference to God and to His servants; yet in a lower sense in the one case than it is in the other. The people plainly did not worship the king in the same way in which they worshipped God; nor could they have cried, "The sword of Gedeon" in the same sense and with the same confidence with which they exclaimed "the sword of the Lord." Indeed, they had confidence in the sword of Gedeon only because it was the sword of the Lord in Gedeon's hands. They worshipped the king because he was the Lord's anointed. They believed Moses because he was the Lord's representative and was invested with His authority. They feared Samuel because he was the Lord's minister. Thus the honour, the fear and the worship which they paid to the servants of the Lord really terminated in the Lord Himself. Why may not the language of Catholic devotion be understood in the same way?

But let us look into one of the passages we have quoted a little more closely, for it contains much to our purpose. It was when God had worked a miracle to vindicate the integrity of His servant Samuel that we read : "That all the people greatly feared the Lord and Samuel." God, at the petition of the prophet, had suddenly sent thunder and rain in the midst of the wheat harvest, that the people might know and see that they had done a great evil in the sight of the Lord in desiring a king over them. "And all the people said to Samuel: pray for thy servants to the Lord thy God, that we may not die. . . . And Samuel said: Fear not; you have done all this evil; but yet depart not from following the Lord, but serve the Lord with all your heart, and turn not aside after vain things, which shall never profit you, nor deliver you because they are vain, and the Lord will not forsake His people for His great name's sake. . . . .

And far from me be this sin against the Lord, that I should cease to pray for you, and I will teach you the good and right way. Therefore fear the Lord, and serve Him in truth and with your whole heart, for you have seen the great works which He hath done among you. But if you still do wickedly, you shall perish."

This passage contains all the principles on which the cultus of the saints is founded. God glorified His faithful servant by a miracle, to teach the Israelites that the one thing great is submission to Himself. Those who witnessed the power of the saint with God "greatly feared the Lord and Samuel;" and the immediate result was consciousness of sin and fear of its chastisements. This was taken advantage of to bring about reformation of life by the promise of pardon, conditional on two things, the intercession of the saint and fidelity in God's service.

The worship of the saint then neither excludes nor encroaches on the worship of God. It is part of it, and a very important part. The people who greatly feared the Lord and Samuel, and who asked Samuel to pray for them to the Lord his God, practised the only kind of worship of the saints which ever found encouragement in the Catholic Church. And Samuel at least saw no contradiction between such worship and serving God in truth and with the whole heart.

But we have already said more than we intended in the way of explanation and defence of the Catholic doctrine and practice with regard to the honour paid to the saints. It is time that we should turn our attention to that which is the more immediate object of these pages, viz., to show that the ancient Church of this country did not in any way fall short of the practice of the rest of the Catholic Church in her devotion to the Blessed Mother of God as the Queen of all Saints.

Collier, one of the fairest Anglican writers of Church history, has said "that the practice of immediate address to the saints, as far as we can discover, did not prevail in England until the tenth century. At this time, in the Homily of the Assumption of the Blessed Virgin, there is a direct prayer to the Blessed Virgin to intercede for them." Collier would not, I think, have made an assertion which he did not believe to be true. Yet his statement is a striking example of the power of prejudice, to keep people from looking into facts. He found himself as an Anglican committed to the position that Invocation of Saints is "a fond thing vainly invented," and he liked to fix the time of its invention as late as possible. He did not feel the absurdity of supposing that a practice like that of invoking the saints was suddenly adopted without opposition—nay, without consciousness of innovation, by Christians whose vital principle was to make no change in the traditions of their fathers. He did not see the utter impossibility that the Saxons, ever travelling to Rome and back, should have differed in faith or practice from the nations of the Continent. He had a controversial position to maintain, and he seems to have turned his eyes from evidence, or else to have persuaded himself that the writings of St. Aldhelm and Alcuin, though admitted to be genuine by all scholars, were really forgeries of a later age.

However this may be, it is certain that much more evidence than was possessed in the time of Collier has since been brought to light: *e.g.*, a MS. in the University Library at Cambridge, called the Book of Cerne, which belonged to Ethelwald, Bishop of Sherbourne in 760, contains the following prayer to the Blessed Virgin,—a clear monument both of the faith and devotion of the Anglo-Saxons as far back as the days of Venerable Bede: "Holy Mother of God, Virgin ever blessed, glorious and noble, chaste and inviolate, O Mary immaculate, chosen and beloved of God, endowed with singular sanctity, worthy of all praise, thou who art the Advocate for the sins (peril) of the whole world; O listen, listen, listen to us, O Holy Mary. Pray for us, intercede for us, disdain not to help us. For we are confident and know for certain that thou canst obtain all thou willest from thy Son, Our Lord Jesus Christ, God Almighty, the King of Ages, Who liveth with the Father and the Holy Ghost for ever and ever. Amen."

Venerable Bede himself calls her "the Mother undefiled, the Virgin blessed beyond compare," and, in his discourse on the Visitation, manifests the exalted idea he had conceived of her sublime sanctity.

St. Aldhelm calls her "the garden enclosed," "the fountain sealed up," "the one dove amid the three-score queens," and many other titles culled from the mystic Canticle of Canticles.

The grave Alcuin writes verses in which he names her, "his sweet love, his honour, the great hope of his salvation, the Queen of Heaven, the flower of the field, the lily of the world, the fountain of life," and calls upon her to help her servant.

Ælfric (10th century) bids us "be mindful of how great dignity is the holy Maiden Mary, the Mother of Christ. She is blessed above all women; she is the heavenly Queen, and the comfort and support of all Christian men. Our old mother Eve shut to us the gate of heaven's kingdom; and the holy Mary opened it again to us, if we ourselves by evil works shut it not against us. Much may she obtain of her Child, if she be fervently thereof reminded. Let us, therefore, with great fervour pray to her, that she mediate for us to her own Child, who is both her Creator and her Son."

St. Aelred, two centuries later, commenting upon the words of Ezechiel (xliv. 1) as to "the gate which looks towards the east and was shut," says: "The most holy Mary is this eastern gate. For a gate which looks towards the east is the first to receive the rays of the sun. So the most Blessed Mary, who always looked towards the east, that is, towards the brightness of God, received the first rays or rather the whole blaze of light of that true Sun. This gate was shut and well guarded. The enemy could find no entrance, no little hole what-ever." And again: "She was the first of the whole human race who escaped the curse of our first parents."

St. Aelred writes also elsewhere as follows: "Our great care should be that we so conduct ourselves towards the Blessed Virgin as that she may be willing to undertake our cause with God. What then shall we do? What offering shall we present to her? Oh! that we could only pay her at least what we strictly owe! We owe her honour; we owe her service; we owe her love, and we owe her praise.

"1. First we owe her honour, since she is the Mother of our Lord; for he who does not honour the Mother, without any doubt dishonours the Son. Again the Scripture says: Honour thy father and thy mother, and is not Mary our Mother? Certainly she is most truly such. Through her we have been born, through her we are fed, through her we grow. Through her, I say, we have been born, not to the world, but to God; through her we are fed, not with natural milk, but with that of which the Apostle says: I have given you milk, not strong food (1 Cor. iii. 2); through her we grow, not in size of body, but in strength of soul. Let me explain this birth, this milk, this growth.

"We were once, as you believe and know, in death, in decay, in darkness, in misery. But through the blessed Mary, much better than through Eve, we have been born, because from her Christ was born. She is the Mother to us of life, of incorruption, and of light. Does not the Apostle say that " Christ is made to us by God wisdom and justice, sanctification and redemption?" (1. Cor. 1. 30). She then, being Mother of Christ, must be mother of our wisdom, of our justice, of our sanctification, of our redemption. Is she not then more our Mother than the Mother of our bodies? And does she not also feed us with milk? The Word of God, the Son of God, the Wisdom of God, is bread; He is solid food. Only strong ones, like the Angels, could eat of that food; we who are little ones, could not partake of food so solid; we were on earth and could not ascend to eat of that heavenly bread. What then has been done? That bread descended into the womb of the Blessed Virgin, and there was made milk, such milk as we could drink. Think of the Son of God in Mary's lap, in Mary's arms, at Mary's breast, and He has become milk to you. And this our good Mother provides for us. Again, think of Mary's chastity, her charity, her humility; and after her example grow in chastity, in charity, in humility; so imitate your Mother.

"2. But, secondly, we owe Mary service, since she is our Lady. The Spouse of our Lord is surely our Lady; the Spouse of our King is surely our Queen. Therefore, let us serve her, for the Apostle commands: " Servants, be subject to your lords in all fear." (1. Pet. ii. 18.) And, if he disobeys God's precepts who does not serve his carnal masters, without doubt they also deserve blame who do not serve the spiritual mistress. But how must we serve her? Brethren, no service pleases her so much as this—that with all love and affection we humble ourselves before her Son; for all the praise and service we give her Son she counts it as her own. Let no one say: "Though I should do this or that against the Lord, I do not care much; I will serve holy Mary and be safe." It is not so. When a man offends a son, he thereby offends the mother. But if, after our sins, we wish to be reconciled with our Lord, then we must needs have recourse to her and commit our cause to her.

"3. Thirdly, we owe her love. She is our own flesh; she is our sister. Do I seem presumptuous? Nay, the Son of God, because He is the Son of Man, is our brother. Let us love her, since she loves us. Indeed, we ought to love that sister whose sanctity, whose benignity, whose purity, have profited not her only, but all of us.

"4. Lastly, we owe her praise. Scripture bids us praise God in His saints. If the Lord is to be praised in those saints by whom He works miracles, how much more is He to be praised in her in whom He—the wonder of wonders—was made flesh! If they are to be praised who keep their chastity, how much she who chose virginity and received fruitfulness as its reward! If they are to be praised by whom God raised the dead, how much more she by whose sanctity the whole world has been raised from death eternal! Let us then praise her with our mouths and beware lest we insult her by our acts. He gives but feigned praise who cares not to imitate what he praises. He truly praises Mary's humility who strives himself to be humble. He truly praises her chastity who execrates and scorns all impurity and lust. He truly praises her charity whose whole desires and efforts are to love both God and his neighbour with a perfect love."

In this passage St. Aelred does not speak of asking our Lady's intercession in our needs. I add therefore,

another extract from the same sermon: "With gladness
let us celebrate the nativity of the Blessed Virgin Mary
that she may intercede for us to our Lord Jesus Christ.
Wonderful is the mercy of our Lord Jesus Christ. He
is our Judge, and He knows that we are wretched and
of ourselves can bring no good cause before His tribunal.
He is indeed merciful and wishes to show us mercy.
Yet He cannot but judge justly. . . . . Let us offer Him
our prayers; let us beseech Him; 'Enter not into judgment with Thy servants.' But it is not enough to offer
Him our prayers only. Let us seek her help whose
prayers He will never despise. Let us go to His Spouse,
to His mother, to His perfect handmaid. Blessed Mary
is all this. Therefore with joy let us celebrate her
festival that she may intercede for us with our Lord. If,
by the grace of God, we have done anything good, if
she present it to her Son, He will not despise it; and for
the evil we have done without doubt she will obtain
pardon. . . . . . The greatness of Mary's love for men
is proved by the many miracles and many visions by
which the Lord deigns to show that she especially inter-
cedes with her Son for the whole human race. It is in
vain for me even to attempt to show how great is her
charity; no human mind is able to conceive it."

This and much more we find in the writers of the Anglo-
Saxon Church, and thus they tried to express the
idea of absolute sinlessness and perfect excellence
which had been impressed on their minds by their
first teachers in the Faith, and which was developed
by their constant study of Holy Scripture and their
meditation on the mysteries of Redemption.

There were among them no native heresies to be
refuted, no tongues pretending to honour the Incarnate
Son of God by slighting and depreciating His chosen
mother. Having therefore no controversy to sustain,
they do not refute opinions which it did not occur to them
to imagine, nor make assertions where there was no
denial. They neither assert, nor much less deny, the
exemption of our Lady from the stain of original sin.
They speak of her immaculate purity in terms which
may well include that grace; but not until it had been

denied were English writers zealous in its defence. Then, indeed, many of them wrote learned dissertations against the opponents of Mary's singular privilege, and none were more zealous than the English in celebrating the Feast of the Conception.

It was at the beginning of the second half of the twelfth century that the news reached England that the famous Abbot of Clairvaux, St. Bernard, had opposed the celebration of this feast in the Church of Lyons (1140). As was natural, his opinion would be embraced by many of the Cistercians who were now just celebrating their first foundations in England; and this would arouse the zeal, if not the indignation, of the great Benedictine abbeys which shared the reproach of innovation addressed by St. Bernard to the Church of Lyons.

Among those who took up the pen in defence of the feast and of the doctrine it involved, was Nicholas, prior of St. Albans in Hertfordshire, or perhaps of Wallingford, a cell dependent on St. Albans. His original treatise or letter is lost, but we have part of a correspondence to which it gave rise between him and Peter, abbot of St. Remi, and afterwards bishop of Chartres, more commonly known as Peter of Celles. This correspondence or controversy is very interesting, and shows clearly what were the grounds of the opposition to the feast in the twelfth century, and that it was not until a later period that the opposition had the form of a dogmatic denial of Mary's singular privilege.

Peter begins by the remark that, however beautiful and seductive the things which Nicholas had written about the Blessed Virgin, they were wanting in the solid foundation of authority. He then draws a contrast which will surprise us at the present day between "English levity and too great fickleness in vain and fanciful speculations," and "French maturity which is more solid." After developing at some length his own immovableness from the ancient ways, Peter declares his entire devotion to the Mother of God, and his conviction that the Blessed Trinity never brought from the Divine treasure-house anything so excellent except the Humanity of the Word Incarnate. "This," he says, "I confess in my heart and profess with my lips. You profess the same, though with more vehemence, perhaps with too great vehemence. You pour yourself out in praise of the Blessed Virgin. Well, so do I and even to over-flowing. You wish to honour her Conception, and I even her Predestination. You honour the rose, I even the stalk that bears it. You praise the flower and the fruit, I even the leaves and the bark, &c. I will ever take part in all assemblies in which our Lady is worthily honoured, whether the commemoration is termed Con-ception, or Nativity, or Assumption or called by any other name."

He then explains that his only objection is the novelty of the feast now introduced. "But perhaps you will say, do you, a mere Abbot, dare to fill up the wells of ever-springing devotion, or forbid them to be dug deeper? Do not the moderns drink of the same Holy Spirit as the ancients? The Nativity of the Blessed Virgin was not solemnised at the beginning of the Church; but as the devotion of the faithful increased, it was added to the other solemn festivals. Why then should not the zeal of Christian devotion now add the day of her Conception?

"To this, I reply: I would far more willingly open the cataracts of Heaven, and the fountains of the deep in honour of the Virgin than close them. Nay, if her own Son, Jesus—were such a thing possible—had left un-done anything for the exaltation of His Mother, I, her servant and her slave, would try to make it up if not in effect at least in affection, and would rather have no tongue than use it against our Lady. I would rather have no soul than diminish anything of the glory of hers. No doubt it ever was lawful and ever will be lawful for the Church, the Spouse of Christ during her sojourn in the world, according to the changes of times and of persons and of things, to vary her decrees and to find new remedies for new diseases and to appoint new festivals for her Saints. But gold and silver have a mint in which they must be coined—the seat of Peter and the court of Rome, which holds the principality and the keys of heaven. It belongs to her to open to us, in the dispen-sation of God, the secrets of God's counsels, and the oil of grace runs down from the head (Aaron) to the borders of his vestment.

"This seat of Peter, in which Moses sits, that is, in which resides the immaculate law which converts the soul, this is the Rock which falls and crushes the gatherings of the heretics, which stops all profane novelties of word, which cuts off what is superfluous and fills up whatever is incomplete. I should then be glad indeed, if this Mistress and Directress of Christendom with the authority of truth had weighed in the scales of a general consultation and had approved this festival of our Lady's Conception, and had propagated it from sea to sea. If the sun, that is the Pope, and the moon, that is the Roman Church, had gone before, then no less quickly than securely would I have walked in their light, without fear of slipping or of stumbling."

In a subsequent letter Peter writes: "I believe, I say, I maintain, and I swear that the most Blessed Virgin was endowed with special privilege in her eternal predestination, nor from the moment of her Conception did she suffer the slighest stain but remained ever and persevered to the end in spotless integrity; and as she was blessed beyond human nature, so are her perfections sublime and hidden beyond human thought."

After this explanation, he might well conclude that there was little real difference between his sentiments and those of his friendly opponent.

"You praise the Blessed Virgin; so do I. You say that she was holy; so do I. You exalt her above the Choirs of Angels; so do I. You assert that she was free from every sin; so do I. You maintain that she is the Mother of God and our advocate with God; so do I. Turn hither or thither as you will in your veneration and glorification of Mary, I go with you. But if you wish to strike a new coin different from that which is in common circulation and without the approval of the See of Peter to whom it belongs to approve or disapprove the order of the universal Church, then I hold back nor will I pass the bounds marked out. I believe and confess that there are more things unknown about this most holy Virgin than are known, for her grace and glory are high above our reach. Still I believe in the Gospel, not in dreams: and if in anything I be otherwise minded, that also will God reveal, (Phil iii. 15) when and how He may please."

"SECURUS JUDICAT ORBIS TERRARUM."

" Securus judicat orbis terrarum, bonos non esse qui se dividunt ab orbe terrarum in quacumque parte orbis terrarum."

"The whole world judges, without the least fear of a mistake, that they are in the wrong, who in any place separate themselves from the whole world."

ST. AUGUSTINE, contra *Parmen.* iii. p. 4.

1. Such is the well-known argument of St. Augustine against the Donatists, in refutation of their claim to be called the "Catholic Church." Those cannot be in the right—so runs his argument—who have separated themselves from the communion of other churches which are still in communion with each other. The very fact of one Church being so out of communion with the rest of Christendom is in itself an unerring judgment against that church.

2. St. Augustine has here, as he himself declares, * produced a test applicable to all cases at all times. If ever there should be found an isolated Church claiming to be Catholic, that Church must be able at the very least to find some one besides itself admitting its claim. If such a claim were rejected only by some other isolated Church, against whose counter-claim it was made, there might still remain something to be said for it. But when disinterested parties on all sides throw in the force of their opinions against that claim, and no body

---

* "Let us therefore hold it for an unmistaken and stable principle, that no good men can separate themselves from the Church . . . by the rash sacrilege of schism. And in whatever part of the world this has been done, or is done, or shall be done, while the other parts of the earth yet continue in union with the rest of the world: let this be considered certain, that none could have so acted unless" &c.— *St. Aug. contra Parmen.* iii. 5.

(88)

is found to support it except the claimants themselves, such a claim cannot be anything but a futile attempt to resist the consensus of the world, and carries with it its own condemnation.

3. It is a test which can well be applied to the questions—" With what foundation can the Anglican Church claim to be Catholic?" "How does that Church stand in relation to the *orbis terrarum?*" "Who are those who agree in acknowledging the Anglican claim?"

4. Let us first go to those Churches which are in communion with each other—those whom the whole world, including the Anglicans, acknowledge to be Catholic. What do they say to the Anglican claim?

The Italian Church, of course, denies it; the French, the German, the Austrian, the Spanish Churches, whether in the Old World or the New, repudiate it; and in short, wherever any Church is found in communion with the rest of the Churches, *there* the decision is against the claim of the Anglicans to be called Catholic.

5. " But these Churches," it may be said—"are all *Roman* Catholic—those against whose counter-claim the Anglican claim is made, and whose exclusive pretensions are the very cause of their refusal."

Then let us go to disinterested third parties, both in the East and in the West.

The Anglican clergy have made more than one attempt to enter into communion with the Russian Church, but have never succeeded in getting either Russian, Greek, Armenian, or any other Eastern section of Christianity to admit that the Anglican Church could be called Catholic.

And if it be said that these are infected by the same narrow exclusiveness, we say this exclusiveness is a significant fact : one which does not militate against *their* position, but against that of the Anglicans.

6. But let us come to Western Europe : what say the Lutherans and the Calvinists? They not only deny that the Anglicans are Catholics, but call them *Protestants*, of like origin with themselves.

7. To come nearer home: What say the Wesleyans, the Baptists, the Congregationalists—which of the hundreds of dissenting sects in England or Scotland will admit that in parting from the Establishment they parted from the Catholic Church?

And if these are still ranked as enemies, let us come into the very household of the Anglican Communion itself. A strange kind of Catholic Church would that be which did not acknowledge the present and past verdict of its own members on a question like this! And what do we find? We find not only at present a large section of the Church of England which utterly repudiates the name of Catholic, but the tenor and spirit of the whole past history of that body is against it.

8. In fact, so deeply rooted in England is the consciousness of possessing a *Protestant* National Church that no Anglican claims can make people in practical life think of it as Catholic. Let any one stop in a city street, and ask the way to the Catholic Church. Would any passenger or policeman hesitate where to direct him? Address a letter to "The Catholic Church" in any town. Does any one doubt where it would be delivered? Nay, if one of those would-be Catholic Anglicans were himself asked the way, could he possibly misunderstand where the inquirer wished to go? He would feel himself guilty of an ungentlemanly trick, if he endeavoured to palm off his own parish church as the Catholic Church sought by the inquirer.*

9. "Securus judicat orbis terrarum." Does not all this look like the world's judgment on the Anglican claim to be Catholic? Against such a universal refutation, what witness can be brought forward to support it?

The answer is sometimes made that in spite of the almost universal opposition above stated there are still

* To the same effect writes St. Augustine :—"Whereas the different heretics are all desirous of being called Catholics, yet if any stranger were to ask them ' Which is the assembly of the Catholics?' none of them would dare to point out his own place of worship."—Contra Ep. Fundam. cap. I. So likewise St. Cyril in Jerusalem and St. Pacian in Spain.

men to be found in all quarters of the world who acknowledge the Catholicity of the Anglican Church. But who are these men? Who in Europe, who in Africa, who in America, who in Australia, are these men that uphold the Anglican claim? Why, they are men of their own language and stock, men belonging to the Anglican Church, men of the same party who happen to be distributed there, and who make the same claim for themselves!

Would it be sound reasoning to admit a *universal* consensus in favour of the Jews being still the favoured people of God, because the Jews themselves, who say it, happen to be scattered about all over the world? Then how can any argument be drawn from the fact that those men of the Anglican Church who themselves claim to be Catholics, happen to have distributed themselves over the four quarters of the globe? This distribution does not constitute that grand consensus of nations, of different stocks and languages, of different interests and ways of thought, which is called the "orbis terrarum," by St. Augustine.

9. The difficulty then, is—not to find out who deny the Anglican claim to be called Catholics, but to find any but themselves who admit it. "Securus judicat orbis terrarum." So said St. Augustine, and so say we to-day. Take the votes of the whole world—and, except the claimants themselves, all will be found against them. Exclude the Anglican party itself from the court, and who among the nations has a favourable word for their claim?

——

CATHOLIC TRUTH SOCIETY, 18 West Square, London, S.E.

[Price 1s. per 100.]

THE REUNION OF CHRISTENDOM.

THE Association for Promoting the Reunion of Christendom has for its aim a highly laudable object. It expresses a feeling among Anglicans that the present state of Christendom, divided up as it is into numberless isolated communions, is so unsatisfactory, that every effort ought to be made to bring all these scattered parts into a united whole.

The way by which it proposes to effect this re-union is by mutual compromise between the several churches on so-called minor and unessential points of difference ; and it is hoped that a willingness on the Anglican side to make such a compromise may open the way for the other churches to do the same.

2.   There is, however, one great obstacle standing in the way.   This obstacle is the claim of the Roman Church to be the one and only true Church, in virtue of which claim she declares compromise impossible.   In this claim Rome is unique; for while the Greeks and Anglicans say "We believe in one Church, and we are a part of it," the Romans say "We believe in one Church and we are the whole of it."

" Ubi Petrus, ibi Ecclesia "—where the successor of St. Peter rules, there is the Church, and outside his jurisdiction no true church can exist.

3.   The Anglicans cannot allow this.   They cannot admit a claim which places them at present outside the Catholic Church.   If Rome would only concede that the Church is capable of existing in a divided state— that the Church is now actually existing in that state, and only requiring a mutual concession of unessential points of doctrine and government to become united into one—if Rome would only condescend modestly to call herself a. part of that Church—then nothing insuperable would stand in the way of re-union.   Let Rome only acknowledge her equality with other communions, and the work is done.

(89)

4. Nay, we answer; let Rome but acknowledge that equality, and the work is hopelessly *undone*. It is a startling paradox, but an equally certain truth, that in the very "obstinacy" of Rome lies all hope of re-union. Without it, reunion would be impossible. Without it, the very elements of unity would be hopelessly destroyed. Let Rome only acknowledge that she is *not* the one and only and the whole true Church, and the phrase "One Holy Catholic and Apostolic Church" would become a mere memory of the past.

5. In order to see why this should be so, let us imagine for a moment that the Roman authorities were induced to resign the unique claim of their Church; and observe the result.

At the very moment of that concession, the millions who now believe in the Roman Church would find it impossible to believe in her any longer. The Church in which they have been implicitly believing as in a Divine messenger has acknowledged that she has made a mistake, and that in the very foundations of her credibility—in the knowledge of her own identity, personality, constitution. She used to say that she was the one only true and whole Catholic and Apostolic Church. Now she says she is only a part of it. She used to exclude the Greeks and Anglicans from it. Now she has confessed to having erred in so doing—she ought to have admitted them. She has contradicted herself, pronounced herself fallible, deceived and deceiving—no reasonable man can henceforth believe in her or trust her. There is no alternative before us but to repudiate her, and take refuge in agnosticism or infidelity.

Or to put it another way. The very reason why a Catholic believes in the Church is because he unfalteringly believes that Church to be the one unerring perpetual and enlightened witness of God's revelation, and the one infallible teacher of truth. As a teaching Church, she must necessarily know who and what she herself is. Ignorance of her own identity would be fatal to her claims. And for that Church to reverse her teaching on this point, to acknowledge that she has made a mistake about herself in the past, would *ipso facto* exhibit her incapacity to guide men to truth, and compel every rational being to disbelieve in her. For how can there be any certainty about other points of doctrine, when in one point, and that one so fundamental, she has thus grievously failed?

Or, once more—Reason cannot implicitly submit herself to any but an infallible guide. Yet it is by virtue of the acknowledgment which Catholics make of the Infallibility of the Church as a teaching power, that they repose implicit confidence in her teaching. Let the Church only by a single act disavow this infallibility, and with this disavowal all belief in her would become folly.

Hence it is that the very act which it is hoped would bring the Anglicans into communion with Rome would drive the present Catholics out of it; and no one would be left to welcome the new children of the Church except those very authorities whose concessions had destroyed the allegiance of the old.

6. The truth of this position will be more easily seen by a parallel taken from Holy Scripture.

The writings of the prophet Jeremias abound in the strongest denunciations of those who falsely prophesied good things of Judah. They express more than once a claim on the part of Jeremias to be the one and only prophet whose mission was from God, or whose word was truth. Now suppose that Jeremias had been brought at length to confess that, in condemning his brethren, he had been too severe, and that in limiting the gift of Divine inspiration to himself, he had fallen into a presumptuous error. How instantly that one admission would take away the whole force of his prophecy, and would not only justify, but *compel* all reasonable men to disbelieve in him altogether!

Or again, suppose for a moment that Christ our Lord, after having during His whole ministry taught that He was the sole Messiah, *the Way, the Life, and the Truth,* and that no one *cometh to the Father except through Him*— should finally, on maturer consideration, have modified His claim; have acknowledged that He was not after all the only way, truth, and life—but that some other person, say John the Baptist, really shared the Messiahship

equally with Him.   How would the Apostles have
regarded Him after such a confession ?   How would
St. Peter have answered his own question—"*Lord,
whither shall we go ?*"   Not by saying, "*Thou hast the
word of eternal life.*"   No, they would have seen that
this one admitted error had entirely invalidated His
whole claim to be a teacher sent from God.

Jeremias is not to be called obstinate because he
maintained uncompromisingly the truth about himself.
Nor is Christ our Lord open to a like charge because
He sustained His high claims even in spite of
death.   And as with Christ and His prophets, so is it
with His Church, who, knowing full well her own
constitution, personality, extent of power, and condition
of communion, adheres to her own unchangeable
doctrine with a firmness which no persuasion, no motive
of policy, no threat or persecution, no hope even of
spiritual good, is able to shake or move.   Of her very
nature she can never acknowledge that she is deceived
in this.   To do so would be to acknowledge that she
had no Divine mission to teach, no power of discerning
truth from falsehood, and no right to claim the belief
and allegiance of men.

7.   The Roman Church therefore claims, and must
ever claim, to be the One Church, and the Only Church,
Infallible and Indefectible, and this constitutes in part
her "note" of *Unity*.   It is a claim both peculiar and
notorious ; indeed it is made a matter of opprobrium to
her.   For while the Greeks say "I believe in One
Church, of which I am a part," and the Anglicans
are taking up the same cry,—the Church of Rome says
"I believe in One Church, and I am that Only Church,
and beside me there is no other."   There is no society
on earth claiming either by right or in fact to be The
Church, the Whole Church, and the Only Church,
except the Church of Rome.   And this very claim is
the only basis on which the re-union of Christendom
can ever be brought about.

CATHOLIC TRUTH SOCIETY, 18 WEST SQUARE, S.E.
[Price 1s. per 100.]

"THE BISHOP IN THE CHURCH
AND
THE CHURCH IN THE BISHOP."

" Unde scire debes episcopum in ecclesia esse, et ecclesiam in episcopo ; et si qui cum episcopo non sunt, in ecclesia non esse."

"Whence you may know that the Bishop is in the Church, and the Church in the Bishop; and those who are not with the Bishop, are not in the Church."

ST. CYPRIAN Ep. Florentio lxvi. p. 168. Ed. Oxford, 1682,

1. These words of St. Cyprian form a ground of assurance among Anglicans that they are within the Church of Christ. "We are in communion with our Bishops," they say "therefore we are within the Church."

Now, although the assurance would be well grounded where no doubt was possible about the rightfulness of the Bishops themselves, a serious question arises where there exist two rival Bishops, each asserting against the other his sole rightfulness, and claiming for himself the allegiance of all in their common diocese.

2. Thus we have the Bishop of London holding his jurisdiction from his co-provincials of Canterbury, and the Archbishop of Westminster holding his jurisdiction from Rome; and within the common diocese of both, two men, the one an Anglican, the other a Roman Catholic, living on the same acre of ground, are paying their allegiance to these two Bishops respectively. And while the Bishop of London denies the right of the Archbishop to be established at Westminster, the Archbishop denies the Bishop of London's claim to the episcopacy at all; and each hold that to be in communion with the rival Bishop is to be out of communion with the Church.

There is something strange in all this. They cannot
both be rightful Bishops. One of them must be a
schismatic, and the other a rightful and divinely
appointed Bishop. One must be within and the other
without the Church.

3. "No doubt that is true," concedes the Anglican;
"But which of the two is the rightful Bishop? The
Archbishop of Westminster is evidently an upstart of
modern growth, and an intruder, while the Bishop of
London has held his see by succession for centuries;
and it is this which establishes the Bishop of London's
claim to be the rightful Bishop, and so, according to
St. Cyprian, the medium and criterion of communion
with the Catholic Church."

4. But this conclusion clearly rests on a false
assumption. The mere fact of possessing a see does
not prove the possessor to be a rightful Catholic
Bishop, for a Bishop, however rightfully ordained,
may, by an act of schism, lose for himself and his
successors the right of jurisdiction.

St. Cyprian, fully aware of this, carefully guards us
against such a mistake; for besides speaking of pseudo-
bishops, erected by heretics, and those who are illicitly
constituted,* he also instances a class of Bishops, who,
once rightly constituted and orthodox, have since their
installation fallen away, and by their schism have lost
all right of exercising the episcopal office and power.†

Moreover, he tells us clearly why they lost that right.
It is because they have separated themselves from the

* "That Fortunatianus, once a bishop among you, who since his
most grievous fall wishes now to begin afresh, and is beginning to
claim his episcopate." (Cyp. Ep. Epicteto lxv. p. 162.) See
also Ep. Cornelio lix. p. 131. Ep. Maximo and Nicostrato xlvi.
p. 131, etc.

† "But he could not hold the episcopate, even after his episcopal
ordination, if he should fall away from the body of his fellow bishops
and from the unity of the church. . . . He, therefore, who
keeps neither the unity of the spirit nor the bond of peace, and
separates himself from the bonds of the Church and from the
sacerdotal college, can retain neither the power nor the honour of a
bishop, in that he has willed not to uphold either the unity or the
peace of the episcopate." Cyp. Ep. Antoniano, lv. p. 112.

communion of their fellow Bishops, and deserted the
sacerdotal body. "For a man can retain neither the
episcopal power nor its honour, who has chosen not
to hold to the unity of the episcopate, but to be out of
concord with it." This episcopate being in several
places described as one and indivisible, its different
members cohering together in the closest fellowship.*

St. Cyprian therefore not only tells us under what
conditions a layman is in communion with the Church,
but also under what conditions a Bishop is a proper
medium of this communion—without which latter
conditions, communion with the Bishop on the part of
a layman is of no value.

Now can any Anglican Bishop—say the Bishop of
London—stand this test?

5. "Certainly," is the Anglican's reply, "for the
Bishop of London does not stand alone; he is in
communion with a considerable number of bishops
both in England, America, Australia, and many other
parts of the world. Is not the communion of such a
number of Bishops together enough to satisfy Cyprian's
condition, and to prove the Bishop of London's rightfulness, and establish his claim to be a proper medium
of communion with the Catholic Church?"

6. Yes—if that collection of Bishops is also in
communion with the rest of the episcopate of the
Catholic Church. But the mere multiplication of numbers is not enough. As it is possible for one Bishop to
fall away, so is it possible for many to fall away together,
who, while cohering with one another by a schismatical bond, are yet separated from the unity of the episcopate, and so from the Catholic Church. Of this the
Donatists afford us a notable example. For in that heresy
four hundred Bishops fell away; that is, one-fifth of the
whole episcopate of Christendom.† They split off in

---

* "One episcopate, diffused throughout an harmonious multitude
of many bishops."—Cyp. Ep. Antoniano lv. p. 112. "Whereas the
Church is Catholic and one and is not separated or divided, but is
in truth connected and joined together by the cement of priests.
(Bishops) cleaving to each other. Cyp. Ep. Florentio lxvi. p. 168."

† Newman, Difficulties of Anglicans, Lect. xi. p. 281, Edition 1850.

a body, and persevered for a time in unity among themselves.   Yet this unity did not prevent them from being
as a body condemned by the rest of Christendom—
a condemnation whose force is acknowledged by Anglicans themselves.

The case of the Nestorian party is still more forcible—
"a schismatic communion," we read, " the most wonderful the world has seen, which propagated itself
both among Christians and pagans from Cyprus to
China; which formed the Christianity of Bactarians,
Huns, Medes and Indians; which prevailed over Mala-
bar, Ceylon and Tartary—a vast organization administered by no less than twenty-five Archbishops, and
probably, together with the opposite sect of the Mono-
physites in Syria and Egypt, surpassing in numbers the
body of the whole Catholic Church, and, moreover,
occupying a portion of the world with which the Catholic
Church in those centuries had very little to do."*

If then the Donatist and Nestorian parties, multi-
tudinous as they appear to have been, were yet external
to the Church, it is clear that on score of numbers the
Anglican communion can establish no claim.   It is not
the numerical strength of a body but the relation of that
body and its Bishops to the united episcopate of
Christendom that, according to St. Cyprian, deter-
mines the issue.

7.   Who then are the Bishops who support the Bishop
of London in his claim? and what is their relation to
the rest of Christendom?

They are the successors of that handful of Bishops,
who, three hundred years back, jointly, and by their own
policy, fell out of communion with the rest of the Church
—with the Bishops of Italy, Austria, Spain, Portugal,
France, Germany—in short, of all those countries with
whom they were in communion before.   These few
Bishops, I say, fell out of communion with the rest of
the Episcopacy, while at the same time—a point of
great importance—all those from whose communion
they fell out still remained in communion among
themselves.

* Newman, Difficulties of Anglicans, Lect. xi., p. 282.

8. The isolation to which those few Bishops reduced themselves and their successors will soon be seen by a practical test, which was then, and is now, a conclusive means of determining the limits of communion. I mean the use of commendatory letters (epistolae formatae). It was the test applied by St. Augustine to the case of the Donatists, as he himself says in the following words:—

"Then we began to ask which was the Church in which one ought to be—whether that which, as Holy Scripture had prophesied, was spread all over the world, or that limited to the African race, or to Africa. He (Fortunius) at first tried to assert that his communion was all over the world. But then I asked him whether he could give me letters of communication (which we call formatae) for me to go whithersoever I wished. And I said that (as was clear to everybody), the whole question could easily be settled by the application of this test." *

9. It remains to apply this test to the Archbishop of Westminster and the Bishop of London respectively.

A Catholic priest on the eve of a journey goes to the Archbishop of Westminster, and asks for letters of communion, his "celebret" as we should now call them. He receives them, and sets out on his travels. Now see in how many places those letters will be received as credentials, and admit him to the altar. They will serve him in every town and village of Spain, Portugal, France, Italy, and Austria, in fact, in the whole of Catholic Europe. He, an Englishman, may travel through all the foreign missions of all those foreign nations—in Syria, India, China, Africa, and elsewhere, and in every place his letters will ensure his admission into communion, and to the privileges of the Altar. In short they will be his passport to whatever Catholic church he wishes to introduce himself, from the cathedral of St. Peter's to the mud cabin of a far-off mission land. In no part of the world need he miss his daily Mass, except in those parts where no universally acknowledged Catholic altar is found to exist.

* Aug. Ep. ad Eleus. Glor. and Fel. Tom. ii. Ep. xliv, cap. 2. Venice 1729.

10. How much narrower would be the circuit of the Anglican clergyman who started from England fortified merely by the commendatory letters of the Bishop of London! He might (if he liked to present himself) be accepted by those bodies of German Lutherans, or by the Calvinists of France and Switzerland, who glory in the name of Protestant, and who deny the Catholicity of the Church to which he belongs. He might find here and there in European cities a few English residents with their English minister, and, if he did not himself regard them as schismatics, he could enter into communion there. In the English colonies he would find a number of his fellow-countrymen professing the national religion—in America he would meet those who, a century ago, were English in name also, and who now are still English in language and race, and amongst them he would be received. But if, after declaring clearly who he was and to what communion he belonged, he were to apply for admission to the altar at any of those places at which the Catholic priest had been received into communion, he would meet with an uncompromising refusal. His welcome would be restricted to the various branches of his own Anglican Church abroad, the rulers and worshippers of which were of his own race and language.

11. Contrast the two: the Catholic priest received and acknowledged among the various nationalities of the world, by peoples of all races, languages, and ways of thought wherever he wishes to go;* the Anglican clergyman admitted to the churches merely of his

* St. Basil aptly says: "It is more just that we be judged in what regards ourselves, not by one or two who walk not according to truth, but by the multitude of Bishops who by the favour of the Lord are united with us. Let the question be put to those of Pisidia, Lycaonia, of Isauria, of both Phrygias, of that part of Armenia which borders on your country, of Macedonia, of Achaia, of Illyricum, of Gaul, Spain, the whole of Italy, Sicily, Africa, the sound parts of Egypt, and what is left of Syria. They all send letters to me and receive mine; from which letters whether sent by them or received from us, you may learn that we are all unanimous and think the same thing. So that it will not escape your accuracy, that whoso flees communion with us severs himself from the whole Church." Ep. cciv. ad Neocæsarienses.

own nation, language, and custom, but refused in numberless places where he would give almost anything to gain admittance—where he feels it would be a great triumph to his pretensions to be acknowledged. And as he goes about from place to place in this way, how could he but be impressed with the state of isolation which the Anglican Bishops have inherited through their predecessors having lost the communion of the united episcopacy in the 16th century.

12. Such, then, is the result we arrive at by applying St. Cyprian's and St. Augustine's searching and conclusive tests.* It brings out into full relief the fact that this one national section has been for three hundred years, and still remains, outside the communion of the rest of Christendom, while the other numerous national sections of the Church from which they were cut off are still in as close communion with each other as they have ever been. They merely miss from their united body one nation which formerly belonged to it; whose loss has affected their numbers, but not their unity.

When, therefore, St. Cyprian speaks of receding from the body of the one episcopate, he describes in one word both the Donatist and Nestorian position in the past and the Anglican position at the present day. In all three cases the tests are the same. In all three they lead to the same conclusion.

13. So then it is this universal communion of the episcopacy through all the nations in which it lies outspread, which is the sign of the true and rightful episcopacy. And it is the absence of this communion between one group of Bishops and the rest which decides that group to have lost its episcopal right and power. That group may retain its palaces, its sees, its name, its show of jurisdiction: but the spirit is gone, and the sees are really vacant. It becomes necessary

* Expressed also in the following amongst many like passages:—
" "Again, those who believe indeed that Christ came in the flesh &c., (in short do not err in doctrine) but nevertheless so disagree with His body, that their communion is not with the whole wherever it is spread, but is found in some part, separated, it is clear that such are not in the Catholic Church." Aug. contra Donat. No. 7, vol. 9, p. 342. Venice, 1733.

for a new hierarchy to be set up in that land, so long deprived by schismatic defection of the blessing of Catholic government; a hierarchy deriving its power from the one united episcopacy of the Catholic Church, of which the new extension will form an integral part. And it will be this hierarchy which will stand as the one medium of .ommunion in that land with the Catholic Church.

The Englishman who, following St. Cyprian's test, desires to find himself within the Catholic Church, must pay his allegiance, not to the present holder of the see of London, whose predecessors fell out of communion with the rest of Christendom, but to the Archbishop of Westminster and his fellow Bishops, who are not only one among themselves, but are in communion with the Churches of all the world.

CATHOLIC TRUTH SOCIETY, 18 West Square, London, S.E.

[Price 2*s*. per 100.]

THE UNITY OF THE CHURCH.

" Ecclesia enim Una est, quae una et intus esse et foris non potest . . . nec scindi adversum se aut dividi posse."

For the Church is One, and this One cannot be both within and without . . . nor is it capable of being split up against itself, nor divided. ST. CYPRIAN, Ep. Magno lxix. p. 182. Ed. Oxford, 1682.

This is one of the many passages of the Fathers which say that the Church, being incapable of division, cannot be cut into separate parts by schism; that schism is not a dividing of the Church into parts, but the dividing of a party from the Church, separate from the Church itself; that the Holy Ghost, not being divided, must in case of a breach of unity remain only in one member of the division,—the other part losing Him, just as a limb cut from the body loses the soul which remains in its entirety in the trunk.

The Church is One Body.—What we mean when we say that the Church is one body will be seen by thinking what "oneness" means in other things.

To be "one" is, according to the philosophical definition, to be "undivided in itself"—essentially, of its own nature, indivisible into parts—a something which is no mere aggregation of parts, but which when divided into parts ceases to be.

A few examples will make this clear.

A vast amount of materials lies in a dockyard—timbers, bolts, coils of rope, spars; all things needful to make a ship. You may take away some of these materials, exchange them for others, add to them—there is no "union" here, for there is no essential bond. But when you build up these materials into a ship, a new thing has come into existence—a *one* thing, composed indeed of many things, but forming a constructive unity—realizing a single idea. Divide that ship into

two parts—you have broken its unity : that unity was the
essence of that ship—the ship is no more. Moreover,
the parts of that ship are only such, because they are
intimately bound up with other parts; take a part
away, and that piece of material, useful as it may be
for other purposes, is no longer a part of that ship :
because it belongs no more to its constructive unity.

Again, a tree is a body having the unity of an organic
life.   Cut off a branch, and you have severed it from
the centre of life.   That branch may for a short time
retain a vestige of its former life, but sooner or later it
inevitably dies.   Or it may by grafting into another
tree, or planting in the ground, continue to live, but
not with the same life it had before.   The life it
derived from the original tree dies out and is super-
seded by another and distinct life springing from a new
source outside the parent stock, so that it is no longer
in any sense a part of the original tree.

Thirdly, there is like unity in the body of a man, by
reason of the soul pervading it in every part.   When
the soul goes out the whole body dies.   If you cut off
a limb from the body, what happens ?   You do not, as
in case of the tree, cut off with it a part of the life which
can be continued by grafting into another trunk.   At
the instant of separation, the life withdraws from the
limb.   Henceforward the body is diminished in extension, but the soul which informs it suffers no hurt, for
being essentially one it remains as entire as it was
before, while the severed limb is irrevocably dead.

From these examples it will appear of what sort is
the unity of the Church.   The Church is no mere collection of individuals, or of parts, which added together
equal the whole.   For no one would say that the Church
broken up into isolated individuals would in any sense
equal the Church in a state of unbroken unity.   Nor is
the Church a mere constructive unity like a ship, for
then the disunion of its members would destroy the
Church altogether.   Now no one would admit that the
Church as a church could be so destroyed.

But our Lord Himself has used the simile of
the vine, from which all branches that are cut off

must die. And though such severed limbs may, by grafting into the unity of a national state, continue to exist and flourish, they no longer live with a life derived from the Church, from whose communion they have parted, but with a life derived from a source distinct and new, human both in its character and effect. That in matter of fact such sects, unsustained by any external force, do sooner or later fall into decay, is shown by the history of the Donatists among others in the past, and the Greek Patriarchate at the present day. And that severed branches can retain great vigour of their own kind by becoming identified with a secular government is manifested in the case of the Russian and Anglican Churches.

But the Church is both by Scripture and the Fathers specially symbolized by the human body. The fitness of which parallel is seen by the following paraphrase of the words of St. Cyprian which head this tract:—

"The Church (human body) is one, which cannot be both within and without itself, nor can it be split up into parts acting against itself, nor divided." Of which the same Saint treats as follows:—

"There is One God and One Christ, and His Church One and the Faith One, and the people all joined in the solid oneness of a body by a cementing concord. Unity cannot be sundered, nor can the One Body be divided by a dissolution of its structure, nor be cast piecemeal abroad with its vitals torn and lacerated."— Cyp. de Unit. Eccl., p. 119.

The Church therefore being such in its nature, it must correspond in its mode of existence. That which is essentially one must necessarily exist in a *state* of unity. As in the social order the unity of a club is not destroyed by the loss of a member, who, by separating from the communion of his fellow members, loses the privileges and benefits of the club as soon as the act of separation is formally established, so the unity of the Church is not impaired by defections from that unity; while those falling out of communion are, by the act, cut off from the centre and source of unity, which is the Holy Ghost.

I do not here mean to say that the Holy Ghost ceases altogether to work on the souls of those excluded members; for the Holy Ghost, in his office of Sancti-fier, works on all men's souls alike, regardless of their creed. I speak of the Holy Ghost in His office as Author of Unity in the Church; performing a func-tion like that of the soul in the body, which gives life and unity to all its members; or, according to St. Cyprian's simile, "conserving the unity of an indi-visible and single household." Mark well what kind of household—one, indivisible and united—not one from which it is impossible for a member to depart, for that would be to coerce the wills of men—but one which cannot within its own confines be in dissension —one from which a dissentient by his own act becomes an alien and a castaway.

Such is the unity of the Church, the unity prayed for by Christ, effected at Pentecost, prefigured in prophecy, expressly stated by the Fathers, and asserted to-day by the Roman Church:—

Our Lord prayed :—" Holy Father, keep them in Thy Name, that they may be one, as We also are One. And not only for them do I pray, but for those also who through their word shall believe in Me; that they may all be one, as Thou Father in Me and I in Thee: that they also may be one in Us; that they may be perfected in one, and the world may know that Thou hast sent Me." *

What kind of Unity is this for which Christ prays? For a unity like that of the Blessed Trinity, which we know by faith to be absolutely indivisible, and passing all human understanding. A bond of unity of this kind, not only pervading the Twelve, but also all who through them should believe; so remarkable to the eyes of men, that it should be a standing proof of Christ's divine mission. A prodigy unique on earth, which no passion of weakness, no lapse of time, no effort of hell should bring to dissolution; a unity so far surpassing human capacity, that nothing but the active agency of the Holy Ghost could bring it about.

This was in fact brought about by the coming of

* St. John, xvii, 11-23.

the Paraclete at Pentecost, in that upper chamber where one hundred and twenty individuals were gathered together; united indeed by a common faith, hope and love, but not with a unity adequate to the desires and prayers of Christ. But in a moment, the Holy Spirit, one and indivisible Himself, comes upon them, permeates them, and knits them together in a new bond of fellowship indissoluble as Him Who has effected it. More and more were added tò their numbers, only to be cemented into the Unity of the same Spirit. .Some indeed did afterwards leave that company. But of them, what is written? "They went out from us, but they were not of us." (1 John, ii. 19). No man's will was to be coerced; they who would might enter, they who would might go. But there was a clear line marked between those of the household, and those who were not of it. The household were of one mind in the Spirit. Those who were not of one mind had no place there; they were out of the communion of the United Church.

Here then was fulfilled all that the prophets had foreseen—David calling on all nations to unite in magnifying God—the creation of a new people, "*in conveniendo populos in unum*" (Ps. 101), by drawing together the nations into one great unity. Now was enacted in reality that scene of which Ezekiel describes the type:—The separated joints and limbs of scattered peoples lay in the valley—and at the word of the prophet were brought together, joint to joint, and with the flesh and skin upon them : but they had no life, till the spirit of God came upon them, and they rose up, no longer a collection of scattered members, but an army of living men. Nothing better could be found to picture the change produced by the Holy Spirit when He entered upon His work of unity in the Church of Christ at Pentecost.

This too is the unity so clearly expressed by the Fathers—a unity, which in spite of the troublous times in which they wrote, all alike saw, and felt, and enjoyed.

"Does any one believe," asks ST. CYPRIAN, "that this unity which comes from the divine strength, and coheres in celestial sacraments, can be divided in the Church, and can be separated by the parting asunder of opposing wills? He who does not keep to the unity does not keep God's Law." Cyp., De Unitate, p. 109. Oxford, 1682.

"God is one and Christ is one, and faith is one and the people is one, united into the substantial unity of a body by the cement of concord. Unity cannot be severed nor can the one body be separated by division of the structure." Ib. p. 119.

St. Optatus says that "Schismatics are like branches cut off the vine, doomed to punishment, reserved like dry wood for the fire of hell."—De Schism Donat. lib. i. no. 6-10.

And St. Athanasius that "the holy and veritable among heralds of truth are of one mind, and differ not themselves."—t. 1. de Decret Niceaen. no. 4.

While *St. Basil* declares that "Whoso flees from communion with us, severs himself from the whole Church."—Ep. cciv. ad Neocaesarienses no. 7.

St. Ambrose that "the congregations are not many: there is one congregation, one Church."—t. 1. Hexaem l. iii., c. i., no. 2, 3.

St. Irenæus that "the Church, although scattered throughout the world, yet as dwelling in one house, carefully preserves the faith."—Adv. Haeres. lib. i. cap. x., no. 2.

St. Ignatius tells us that "for this end did the Lord allow the ointment to be poured on His Head—that he might breathe incorruption into the Church."—Ep. ad. Ephes. xvi. xvii.

St. Gregory of Nyssa, that: "if any part be out of the body it is utterly disconnected with the head."—t. iii. de Perfect. Christ. Forma, p. 289; Ed. Paris 1638.

Clement of Alexandria, that "in substance, in doctrine, in origin, in excellence the ancient and Catholic Church, is unique. . . but the excellency of the Church like the principle of everything concrete, is in unity surpassing all other things, and having nothing similar or equal to itself."—t. i. Strom. lib. vii. p. 899. Venet. 1757.

While finally St. Augustine (for we can give but a few out of numberless quotations) says that "the whole Christ consists of Head and body. The Head is the only begotten Son of God; His body is the Church; husband and wife, two in one flesh." And after dealing with the case of heretics he turns to that of schismatics, saying, that "even those who believe all the doctrines of Christ, but nevertheless so disagree with His body the Church, that their communion is not with the whole, wheresover it is spread, but is found in some place separated—such are manifestly not in the Church." Contra Donat. no. 7. vol. 9. p. 342. Venice 1733.

We have now seen in what consists the unity of the Church; for which Christ prayed; with which the Early Church was endowed, and which the fathers of the Church enjoyed and described. We have seen it to be 1, *Indestructible*, so that there can never be a time in which the Church is not really united, and 2, *Clearly visible* both to those outside and those within its boundaries. So that the Church can never be split up into sects or isolated communions in such a way as to nullify or obscure this unity, or to make it a matter which the world may doubt. And in the face of this conclusion surely it is impossible to hold any longer a persuasion that the Church can consist of three or any other number of separate communions, each one isolated and in opposition to the rest. For now we see clearly that the Holy Ghost can abide in but *one* of these, and that only one of them can be the Church of Christ.

Which of these three that Church is, there can be left no room to doubt. The eight or ten divisions of the Eastern Church make no pretence of corporate unity at all. The Anglican Church, with its perpetual variations and differences between bishop and bishop, party and party, cannot dare to claim a unity such as we have seen the unity of the Church to be. But the vast Church which is in communion with Rome, by the very testimony of her enemies is *One*,—severely, tyrannically one, they would call it—yet without question phenomenally one. One, we may add, indefectibly and without compromise, is the Church in communion with Rome; one with a unity which no human organization can change or destroy, because it is the oneness of the Holy Ghost.

"And since Christ in His Gospel says that there is great joy in heaven over one sinner that repenteth, how much more joy both in heaven and on earth would there be over confessors of Christ returning, to their own glory and honour, into the Church; and, by the fidelity and uprightness of their example, opening out a way for others also to return. For not a few have been persuaded to remain in error, because in this they seemed to be following in the company of confessors. But when this error is done away a light is infused into every breast, and the Catholic Church is shown to be really one, and incapable of being cut asunder and divided, and when it is proved that good and noble soldiers of Christ cannot long be detained outside the Church by fallacies and frauds, it will be impossible for anyone to be deceived by the specious arguments of schism."—CYP. Ep. Cornelio li., p. 95.

CATHOLIC TRUTH SOCIETY, 18 West Square, London, S.E.
[Price 2s. per 100.]

THE CHURCH OF GOD

VINDICATED BY NON-CATHOLICS.

BY

H. MORDEN BENNETT, M.A.

PART I.—MARKS OF THE TRUE CHURCH.

Introduction.

As in the life of her Divine Founder, so in the history
of the Catholic Church in every age, misrepresentation
has been actively at work in setting those who might
otherwise be influenced for good against the light of
Divine Truth. It is, therefore, a great relief occasion-
ally to come across statements,—sometimes intentional,
sometimes unintentional,—in the writings of those not
in communion with the centre of unity, which, in one
way or another, support the distinctive doctrines or
practices of the Catholic Church, or defend the unique
historical position which she holds, and the form of
government which she adopts.

In the following pages an endeavour has been made
to arrange a few quotations from leading writers, mostly
of the Anglican communion, at various periods, which,
running counter to the ordinary attacks against everything that savours of Rome, show the soul of the Christian
to be naturally Catholic, just as the soul of the heathen
was pronounced by the apologist of old to be "natu-
raliter Christiana." In the present pamphlet, subjects
relating to the nature of the Catholic Church and her
government are exclusively treated ; leaving many other
subjects, on which equally forcible quotations have been
collected, to depend on the favour with which these are
received ; and in the hope that, eventually, with the

help of those interested in the research, a more important compilation may be made. The use of italics for
emphasizing has been entirely avoided, except where
the authors themselves have used them ; and thus no
unfair estimate is given of the exact meaning of any
passage.

The compiler will be very grateful for any assistance
towards such a collection of extracts as may be of substantial and permanent use in forwarding the cause of
peace and re-union.

MANOR LODGE,
            BOURNEMOUTH.

The True Church is One, Visibly.

BINGHAM, in his 'Christian Antiquities,' vol. v., bk.
xvi., chap. i., sec. i., p. 369 (Straker, London), says :
"The ancients accounted both the unity of faith and
obedience necessary, as fundamentals, to the very being
of the Church."

Again, sec. vi., p. 398, he speaks of "the standing
rule of the Catholic Church, which was to have but one
Bishop in a Church, as the centre of unity." Again,
sec. vii., p. 405, he says : "To preserve the unity of the
Church in its well-being, it was required that every
member of a Church should submit to the ordinary rules
of discipline." And again, sec. xvii., p. 431 : "The
Church went by this rule, to judge none to be in her
perfect unity, but such as were in full communion with
her."

ANTHONY GRANT, D.C.L., in his 'Bampton Lectures,'
(Rivingtons, London, 1845), lec. ii., p. 65, says :
"Unity is the law of Truth . . . . for evil dissociates
and separates, and holiness unites, because it draws to
God ; so that unity becomes the evidence of the presence
of God, disunion a witness to the presence of evil."

Again, lec. iv., p. 134: " We must admit that the
fact of such a power (that of Rome) having been established, proves at least the prevalence of a conviction
that Christianity was a system, that Christians were a
body, and that unity was a token of that body."

Again, as to the visibility of the Church, in lec. iii., p. 76, he says: "Holy Scripture bears on its front that God has ordained such a visible system, a holy society, the Church; to which are entrusted the oracles of truth and the means of grace." And again in lec. iv., p. 132: "Throughout these periods, it is to be observed, the Gospel was presented to the heathen as a system, in the form of a visible body, within which, as it were, Christ was to be found, and in Him the new life of their whole being acquired."

HOOKER in his 'Ecclesiastical Polity' (Oxford, 1836), vol. i., bk. iii., p. 426 et seq., says: "That Church of Christ which we properly term His Body mystical can be but one . . . . and this visible Church in like sort is but one. . . . The unity of which visible Body and Church of Jesus Christ consisteth in that uniformity which all several persons thereunto belonging have, by reason of that one Lord whose servants they all profess themselves, that one Faith which they all acknowledge, that one Baptism wherewith they are all initiated."

Compare and contrast with the above statement what he says in vol. ii., p. 765, as to the disunion amongst the 'reformed.' "If our communion with Papists in some few ceremonies do so much strengthen them as is pretended, how much more doth this division and rent among ourselves; especially seeing it is maintained to be, not in light matters only, but even in matter of faith and salvation."

DR. MILMAN, in his 'History of Latin Christianity' (ed. 1867), bk. ii., chap. i., vol. i., p. 104, affirms that "the unity of the visible Church . . . . seemed to demand or, at least, had a strong tendency to promote and to maintain the necessity for one supreme head."

Again, he asserts in bk. xiv., chap. ii., p. 53, that "Latin Christendom, or rather universal Christendom, was one . . . . not only in the organization of the ruling hierarchy, and the admission of Monkhood; it was one in the great system of belief."

DR. MOBERLY, in his "Discourses on the Great Forty Days" (Rivingtons, 1846), pp. 68 and 69, tells us that our Lord speaks of His disciples' unity "as being a sign to

the world of His mission.   He speaks of having given
them His glory with a view to their unity . . . . He speaks
of His Apostles as sent, even as He was Himself sent by
the Father, into the world, to be instructed, inspired,
comforted by the Holy Ghost: to succeed to His own
glory . .   to be united with each other, and with
Himself, even as He is one with the Father."

BISHOP PEARSON 'On the Creed' (Bohn's Standard
Library), under Art. ix., p. 547, says: "The Church is
therefore one, though the members be many, because
they all agree in one Faith."

BISHOP WILSON, quoted in his 'Life' (Library of
Anglo-Catholic Theology), p. 447, says that "if the
unity of the Church is once made a light matter, and he
who is the centre of unity and in Christ's stead shall
come to be despised, and his authority set at nought ;—
if the Bishops and Pastors of Christ's flock should not
be careful to preserve inviolably the sacred rights
committed to their trust; then will error and infidelity
get ground, Jesus Christ and His Gospel will be despised,
and the kingdom of Satan set up again."   In his
'Parochialia,' p. 210, he declares that "the necessity of
believing this article (the Holy Catholic Church) is
plain, because it is the only covenanted way to eternal
life."

It is, of course, easy to find statements of recent High
Church authors of equal force with the above as to the
essential and visible unity required of the true Church.
It will be sufficient, therefore, to quote, simply as
samples, a few statements by them of a yet stronger
character and more instructive import.

REV. W. J. E. BENNETT, in his 'Plea for Toleration in
the Church of England' (Hayes, London, 1867), for
instance, tells the truth concerning the unity to be
found only in communion with Rome, when he says,
on p. 100: "In the Church of Rome, which numbers
far more souls within her communion than ours, while
unity of doctrine is strictly maintained, uniformity of
worship is a thing not insisted upon."   And on p. 101,
"The pomp of St. Peter's does not discard or drive out
the poor Cistercian, neither does the simple-minded

Cistercian anathematize the glories of St. Peter's; they remain as brethren."

BISHOP HAMILTON in his 'Charge' (Rivingtons, 1867), p. 31, asserts that "the whole Church . . forms one visible polity or kingdom."

KEBLE in his 'Sermons, Academical and Occasional' (Parker, Oxford, 1847), p. 258, says: "One great object of our Lord's intercession is the visible unity of all believers in Him, and through Him with the Father; such unity as the world might see, and believe that God had sent Him;" and, on p. 267, "the prayer of the Only-Begotten could not be in vain."

And again, p. 299: "Who shall deny that such descriptions as these (of the Church, in the New Testament) imply an outward and visible unity, such an unity as the world can take notice of, else how should it thence learn belief? such an unity as should be no more doubtful or equivocal . . than the form of baptism, or the faith connected with that form," etc.:

ISAAC WILLIAMS, in his 'Sermons on the Catechism.' (Rivingtons, 1851), p. 181, says: "This Church is like our Saviour's robe, woven without seam from the top throughout, which cannot be divided."

Again, on p. 184: "It is to unity, to union, to unanimity, that God has promised His blessing." And on p. 185: "It is evident throughout the Scriptures that the Church of God must be one; and how can we be safe unless we belong to the one true Church?"

Glancing for one moment abroad, we are told by HALLAM—"History of the Literature of Europe," pt. iii., chap. ii., sec. 13, p. 409, (ed. 1860,) that Grotius, on account of the ill-usage which he sustained at the hands of his fellows, became "gradually less and less averse to the comprehensive and majestic unity of the Catholic hierarchy."

This is the unity of which RENAN speaks in his 'Hibbert Lectures,' 1880, Eng. trans., p. 164, where he says: "The phrase 'Catholic Church' breaks upon us from all sides at once (in the 2nd century) as the name of the great communion which is destined thenceforth to come down the ages in unbroken unity."

And this is the unity from which Lutheranism was cut off, for, according to MOSHEIM, 'Ecclesiastical History,' vol. iii., p. 479, " No two systems (than those of Trent and of Augsburg) can be more irreconcileably opposite."

The True Church is Holy.

DR. FARRAR, in his Hulsean Lectures, for 1870 lec. iii. p. 115, remarks: " During this period (5th to 13th century), the Church was the one mighty witness for light in an age of darkness, for order in an age of lawlessness, for personal holiness in an epoch of licentious rage."

J. A. FROUDE, in his Fifth Lecture in New York, 1872, reported in *The Times* of Nov. 16, 1872, said that " he did not question the enormous power for good which had been exercised in Ireland by the modern Catholic priests. Ireland was one of the poorest countries in Europe; yet there was less theft, less cheating, less house-breaking, less robbery of all kinds than in any country of the same size in the civilized world. . . . In the last hundred years at least, impurity had been almost unknown in Ireland. This absence of vulgar crime, and this exceptional delicacy and modesty of character were due, to their everlasting honour, to the influence of the Catholic clergy."

PEARSON, 'On the Creed,' in art. ix., p. 555, tells us that " as . . the Church is truly holy, not only by a holiness of institution, but also by a personal sanctity in reference to . . Saints while they live, so is it also perfectly holy in relation to the same Saints glorified in heaven."

SIR FREDERICK POLLOCK, writing in the *Contemporary Review* of September, 1890, remarks: " In the system of the Church of Rome, the whole of moral duty is included in the Law of God and of Holy Church, and there is no breach of that law which may not be dealt with in a regular and formal manner by the Church's tribunals. Morality becomes a thing . . even of legislative declaration by the authority supreme on earth in matters of faith and morals."

DR. ISAAC TAYLOR, Canon of York, writing in the

Fortnightly for October, 1888, p. 500, bears witness to the sanctity and heroism of Catholic missionaries, saying that . . "General Gordon . . found none but the Roman Catholics who came up to his ideal of the absolute self-devotion of the Apostolic missionary. . . These priests succeed, as they deserve to succeed, while the professional Protestant missionary fails. True missionary work is neccessarily heroic work, and heroic work can only be done by heroes."

ISAAC WILLIAMS, in his 'Sermons on the Catechism,' p. 182, says: "The Head of the Church, Who is in Heaven, is Holy; and, therefore, the whole Body, which is on earth, partakes of His holiness. And it is holy because the Holy Spirit dwells within it, and because, although its members are not all holy, yet they have all been once made holy at Baptism. . . It is, moreover, holy because all things dedicated to God are holy." While on p. 184, he gives us the reverse of the picture: "What is the reason of the numberless religious divisions into which this country is torn? Doubtless," he replies, "it is from the want of holiness."

The True Church is Catholic in every sense.

BISHOP JEREMY TAYLOR remarks in his 'Works,' vol. x., p. 378 (Rivingtons, 1828), that "Bellarmine says 'Ecclesia dicitur Catholica, non solum quia semper fuit, sed etiam quia semper erit;' so we have," he admits, "a rare note for us who are alive, to discern the Church of Rome to be the Catholic Church, and we may possibly come to know it by this sign, many ages after we are dead, because she will last always."

MACAULAY in his Essay ' on Ranke's History of the Popes' (Longmans), p. 131, tells us: " Four times, since the authority of Rome was established in Western Christendom, has the human intellect risen up against her yoke. Twice that Church remained completely victorious. Twice she came forth from the conflict bearing the marks of cruel wounds, but with the principle of life still strong within her. When we reflect," he says, " on the tremendous assaults which she has survived, we find it difficult to conceive in what way she is to perish." And, on p. 142, he approves the wise policy which lies at the root of true Catholicism. ".The ignorant enthusiast whom the Anglican Church makes an enemy, and, whatever the polite and learned may think, a most dangerous enemy, the Catholic Church makes a champion." For he shows his meaning when he speaks further on of " the profound policy with which she used the fanaticism of such persons as St. Ignatius and St. Theresa."

LECKY, in his ' History of Rationalism,' vol. ii., p. 37, acknowledges that " Catholicism laid the very foundations of modern civilization." While DR. MAITLAND in his ' History of the Dark Ages,' p. 393, tells us that " at the darkest periods the Christian Church was the source and spring of civilization " thus fulfilling the outward visible part of her Catholic mission."

PEARSON, 'On the Creed,' art. ix., p. 563, (Bohn), says: " There is a necessity of believing the Catholick Church, because, except a man be of that, he can be of none. . . . . Whosoever is not of the Catholick Church, cannot be of the true Church."

We may turn to KEBLE and PUSEY for yet stronger statements. KEBLE, in his ' Sermons Academical and Occasional,' p. 241, says: " The idea of the Catholic Church is all that in one, which we imperfectly endeavour to shape out by our innumerable and partial, and therefore most unsatisfactory, combinations."

PUSEY, ' On the Minor Prophets' (Parker, 1861,) on Joel, chap. ii., p. 131, utters the true statement, applicable to his own communion as well as those for whom he intended it: " They then are members of the soul of the Church who, not being members of the visible communion and society, know not that, in not becoming members of it, they are rejecting the command of Christ."

The True Church is Apostolic in origin and in government.

BISHOP ANDREWES, in ' A Pattern of Catechistical Doctrine' (Anglo-Catholic Library), p. 357, remarks that the Apostles " betook themselves to residence in

some one place, divers of them, as . . St. Peter first
at Antioch and after at Rome. Which places were
more especially accounted their sees, and the Churches
themselves after a more special manner were called
' apostolic,' ' sedes Apostolorum.' "

BLONDEL, in his treatise ' On the Supremacy,' p. 107,
says: "Rome being a Church consecrated by the
residence of St. Peter, whom antiquity acknowledged as
the head of the Apostolic College, might easily have
been considered by the Council of Chalcedon as the
head of the Church."

DR. DUMOULIN in (Preb. of Canterbury, 17th century),
in his ' Vocation of Pastors,' acknowledges that " those
who read their writings will find those of the fourth and
fifth ages giving the supremacy to the Bishop of Rome,
and asserting that to him belongs the care of all
Churches."

BISHOP GILBERT, in his 'Exposition of the Articles of
the Church of England' (London, 1827), p. 386, on art.
xxxvii., says : " Nor was the doctrine of their (the Popes')
infallibility, ever so universally received and submitted
to in these *Western* parts, as was that of their universal
jurisdiction. They were in possession of it; appeals
were made to them; they sent legates and bulls everywhere ; they granted exemptions from the ordinary
jurisdiction; and took Bishops bound to them by oaths,
that were penned in the form of oaths of fealty or
homage."

GRANT—' Bampton Lectures,' p. 101, says: " The
authority to send is derived from the Lord Himself to
those who bear Apostolic rule in His Church; . . the
method . . the preaching of the Gospel by living
witnesses."

HOOKER, vol. iii., bk. viii., p. 462, is evidently not in
favour of the modern theory that the Church has no
visible head on earth, for he says : " It is not simply
the title of Head which lifteth our Saviour above all
powers, but the title of Head in such sort understood
as the Apostle himself meant it : so that the same being
imparted in another sense unto others doth not anyway
make those others therein His equals." And on p. 476

he says that, "heads endued with supreme power
extending to a certain compass are, for the exercise of
visible regiment, not unnecessary."

JOHNSON, in his 'English Canons' (Anglo-Catholic
Library) pt. i., pref. p. xii., allows that "if the clergy of
England before the Reformation had indeed a zeal for
the Pope's authority, it must have proceeded purely from
their mistaken principles, and the dictates of an
erroneous conscience; for they could have no other
inducement to abet a power so grievous to themselves."
Again, p. xx., he is honest in saying that Augustine "as
all other Western Archbishops in communion with the
See of Rome, received from the Pope a robe called a
pall, which they were to put on as often as they said
Mass; which was in truth designed as a badge of their
dependence on the Pope." Again, p. xxii., he allows
that our early Kings recognized the Apostolic rule of
Rome: "Ine, Offa, Ethelwolf, could find no better
employ for their devotion than to go to Rome," etc.
". . yet . . all the weak zeal of our Saxon and Danish
Kings never proved so injurious to their Kingdom and
people as the management of some of our bravest Kings
after the conquest did. King Stephen and Henry II.,
by permitting the Pope to put his Canon Law in
execution here; the same King Henry II., by submitting
to the penance enjoined him by the Pope's legates;"
etc. And again, p. xxiii.: "It is hard to conceive that
our Kings should stoop so low as to accept grants of
tenths on the clergy from the Pope . . if they had
thought themselves independent. . . It is not only
certain in fact that our Kings countenanced Papal
provisions, but that they sometimes requested the
Popes to make use of this . . prerogative."

As to derivation of power from an Apostolic source,
he says in Part II., p. 446: "As the Popes had made
the Archbishops seem to act with authority derived from
Rome; so every suffragan Bishop might be thought to
derive his power from Canterbury."

DEAN CHURCH, in his 'Life of St. Anselm,' p. 167,
says: "Then it was most natural for Christians, hating
the pride that defied God's Law and the licence which

trod its sanctities under-foot, to rally round the conspicuous and traditional centre of Christendom, and
seek there a support which failed them at the extremi-
ties." And p. 199: " He (Anselm) especially appealed
to his brethren the Bishops, that they would shew him
how he might neither do anything contrary to his obedience to the Pope, nor offend against the faith which he
owed to the King. . . It was a fair question to men
with the inherited and unbroken convictions of the
religion of that age." On p. 215: " What every one
looked upon as St. Peter's gift (the pall), it did not
belong to the royal dignity to convey to him. His view
was the natural one." On p. 233, he says that Anselm
began appeals to Rome "not only in good faith but
with good reason."

He tells us, on p. 225: " There was a very real and
living law in Christendom. . . On it Anselm cast himself." And again, on p. 226, he says that " the quarrel
was . . one between true sense of duty and belief in
spiritual truth on the one hand, and brutal irresistible
force, professedly contemptuous of truth and duty, on
the other."

DEAN MANSEL in 'The Speaker's Commentary,' on
St. Math. xvi., 18, 19 (Murray, London, 1878), says on
the subject of the declaration to St. Peter: " The Greek
can hardly be naturally interpreted except as referring
to the person of St. Peter, and the fulfilment of the
prediction is to be found in the fact that St. Peter was
the chosen agent in laying the foundation of the
Christian Church, both among the Jews and among the
Gentiles. . . By the Keys of the Kingdom will . .
naturally be meant the power of admitting to, or ex-
cluding from, the communion of the Church. Here
again, as in the figure of the rock, an office is in a
secondary sense assigned to Peter, which primarily
belongs to Christ."

DEAN MILMAN, in his ' History of Christianity,' Book
iv., chap. vi., p. 307, affirms that " reverence for Rome
penetrated with the Gospel to the remotest parts."
And in Book vii., chap. i., p. 4, he says: " With all the
Teutonic part of Latin Christendom, the belief in the

supremacy of the Pope was co-eval with their Christianity."

PEARSON in 'Opera Posthuma' (London, 1688), demonstrates by innumerable arguments that St. Peter was at Rome, and that the Popes are his successors. And 'On the Creed,' art. ix., p. 542, he says: "Then (Acts ii., 41), was there a Church, and that built upon Peter, according to our Saviour's promise."

JEREMY TAYLOR, vol. xiv., p. 21, says that the Apostles "were representatives of all the whole ecclesiastical order in some things, and of the whole Christian Church in others; and, therefore, what parts of duty and power and office did belong to each, the Apostles must teach the Church, or she could have no way of knowing without particular revelation."

WHITAKER, in 'Contra Bellarminum Quæstio,' cap. ii., p. 554, says of the Petrine claims: "We deny not that Peter was the foundation and governor of the Church; and, if required, we will grant that it was promised to him in the text, 'Thou art Peter,'" etc.

WHITBY, in his 'Paraphrase,' tom. i., p. 143, has: "I say to thee that thou art by name Peter, *i.e.*, a rock, and upon thee, who art this rock, I will build My Church, and I will give thee the power of making laws to govern My Church."

In his 'Lyra Innocentium,' p. 247, KEBLE writes:

"From Godhead made Man
  The virtue goes out the whole world to bless,
O'er lands parch'd and weary that shadow began
  To spread from St. Peter, and ne'er shall grow less."

From DR. LEE a multitude of very strong passages might be quoted for the Catholic idea of the Apostolicity of the Church, but to these a few references only shall be given.—' Life of Cardinal Pole,' (Nimmo, 1888), Prologue, p. xii., and p. xxxiv.: in the book itself, p. 145 and p. 274. 'The Church under Queen Elizabeth,' (Allen, 1880), Introduction, pp. xli. and xlii.; and in the book, vol. i., pp. 188, 189, 190.

BENGEL in 'Gnomon Novi Test.' (Tubingen, 1855), on St. Matt. xvi., 18, says: "Certe super apostolos ædificata est ecclesia Christi . . qua in re præcipua quædam sane Petri, salva Apostolicæ potestatis æqualitate prærogativa extitit. . . Præterea hic potissimum fratres suos confirmare, ovesque et agnos Domini pascere jussus est." And, v. 19: "Comprehenduntur omnia ea quæ Petrus in virtute Nominis Jesu Christi, . . apostolica potestate, gessit; docendo, convincendo, remittendo, sanando, resuscitando, puniendo," etc.

Foreign Protestants can be quoted largely against the modern Anglican theory that St. Peter had no real connection with Rome. Among others, CHAMERIUS, lib. 13, c. 4, §2, states that "all the Fathers with great accord have asserted that St. Peter went to Rome and governed that Church." And GROTIUS, in 'Synopsis Criticorum,' p. 1540, goes so far as to say that "no Christian ever doubted that St. Peter was at Rome."

The Apostolic work of the Papacy in the Church and the world is shown by ANCILLON, in his 'Table des Revolutions du Système Politique de l'Europe,' vol. i. Introduction p. 133: "The Papacy alone perhaps saved Europe from utter barbarism."

CAPITO (a colleague of BUCER at Strasburg), in his Epistle to Farel (A.D. 1537), says: "The Lord grants me to learn . . what great harm we have done by our hasty judgment and inconsiderate vehemence in throwing off the Papal authority."

Many quotations might be taken from MOSHEIM in support of the evidence in favour of Roman Apostolic authority in early times; as, for instance: for the third century—Eccles. Hist., vol. i., p. 194: for the fourth—p. 259; for the fifth—p. 339 and p. 375; for the eighth—p. 487; and for the ninth—vol. ii., p. 35, where he says: "Even so early as this century many were of opinion that it was proper and expedient, though not absolutely necessary, that the decisions of Bishops and Councils should be confirmed by the consent and authority of the Roman Pontiff, whom they considered as the supreme and universal Bishop."

RANKE, in 'Opera' p. 12, says that "Boniface, the Apostle of the Germans, was an Anglo-Saxon; this missionary largely sharing in the veneration professed

by this nation for St. Peter and his successors, had from
the beginning voluntarily pledged himself to abide faithfully by all the regulations of the Roman See," etc.

RENAN, in his ' Hibbert Lectures,' declares that "the
Pope of Rome has made it (Christianity) the religion of
the world."   On p. 124, he calls St. Clement "the first
type of Pope which Christianity presents to us."   And,
on p. 148, he asserts that "in the reign of Antoninus
(A.D. 138 et seq.), the germ of the Papacy already exists
in a very definite form."

SALMASIUS, in ' Eucharisticon,' p. 644, even went so
far as to say : " The Bishop of Rome is the great Pontiff,
the Father of fathers, the Ruler and Governor of the
Universal Church.   He is, in fine, the successor of St.
Peter, the Vicar of Christ upon earth."

The True Church has authority to govern and to teach.

GRANT, in his ' Bampton Lectures,' lec. iii., p. 92,
says : " In the Church we may recognise such a teacher
as is needed to communicate . . first principles ; to
stand by and remove difficulties ; to satisfy enquiries,
and solve doubts ; to speak with authoritative voice,
as commissioned to teach."   Again, on p. 98, he says
that " we (*i.e.*, Anglicans) have lost too much a sense of
the allegiance we owe to her ; we have not looked to her
for guidance, nor shown our readiness to obey."   And
again, in lec. iv., p. 134, his witness may be quoted to
the effect that the Church of Rome was "the means
whereby the idea of a spiritual rule on earth was tangibly
impressed on minds which would have been unaffected
by the purer and simpler garb which the Gospel wore
in primitive ages ; . . it did overcome the cruelty and
tyranny of monarchs ; . . did frequently check the
career of guilty power, and uphold the cause of justice
and of virtue."

HOOKER, in his ' Ecclesiastical Polity,' vol. i., bk. i.,
p. 357, speaking of fasting, says : " Here men's private
fancies must give place to the higher judgment of that
Church which is in authority a Mother over them."
And again, in vol. ii., bk. v., p. 44, he says : " That

which the Church by her ecclesiastical authority shall
probably think and define to be true or good, must, incongruity of reason, over-rule all other inferior judgments whatsoever."

The True Church is based on Divine Faith, and Infallible.

BISHOP ANDREWES, in his 'Pattern of Catechistical
Doctrine,' p. 57, says: "There is a certain and infallible interpretation; else, if we were always uncertain,
how should we build on the rock? As we must take
heed of private interpretation . . so must we . . hold
that God hath given the gift of interpretation, which
gift is not given to any but those which are in the
Church."

BISHOP BAIL, quoted in 'The Catholic's Manual, by
Bossuet, with notes by Rev. J. Fletcher,' (Newcastle,
1817), cap. xx., remarks: "Religion must essentially
rest upon certitude . . if faith be uncertain, no one
will obey its laws."

BINGHAM, in his 'French Church's Apology,' p. 404,
says: "A voluntary error in faith may prove as fatal as
an immorality in practice."

BISHOP BULL, in his 'Defensio Fidei Nicendæ,' Proem.
No. ii., p. 2, speaking of the great decision in the
Nicene Council, asks "if, in a matter of such importance,
all the Pastors of the Church could fall into error, how
shall we be able to defend the word of Christ, Who
hath promised His Apostles and, in their persons, His
successors to be always with them? Which promise
would not be true, the Apostles not being to live so
long, were it not that their successors are here com-
prehended in the persons of the Apostles themselves."

DR. FIELD, 'On the Church,' bk. i., cap. 13, is very
explicit: "That the Catholic Church should err in anything within the compass of revealed truth is impossible: nay, in things not absolutely necessary to be
believed expressly, we believe that the Church can
never err, and that the visible Church never falleth into
heresy we most willingly grant."

On the other hand, BISHOP JEREMY TAYLOR, quoted

in 'The Catholic's Manual' mentioned above, cap. **xx.**, says of his co-religionists: "We have yet no positive points among us, settled for undoubted truths; there being rather a medley of all religious Christian sects professed among us; or a negation of those tenets of the Church we went out of."

DR. WHITAKER (a violent Calvinist), in his 'Controversy II.,' question v. cap. 13, says: "The Church cannot hold any erroneous doctrine and remain a Church. Truth constitutes the Church, and the Church shows where truth is to be found. . . Other societies may err, this society never can err."

ISAAC WILLIAMS, in his 'Sermons on the Catechism,' p. 177, tells us that "the Church of God alone, so far as she continues the same from the beginning, keeps the whole truth in all its parts."

KEBLE, too, in 'Sermons Academical and Occasional,' p. 300, says: "In the Church we naturally look for a guide in all material points, both of doctrine and worship. She is the pillar and ground of the Truth . . to which exclusively and properly belongs the Truth of whatever was shadowed in the former dispensations."

Thus also DR. NEALE, in his 'Sermons in Sackville Coll. Chapel,' vol. iii., p. 147, says: "The Church, like the Head of the Church, will have all or none. She does not say, 'though mine is the better religion, yours will do well enough;' but she says, 'I am right and you are wrong.'"

So PUSEY, in his 'Eirenicon' (Parker, London, 1865), p. 7, allows that "the question . . is not whether the doctrine laid down in General Councils and received by the whole Church is certain truth,—for this both agree (*i.e.*, Catholics and Anglicans); nor whether an Œcumenical Council, if such were now held and received by the whole Church, would, by that reception, have the seal of infallibility (on this too, there is no question)."

How I Came Home.

By LADY HERBERT.

I WAS brought up in what we should now call the "High and Dry" school of the Established Church of England. It was utterly and entirely distasteful to me. I was eager, energetic, and enthusiastic; and I found myself surrounded by cold and formal services, high pews, long puritanical hymns, and intolerably dry sermons. My Sundays were a perfect terror to me. I was made to learn long portions of the *Christian Year* by heart (some of which, even now, I cannot understand), in addition to the Epistle and Collect for the day: the rest of the time was to be spent in reading sermons, or in church, where kneeling bolt upright always made me faint. I had the greatest difficulty in learning poetry by heart, so that I could never say my lesson, and my evening was consequently generally spent in tears. Even now, I sometimes have the recollection of what I felt on waking in the morning when I remembered it was Sunday.

Then came my Confirmation, for which I can only say that I was simply not prepared at all. A clergyman came and asked me to repeat the Creed, which I did; after which he shook hands with me, and said he was quite sure I had been too well brought up not to be prepared, and gave me my ticket. I went through the service as in a dream. Then came my First Communion, and I was simply horridly frightened. I did not understand what now I see and feel. But I kept on repeating to myself "*verily and indeed taken;*" and wondering if those words were to be taken in a literal or in a non-natural sense: and, if the latter, why they were left in the Catechism? For two years after that I recollect no change in myself, or in the dreary round of my religious duties.

Then came the "Oxford Movement," as it was called. This was my first view of real religion. I found in the writings of that new school all that my heart and mind had longed for and hungered after for years—I found life, and warmth and practice. But what really attracted me, although I knew it not, was their Catholicity. I devoured every book of the kind that came out. What I could not afford to buy I borrowed. The son of an old friend of mine (afterwards superior of a religious house), was then at Oxford, and he supplied me with all I required— the *Tracts for the Times*, Dr. Newman's and Manning's Sermons, the *Library of the Fathers*, and the many lighter contemporaneous works of Faber and Churton, Froude and Mozley, Sewell and Yonge, Williams and Paget, Gresley and the like. I began really to pray and watch, and fast, and examine myself, and try and deny myself in little things. I longed, as all girls of my temperament do, for the life of a Sister of Charity. About this time, I was immensely startled and pained at my young Oxford friend and companion announcing to me his intention of joining the Church of Rome. "It would be almost a death-blow to his mother," he said, "and *that* was what grieved him most. But he could not help himself—he could not remain where he was." My father was very indignant, and forbad all further intercourse between us. And so we parted, never to meet again till, twenty years later, I saw him in the cloister of his monastery.

Soon after this event we removed from the west of England to a property in the midland counties, which had been left to us by a distant relative. Here I found a scope for my activity in a hitherto neglected village, which formed part of the property, where there was

neither church nor schools. There was the gable-end
of an old chapelry, dedicated to St. Edith, with a bell
turret, close to the wall of which the rector of the parish
church (which was three or four miles off) used to come
and recite the Morning Prayers four times a year, so as
to be entitled to the tithe. But, except that occasional
service in the open air, the poor people had no " Church
privileges, " as it was called, unless they were young and
strong enough to walk to the parish church. I began by
opening a school, and by degrees, through painting and
selling my sketches, and the kindness of friends, I raised
enough money to build on a chancel to that neglected
gable-end ; and never shall I forget the joy of seeing
the first communions and baptisms in that little place
—many having come who had neglected the Sacraments
for years. In all this work my chief encourager was the
Rural Dean—a very excellent Anglican clergyman—who
with his wife became my greatest friends. They, too,
were drawing nearer and nearer towards Catholic truth,
and helped me far more than they were themselves
aware of. But my father became alarmed at our intimacy, and especially at my religious views. He said,
and said truly, that they were incompatible with Protestantism, and my visits were discouraged, and finally
stopped.

It was in the autumn of 1844 that a great friend of
mine sent me some letters she had received through a
mutual acquaintance, written by Dr. Newman. They
were of engrossing interest to all those who, like myself,
were dissatisfied with their present position, and
hungered after greater certainty and guidance in
matters of faith. These letters insisted, however, a
great deal on not going by one's own taste and inclination, or by one's own feelings in so grave a matter. One
of them has been published in his *Apologia*, and runs as
follows :

"This I am sure of, that nothing but a simple, direct
call of duty is a warrant for anyone leaving our Church ;

and no preference for another Church, no delight in its
service, no hope of greater religious advancement in it ;
no indignation, no disgust at the persons and things
among which we find ourselves in the Church of England.

"The simple question is: Can I (it is personal, not
whether another, but can *I*) be saved in the English
Church ? Am *I* in safety were I to die to-night ? Is
it a mortal sin in *me*, not joining another communion ?"

It is impossible for me to say the effect which these
letters, and many others of the like kind, had upon us.
They were copied and treasured up (in secret, of course,)
and pondered and prayed over by hundreds of souls of
whom the writer little dreamed, but who were going
through minor throes of the same agony of doubt and
suspense as himself.

A year later I married, and strangely enough my
new home had been St. Edith's old monastery: so
that it seemed as if she were to follow and form part of
my life. Probably her prayers (in return for the imperfect service I had ignorantly paid her by restoring her
ruined shrine) helped me in my coming struggle. Dr.
Newman, F. W. Faber, and many others whose names
were household words among us, had by that time joined
the Church of Rome. I felt that they had carried our
principles to their legitimate conclusion. But I was too
full of my new-found happiness at that time, and too
much engrossed with the intense joys of life, to give
much thought to religious questions or duties. However,
it soon came back to me that this was an unworthy
return to make to the Giver of such untold blessings, and
I resumed my inner life and active works of charity as
before. Then began my intimacy with one who so
greatly influenced my future course.

I had been married about four months when my
husband one day brought to introduce to me one
whom he called his "oldest school and college
friend;" adding: "He is the holiest man I have

ever met." It was quite true. There was a something about Archdeacon Manning which made one ashamed of an unworthy thought or a careless word; and yet he was always loving and tender as a woman. We went abroad the following year, and he accompanied us and spent the winter, partly in Rome and partly in Naples. He and my husband used to take long walks together almost daily, and then he would either dine with us or join us in the evening and continue the conversations which to us all were of such engrossing interest, relating, as they did, to the political and religious state of Rome. At that time I was anxious and disappointed at having no prospect of a child; and some cousins of my husband's who were nuns of the Sacred Heart in a convent in Rome, offered to make a novena for us for that intention, which we gratefully accepted. The Archdeacon suggested that we should go together and pray at the Ara Cœli for the fulfilment of our wish; or rather, he added gently: "That the Will of God may be done in you and by you." He gave me at the same time a little terracotta statuette of the Blessed Virgin, with the hands crossed in submission, and the words: *Ecce ancilla Domini!* underneath; saying: " When you can feel as *she* felt, when you can give up your will and have no wish or will but *His*, then, and not till then, will the blessing you seek be granted to you." Another day, I recollect tormenting myself with the fear that I was not clever or amusing enough to be a fit companion for my husband. His answer I feel should be engraved in every young wife's heart: " Your business is not to make your husband's home *brilliant,* but *blessed.*"

Our intimacy went on increasing; he virtually became my confessor; drew up for me a plan of life; gave us both prayers to use; directed our spiritual readings; and helped us in all the little difficulties which a conscientious mind must ever feel even in the happiest path. He got me to make a review of my past life; dividing it into portions of eight years, and marking the faults of each period, so as to give me a better insight into my own character, and to teach me to detect and struggle against my besetting faults more vigorously. Dr. Newman was at that time at Rome, living very quietly in the Benedictine Monastery of S. Paolo fuore le Mure. My husband had been his old and favourite pupil, and went to see him, taking me with him. I was much struck by that interview, although he did not say much on the questions in dispute.

From that year until 1851 our friendship with the Archdeacon increased in proportion to our more frequent meetings, both at his house and ours. "The child of many prayers" (as he called her) was born, and received (as we had promised) the name of Mary. I was very ill before her birth, and the Archdeacon came to me constantly to strengthen and cheer me in my coming trial. Again, the following year, when a son was given to us, who nearly died a few months after his birth, he was again by our side to share in our anxiety as in our joy. Then came the Gorham decision on the question of baptism; the efforts made by my husband and his friends to counteract its effects; their protest against it, signed by all the best and most influential members of the Church of England; and Bishop Blomfield's bill to confine ecclesiastical questions to ecclesiastical courts, a bill thrown out in the Lords mainly owing to a clever speech of Lord Brougham's, in which he asserted that "so great was the disunion among the right rev. prelates on the Bench that no question brought before them would have the chance of a peaceable solution; and even if it had, that the minority would never obey the majority in such matters."

I have a vivid recollection of a discussion the following day at our house, in which two or three of the speakers openly declared their conviction of the impossibility of remaining in a Church in which even the Sacraments were treated as open questions: that the late assertion of royal supremacy in matters of faith was contrary to the law of our Lord; and that the theory of the Church of England being a branch of the Church Catholic was entirely set aside by such decisions. Moreover, that in spite of all the special pleadings upon the subject and the words of individual writers, the Catholic Church distinctly repudiated Anglican Orders as invalid, and proved it by insisting on re-ordaining all Anglican ministers, no matter how high their position or how great their ability; an act which in the case of a real ordination would be sacrilegious, and which was never done to converts from the Greek Church. Day after day these subjects were renewed with the earnestness of men who had nothing to gain but everything to lose by a change of creed, and who yet felt that they could not remain where they were. How it all ended is a matter of history. The best of the clergymen, and many of the laymen present on these occasions "went over to Rome," as it was called. Those that hesitated, did so less from conviction than from that wonderful theory, to which so many still cling, of "going over" in a corporate body, *i.e.*, of the whole Church of England shaking off the errors of the Reformation and returning to the One Fold.

As to ourselves and the Archdeacon, he voluntarily broke off all communication with us, writing to us both "that it would not be right for him to continue an intimacy which might be prejudicial to my husband in his present position; that we had been too nearly drawn together to meet as ordinary friends; and that he would never seek either of us unless we first sought him."

We both of us felt the separation most keenly: but to me it was a sort of religious shipwreck. If I had had doubts before as to the validity of Anglican Orders, the fact of the Archdeacon's utter disbelief in them and his refusal, even before he took the final step, to give absolution, would have settled that point with me for ever. And if Anglican Orders were invalid, what were the Sacraments? I tried to console myself by laying great stress on the doctrine of Intention, and by making frequent spiritual communions. I wrote to the Bishop of ———, asking him to take the Archdeacon's place

as my confessor.   He refused, alleging the usual
Anglican reasons, and throwing me back on myself.   I
have since been most thankful for this refusal; for
nothing can be more dangerous and injudicious than
the way in which direction and confession are abused
in the Anglican body.   Neither are legitimate; neither
are recognized by the Bishops or the formularies of the
English Church; so that all the evils which the wildest
imagination may attribute to the practice in the Church
Catholic, are almost inevitable under circumstances
where no check whatever is placed on the exercise
of authority.   I speak from actual knowledge when
I say that this authority is exercised on weak and
timid women to an extent which would be not
only incredible but utterly impossible in the Catholic
Church.   Each of these clergymen is a pope in his own
proper person.   His decisions are infallible, and as he
recognizes no ecclesiastical superior there is no limit
whatever to the exercise of his powers.

But to return to myself.   My only resource was to
fall back upon my old rule of life, to try as far as
possible to be in the mind of the Church if I could not
be outwardly of its body; above all, to wait and pray
for further light and guidance.   My Catholic longings,
however, were not satisfied: I could not forget what I
had heard.   Dr. Newman says truly: " He who has
once seen a ghost cannot be as one who has never seen
it."   Doubts as to the truth of the Church of England
had been sown broadcast in my mind; and I could not
but feel that the only legitimate and honest conclusion
to which the High Church teachings of my life could
lead was the one at which the Archdeacon and Dr.
Newman had already arrived.

Whenever we went abroad, we used to go to Benediction or early Mass, and I often discussed the whole matter
with my husband.   He knew perfectly what my feelings
were, for I never had a secret from him in my life.   He
admitted that the Catholic religion was more suited to
some temperaments than the Protestant; that one's

religion was, after all, very much what a clever writer
has called "a geographical accident;" by which he
meant that if we had been born in Russia, like his
mother, we should have been brought up in the Greek
Church; if in France or Italy, Austria or Spain, in the
Catholic, and so on. But he always maintained that as
long as the Anglican Church did not force us to believe
anything contrary to Catholic truth, we were bound to
remain in her communion in spite of her many heretical
teachers: that it was, in fact, "good for the present
distress;" and that as everything Romanist was looked
upon with such distrust and aversion in England, all
hope of doing good, or of influencing others and being
of use in one's generation, depended on our staying
where we were and making the best of it. This was
the result of hundreds and hundreds of such conversations. I found it worried him, and I left off talking of
it; but my own feelings underwent no change. I had,
deep down in my heart, the conviction that had dawned
upon me before my marriage and kept growing upon
me ever after, that the Church of England was but an
offspring of the Reformation and not the Church of
Christ; that it was a national establishment, in fact, and
nothing else. And if it were indeed a branch of the
true Church, where was the harm of going to the
parent tree? In the meantime, I read every book that
came in my way *against* these convictions—Wordsworth
and Burnett, Sewell and Goulburn, Bennett and Burgon,
and half-a-dozen others—and laid each down in disgust,
because I felt that they made *ex parte* statements, that
they quoted isolated passages from the Fathers and left
out the context, that they gave you garbled extracts
which perverted the original meaning of different
passages; in fact, that they were, like lawyers, pleading
a bad cause and feeling it to be one all the time. My
husband used himself to speak of the "curse of the
Reformation," which in so many cases had destroyed
where it ought only to have amended; and especially
regretted the substitution of the Morning Service with

its wearisome " dearly beloved," Ten Commandments,
and reiterated prayers for the Queen and the royal
family, for the simple Eucharistic service of the
Catholic Church.

But work thickened upon us. The Crimean war came ;
and for the moment, I laid aside my racking doubts
and fears and bent all my energies to trying to help my
husband.   During the war, I saw my old friend, the
late Archdeacon, two or three times.   He was
then living in " a little chamber in the wall "
like the prophet, in ————— Street, of which the
sole ornament was a bronze head of Christ which
we had given him at Rome.   I recollect nervously con-
fining myself to the business on hand ; but at the end,
I could not resist kneeling to ask for his old blessing.
He gave it me without comment, kindly but sadly ;
and then we did not meet again for months.

I pass over the intervening years of my life till my
husband's death.   They had been passed in arduous
work and in ever-increasing anxiety for the health of
one who was dearer to me than life.   At last, the blow
came ; and then it was that I fully realized what it was
to be in a Church in which I did not believe, and which
did not recognize prayers for the dead.   My mother-in-
law had once said to me (in speaking of my sister-in-
law's death), that it was the only thing she could not
bear in the Church of England.   And to me, it was
simply impossible.   I had prayed for him daily for
twenty years.   How could I leave off now ?   Besides, if
there were only a chance, however remote, however
doubtful, that such prayers could benefit him, how could
I withhold them ?   I had a very touching letter from
our old friend, speaking of him as I felt and knew he
would do.   In reply, I asked him where I could find
such prayers as I had sought for in vain among Anglican
manuals of devotion, begging him likewise to say some
Masses for my husband's soul ; for he was then a priest.
He complied with my wishes in both cases, but never
attempted any renewal of intercourse either in person
or by continuing the correspondence.

That year of overwhelming misery went by. I spent it in the south of France; seeing no one scarcely but my children and the poor, and holding no conversations on religious subjects. I went once or twice to the Catholic Church of the place where I was living; but I was rather discouraged than otherwise by so doing; for I found it next to impossible to follow the services from the rapidity of the priest's utterance and my own ignorance of Latin. This I resolved to remedy by taking lessons ; but I had no one to help or explain to me the ceremonies of the Mass or Benediction, and got hopelessly puzzled at the rapidity with which the former was said. Even at that time, reports were spread in England of my having been received into the Church. I repelled them almost indignantly. I had come to no such decision. Yet, being miserable and dissatisfied with the Anglican establishment, my mind was ever insensibly working onwards in that direction.

The following year, I went to Rome for the winter for the health of two of my children. Dr. Manning was there and preached ; but I did not go and hear him or try to see him. In the first place, I did not like to make people talk ; and in the next, I was so peculiarly situated with regard to my children, that I felt I could not ask him to my house. I had, therefore, been three months in Rome before we met; and he then spoke of nothing but my sorrow and his great love for my husband, and begged to hear all details of the end. These I gave him ; but we did not touch on religious subjects.

In spite of all my caution, however, the reports of my conversion were renewed. I had not only done nothing to give rise to them; but I had carefully abstained from going to services (as I had always done before with my husband) lest people should talk and make mischief. The only thing I used to do was to go and pray and cry at that same little convent in the Lungara, where my cousins had had the novena for the birth of my child. No one was admitted into the " clausura " of this convent but relations of the nuns ; but as I was

thus related and the Superior knew and felt for my
sorrow, she let me come whenever I pleased.   I felt
shy and unworthy to join in their services, but I used
to steal in from the garden towards dusk and pray
before the little light telling of the Presence, and felt
inexpressible comfort there.   I often wished at this
time to have talked to my Anglican chaplain, who was
my boy's tutor and lived with us.   But his notions
about women were peculiar.   He had a firm conviction
of their being all "inferior beings ; " that, as Pope says,
"most women have no character at all ;" that our
business, if we had doubts, was to go about our daily
duties and stifle such feelings as a temptation.   Now, in
some cases, such advice might have been wise and right.
No one feels more strongly than I do how absurd it is for
a woman, however carefully educated, to discuss theological questions.   They can only read books in translations and extracts ; and my old work for my husband
long ago convinced me of the extreme difficulty of
judging any questions fairly by such means.   But in
my case, I had always lived with and been treated as
the equal and companion of clever men ; I had not
had the education or training of an ordinary woman ;
and the religious doubts and difficulties which troubled
me had been put before me by really able and first-rate
minds.   So that to tell me, as this good man once
did, to stifle without solving them, was a moral impossibility.
   Circumstances at this time made me acquainted with a
Hungarian lady, a very fervent Catholic, to whom I now
became intimately and warmly attached.   She took me
with her to a retreat she was attending at the Villa
Lanti, which was preached by the Père de Damas,
of whom I had heard a great deal during the Crimean
war.   I was struck by the very practical nature of his
teaching.   There was not a word with which I did not
entirely agree.   And this was the more important for
me at that time, because I was just in that state in
which so many people are before they *quite* make up

their minds to submit to the Catholic Church—that is,
I was inclined to cavil at everything. People imagine
that they must understand everything, and that all their
doubts must be cleared up before they take the final
step ; whereas you must take the plunge in order to see
and understand ! God in that way rewards our faith and
simplicity ; and as Dr. Newman well observes : "The
Church is like a painted glass window—all darkness
and confusion without ; all order, beauty and light
within."

But to continue. My Hungarian friend introduced me
to all that wonderful hidden life of Rome which is utterly
unknown to ordinary visitors—I mean the beautiful net-
work of charitable institutions which nowhere exist in
such perfection as in the Eternal City, and of which, as
an English Protestant, I had hitherto seen nothing. In
this way I became acquainted with many eminent and
holy souls, both men and women, who did more to
remove my prejudices by their daily lives than volumes
of controversy would have done. Still, I had difficulties,
especially with regard to devotion to our Lady. I
remember perfectly well having been given a Catholic
manual, and carefully cutting out and pasting down all
such portions of it as treated of the Rosary or the
Immaculate Conception ! On one occasion, at Countess
A——'s House, I again met Dr. Manning. But he did
not encourage me in any way, and I felt that if I wanted
his advice I must seek it directly ; he would not be the
first to open the subject. At last, wearied with the
struggle which had been going on for so many months
in my own mind, and intensely anxious for explanations
which would clear away my doubts and difficulties, I
wrote to him and asked him to see me. Even then he
hesitated ; and I mention this because it is the fashion
for Protestants to affirm that he moved heaven and
earth to make converts ; whereas, as far as I was
concerned, the reverse was the fact. He emphatically
left me alone. And although, at my earnest request, he
at last consented to give me some instruction on certain

points, and met me at a convent for that purpose once
or twice during my stay at Rome ; yet, in each and all
of these cases, it was I that sought him, not he me!
Even later, what I have learned has been principally
from books to which he referred me, and which I was
to study and work out the conclusions for myself,
without his aid. I think he was afraid of his personal
influence over me from old associations, and wished me
to be thoroughly persuaded in my own mind without
any human motive. He did me the greatest possible
service, however, at this time, by kneeling by my side at
Mass once or twice, and pointing out to me the exact
places in the service, which ever after I was enabled
to follow with ease and comfort. If Catholics who
are helping Anglicans into the Church would only
do this more often, one of the greatest stumbling-
blocks of Protestants would be removed. I think
that Catholics who have been used to the service of
the Mass from their infancy, and can never recollect
the time when they did not understand it, have no
idea of the difficulty it presents to Anglicans as Protestants; they have not a notion of following the
intentions of the priest without the words; and I do not
think they can arrive at it either, till they have thorough
ly mastered the sense of the whole. To do this, they
must begin by following the service exactly, and seeing
how each part forms one beautiful and sublime whole,
culminating in the Great Sacrifice.

The result of my visit to Rome was that I resolved to
halt no longer between two opinions, but to try by every
means in my power to arrive at the truth. I felt, in
fact, that I could no longer set it aside—that to do so
would be resisting grace, and imperilling my very
salvation. When I returned to England I found
several of my most intimate friends in the same state of
mind as myself, and we agreed that all we could do was
to go on studying the question, and above all to pray
earnestly for light and guidance. One practice we
followed, which I would earnestly recommend to all

honest seekers after truth and the Divine will, namely, the daily repetition of the prayer to the Holy Ghost, "Deus, qui corda fidelium," &c., and of the *Veni Sancte Spiritus.* I have known many people helped into the Church by this means. After all, it was not a question for A. or B. It concerned the individual soul of each one, and could not be decided for us. Also, whatever may be the effect of arguments or logic on the human mind, I am more and more convinced that conversions are not brought about by those means. I have seen people entirely convinced intellectually and yet remain outside the Church. "The wind bloweth where it listeth," and it is the gentle wind of God's Spirit which moves a soul to follow its inspirations. That is what people mean when they say, "they believe not with the intellect but with the heart," and that "they have an instinct of what is true or false before they realize the matter as a fact." They do not mean that the Catholic Faith does not approve itself to their intellect or their reasoning powers, but that there is a Spirit stronger than theirs—even the Holy Spirit of God, which touches them to the quick, so that they can find no answer but in the words of Samuel; "Speak, Lord, for Thy servant heareth."

With me (as with so many others at this very moment) all human considerations were perpetually urging me the other way. I had been left sole guardian of my children by my husband's will; but I had already received notice that if I took this step my husband's family would either remove them from me, or, at least, make them wards in Chancery. Of the justice of such a course this is not the place to speak. Enough that it is the law of England that children can thus be forcibly estranged from their mother and natural pro-tector, in spite of the will of the father, if that mother, by following the dictates of her conscience embraces a different faith. I had promised my husband on his death-bed that I would never leave his children; nor entrust them to the guardianship of others. And I found myself therefore in a great strait, not knowing exactly what the powers of the Court of Chancery might be; and dreading, as all mothers would, that my children would either be taken from me (in which case my promise would be broken) or that they would be exposed to influences which above all others I most dreaded, while I should be powerless to interfere; and that, from my own act. In this great moral difficulty, too, I had no one to advise or help me. I felt strongly also how useless it would be to seek counsel from either side. My Anglican friends would, of course, say one thing, and my Catholic ones the other.

But there were other circumstances which increased my difficulties. With the Catholic yearnings of my whole life, I had induced my husband to begin, and had myself completed, the restoration of all the churches on the property. We had taken away all the pews, put in large altars, restored the patron saint in each church; and, as crucifixes were not possible, had put a representation of the Crucifixion, not in small medallions but in large and separate figures, in all the east-end windows we could find unfilled with stained glass; so that the people might, at any rate, have their thoughts led up to that great Mystery of our Redemption. Moreover, since my husband's death, I had restored and fitted up, in the most Catholic manner possible, the chapel in the house, which formed part of the church of the old Benedictine Monastery which formerly stood on this site. Here I had persuaded the chaplain to use the Compline service on Sunday evenings; and other prayers on Fridays, taken from Catholic manuals. I was organist, and I had carefully selected none but Catholic hymns; while the Bishop had given us leave to have holy communion on all saints' days and festivals, on which occasions the chapel was always beautifully decorated with flowers and lights. All this, if I became a Catholic, I must give up.

But there was one thing which touched me even more nearly. My husband had built a beautiful church in the village at the cost of £30,000. He and I had completed its adornment by bringing the rarest marbles and mosaics from Italy ; beautiful lamps from Venice, and carving and painted glass from Germany. Here too he was buried ; and my greatest consolation, since his death, had been to pray in this church and in the crypt where his dear coffin lay, and which I had fitted up almost as a private chapel. How great would be the struggle before I could give up the daily service in this church, associated as it was with all the happiest years of my life, and now sanctified by being his last resting-place, no one but myself and God knew. In all my church works, also, the bishop of the diocese had been my constant adviser. He was to me as a very dear brother ; how then could I take a step which I knew would not only injure him in the estimation of his flock, but also wound him to the very heart ? Besides all these reasons, human pride came in. How was I to give up the position I held in the whole neighbourhood, where I was looked upon as the promoter of every good work, and consequently admired by good people of every class ? How exchange this for scorn and obloquy, and the contempt and distrust of all those whose good opinion I most valued ?

I dwell upon these temptations (for such they were) because I see them reproduced more or less in almost every case of conversion ; and I know that hundreds are kept back at this moment by similar considerations. To me, the suffering was peculiarly great, because all my life long I had leant so much on human sympathy and human approbation. I had been the spoilt child of my father, the spoilt sister of my only brother, the spoilt wife of one of 'the best and noblest of men. Since his death the same affectionate love and appreciation had surrounded me, both for his sake

and my own.   And all this I felt I must relinquish if
I became a Catholic, and go out, emphatically alone, in
the cold!   My whole nature shrank from it to such a
degree that I recollect saying to a friend who was
talking on the subject of the difference between the
two Churches : "Don't enquire, don't try and see if
you would not be as utterly miserable as I am !"   For
all these Anglican services had now become utterly
distasteful to me.   I felt their unreality : that they
were a sham; the imitation of the truth and not the
truth itself.   But above all, my communions in the
Anglican Church had become a perfect misery to me.
Ever since I had perfectly entered into the spirit of the
Mass and understood the sublime mystery of the Holy
Sacrifice, this cold imitation of it, without the Presence
and without the Substance, became to me the most
horrible mockery and sacrilege.   Dr. Manning had
advised me to leave off communion : but to do so,
would have been at once proclaiming my intention of
leaving the Anglican Church.   I was not in the
position of an unknown person, who could do what
she pleased without remark.   I was the head of a great
house, "as a city set on a hill."   I had laboured hard
to establish weekly and early communion in the
parish and succeeded; and of course, I had always gone
to these communions myself, both from inclination and
to set an example.   Now they were, as I said before, a
positive torture to me, from which, however, in the
country, there was no escape.

In London I was happier.   It had always been my
custom to go to daily service early and alone; and so
it excited no remark when I went out as usual; only instead of going to the Anglican services, I used to make
a great détour and creep into a Catholic Church,
where alone I found what I sought.   There are
several "houses of refuge," as I used to call them,
in London, where people in my position could
go, as to a private house, and find a window or a
gallery looking into a chapel, where, without being

yourself seen, you can have the inexpressible comfort
of hearing Mass. At Harley House and Kensington
Square also, the perpetual Exposition and daily Bene-
dictions were an untold blessing. These I used
regularly to frequent, and also churches in outlying
parts of London where there was no fear of my being
recognized. That of St. Mary and the Angels, at
Bayswater, was my great favourite, as being more
Roman than any other in London, both in its decora-
tions and in the arrangement of its side chapels. As I
never dared take my own carriage to such places, I
used to have all sorts of adventures in going to and
fro ; and from being unused to walking alone in
London or going in cabs, I was very often much
frightened. I recollect one night having been insulted
on my way back, and not returning till midnight, scared
very nearly to death and having run nearly the whole
way ! Another time I came up from the country by a
night train, and sat outside the church door on the
steps in pouring rain and in pitch darkness for two
hours till the doors were opened, so that I might not
lose a Mass on All Souls' Day for my husband.

I do not think I was ever attracted to the Catholic
Church by the gorgeousness or beauty of its services.
I always prefer a Low to a High Mass ; it is to me more
devotional, and the singing during the solemn parts
of the service disturbs and bothers me ; and I do not
care for music enough to make that a snare to me.
But the Adoration of the Blessed Sacrament ; the
little light telling of the perpetual Presence in the
Tabernacle ; the inexpressible relief of Confession ;
and the intimate union with and nearness to the Sacred Humanity of Our Divine Lord which breathes
in every form of Catholic worship, these had from the
first the strongest possible hold upon me. People were
always talking to me about the " Church of my baptism."
What Church is that but the Church of our Baptismal
creed—the One Holy Catholic Church ? Our baptism
binds us to *this*, not to the Church of England, except

so far as the Church of England is one with the Church Catholic; and if you feel convinced that the Anglican Church is at variance with the Catholic Church throughout the world, your very baptism, as it appears to me, binds you to leave it.

Towards the close of that year the health of my children again required a warmer climate, and we went to the Nile. I had obtained letters of introduction to the Franciscan Fathers at Cairo, who gave me a list of all their Missions up the river, where I found frequent services, and was, I believe, looked upon by them all as a Catholic. During those months of leisure, I studied Latin and worked hard. I read works in the original which I had before only gone through in translations, and my faith was strengthened by every line I read. But it was not till we left Egypt and went on to Syria that my doubts and difficulties really began to clear themselves. At Jerusalem I had much time for thought and prayer. I had no teaching or influence of any sort except what the services of the place and season afforded, for it was Lent; but they were all-powerful. I cannot understand anyone going there, and joining heart and soul in those services as I did, and remaining an Anglican. The scales seemed to fall from my eyes; and I saw in a way I never did before the eternal truth of the One Holy Catholic Church. Still, I did not act upon this conviction at once. I asked advice of one or two persons, and they implored me to wait a little, for my children's sake. I recollect, however, the inexpressible misery I felt of being unable to share in the Communion of Holy Thursday at the Holy Sepulchre, which was administered to between seven and eight hundred of the pilgrims kneeling round me; and of the bitter tears which I shed at being the only one left out at that blessed Feast. Once or twice also, the good Franciscan Father who acted as our guide to the holy sites (which are all indulgenced) would mutter, "What a pity! you have come all this way and gone through all this toil and *all for nothing*." "Outside the fold" I felt myself indeed on such occasions; but human reasons and human prudence were yet too strong for me, and I waited.

I resolved, however, henceforth, that, except in the matter of communion and absolution, I would not be excluded from Catholic services, that I would lead a strictly Catholic life and conform to all the rules of the Church. I had been regularly to confession (though without receiving absolution) ever since I was at Rome. People will think that ridiculous; but it helped me very much as giving me a guide, though without its consolations. I resolved also, on my return to England, to tell those towards whom I felt bound not to act a dishonest part that I was only waiting, on account of the children; but that I was firmly convinced of the truth of the Catholic faith and determined to embrace it sooner or later.

I do not think that any preference for the ritual of the Catholic Church, any charm in its services, any increased help even which these services may give to the working of God's grace in your own soul, can justify one in leaving the Church where God's Providence has placed one, if one can believe in it. But I could no longer believe in the Anglican Establishment. I had tried it by every possible test, and with the most earnest wish and hope to be enabled to remain in it; but on all essential points I found it wanting.

I only waited, as I believe every considerate and responsible person ought, till I had ascertained the truth of the grounds on which my convictions rested. I was bound to do this, lest I should act hastily and then find that I was wrong. Convictions had to be tested and tests demand time. All this I had now passed through. My mind, therefore, was irrevocably made up, but the only thing which kept me back was the thought of my children. I said so that summer, when on one occasion, I again spoke to Dr. Manning. He answered after a pause: "Did you ever read the life of Madame de Chantal?" I replied that I had.

He continued, "Well then, you will have seen that she walked over the body of her son when she made up her mind to follow the inspiration which God had given her."

He did not urge me further, and so those weary months passed by. My intention, however, was no longer a secret to my intimate friends, and of course their opposition increased in proportion. A very eminent and excellent doctor in the English Church entered into a correspondence with me on the subject. But his arguments rested on historical points; all of which I felt I could have disproved if I had had sufficient knowledge; but they did not touch the main things, I mean the unity and sacramental life of the Church, in which the real divergence lies.

One argument was made use of to me (not by him, but by others) which I mention here, as I find it has been a stumbling-block to many. I was told that to leave the Anglican Church for the Catholic, would be to condemn all those (whether living or dead) who had died or lived in that Communion. Now this is a complete misrepresentation of Catholic doctrine.

The Catholic belief is that no penitent soul can perish, and that no one who really loves God can be lost; and there are holy and penitent and loving souls in the most erroneous systems.

"I have no doubt" (writes an eminent Catholic ecclesiastic) "that through imperfect ministries and irregular systems, God shows His mercy on every soul which has the right dispositions. Therefore, no doubt would be cast upon the reality of the work of grace in human souls in the Church of England or any other Church, by being convinced that its position is schismatical and its acts irregular. When convinced of this, however, it is a vital duty to submit to the law of unity and authority in the Church of God."

As to "dishonesty" in the matter, a term which both sides are too fond of using, I believe the mass of English people to be blameless. Henry VIII. robbed us of our birthright; Queen Elizabeth sanctioned and confirmed the theft. All literature and history fell into Protestant hands. Every child is brought up in these errors, and simply believes what it is told from its cradle; and what is further impressed upon it in every class and school book. It requires a direct operation of the Holy Spirit of God to clear away these mists and and show people the truth "as it is in Jesus Christ."

But the same high ecclesiastical authority continues:—" I believe with all firmness and with my whole heart, that those dear to me and thousands of others, who fell asleep in full faith of the Church of England, having had no other light and no doubts of its truth, rest in Jesus and are safe in His everlasting arms. And of all sincere souls who remain, I believe they receive grace according to the measure in which they act up to their own light and convictions."

Therefore, if any Anglican minister dare affirm, as one did the other day, in writing to a poor lady whom I know, that by following the inspiration of God's Holy Spirit, she was damning the soul of her own child lately dead, he is guilty of a direct contravention of the truth of the Catholic Church, and telling a wicked, cruel, and unfounded lie besides.

The gist of the whole matter is this: "Whatsoever is not of faith is sin." If people are content with Anglicanism, and have no doubts or fears of its truth, they are comparatively safe. But to remain in it, when you are convinced that she is in error, or when you have grave doubts of the validity of her orders, and consequently of her Sacraments and authority, is imperilling your own salvation; to stifle such doubts is immoral; and this was my case at that time. Certainly on coming to a decision on so vital a matter we must use all the faculties God has given us, and in that way incur the reproach of acting on our private judgment. But if people remain in the Church of England, they must live and die in a perpetual exercise of private judgment upon every doctrine in the Thirty-nine

Articles.   There are no two Bishops and scarcely two
clergymen who think alike or teach alike on the most
vital and important doctrines.   Anglicanism professes
to include within her pale all extremes, from the
Calvinist to the highest Ritualist; and the latter
utterly contemn all ecclesiastical authority, have
made to themselves a sect and a Church of their own
within the Establishment, and then call themselves
Catholics!   On the other hand, by submitting, once for
all, to the Church of God, we rest our faith for ever on a
rock, and form one of a body which through the con-
tinual presence of Our Divine Lord and the teaching of
His Holy Spirit, is infallible and unchangeable to the
end of the world.

But to return to myself.   That winter we spent in
Sicily.   I took a house in a garden outside the town
close to a convent where I could hear Mass every
morning at 6 o'clock, before any of the family were
stirring.   I was more and more unhappy in my mind
at being deprived of real Communion, but Dr.
Manning had spoken to me very strongly on the sin
committed by High Church Anglicans, who, abroad,
often receive the Sacraments sacrilegiously, that
is, without the priest having an idea that they are
not Catholics, and, therefore, giving them unwittingly
Absolution and Communion.   There was no Protestant
Church however, in the place, so that I was at least
spared the infliction of services which was so painful to
me.   On Christmas Eve, I begged to be locked up in
the Church of the Oratorians after Vespers till the
midnight service, and there, in the stillness and the
darkness of the night, I took a review of my whole
position before God and felt that it was untenable.
Midnight came and with it crowds of worshippers to
the crib of the Infant Jesus, which was beautifully lit;
and the number of communicants made me feel
more than ever my utter misery and thorough isolation
from the body of His faithful people.   I came home
utterly wretched, and spent the following week in a

state which only those can understand who have gone through such mental agony.

Then came the eve of the New Year, and the *Te Deum* at the Jesuits' Church, which was lit up from floor to roof like that of the Gesù at Rome, and where there was likewise Exposition of the Blessed Sacrament, to be followed by Benediction. I had gone with some Protestant friends who wanted to see it as a sight; but I slipped away from them and on to the floor among the poor, and then what happened to me I do not know. It seemed to me as if all the people and the lights had disappeared, and that I was alone before Our Lord in the monstrance, and that He spoke to me directly, and lovingly, asking me "Why I waited?" and "Why I did not come to Him at once?" And that then a sudden light or illumination fell upon me, and I felt such a joy that all human considerations, even my children, were forgotten, and my only answer was in the words of Saul: "Lord, what wouldst Thou have me do?"

I can hardly remember, though I have often tried to do so, all that passed through my soul during that time; all I know is, that at last some one touched me on the shoulder, and I looked up and saw that everybody was gone, and the lights were put out, and I had missed the moment of Benediction (which gave me a pang for a moment, but I was too happy to mind much); and that the sacristan was standing by me, and saying that he was going to shut up the church, and "would not the Signora rise also and go?" I got up mechanically, and walked home as if in a dream. I recollected nothing but that I had somehow made a promise to Our Lord which I must not break, and that I must do what I had to do at *once*. The manner and way of doing it was the difficulty; I knew no one in the place at all intimately; though I had a slight acquaintance with one old priest, in consequence of having enquired on my first arrival for a confessor for my maid. (I had for many years had a Catholic maid, as I had always

a horror of being taken ill and perhaps dying without the Sacraments, or worse still, with an Anglican
minister. And I had always charged her, if I was ever
suddenly or alarmingly sick, to send for a priest.)
This old man was a very holy Canon living near
the Cathedral, who did not go into society much,
but spent his time among the poor and in writing
devotional books. He had once called upon me, and
so I resolved to go to him. I did not go to bed that
night; but walked up and down my room thinking over
the step I was about to take and counting the cost. But,
I never hesitated or felt the least inclined to go back;
after what had passed so strangely in that Jesuit church,
I felt a light and happiness and an inward joy which I
cannot express, and in spite of all the misery which I
knew the step would entail upon me in every kind of
way, it never occurred to me that I could do otherwise
than follow the light thus vouchsafed. It was like having found the "pearl of great price," which I had long
sought in vain; and my only feeling was an intense
anxiety to secure it.

The next morning after going to Mass as usual and
hearing the boy's French lessons, I walked down alone
to the town, and found out the Canon's house. I do
not say that my heart did not beat a little quicker than
usual, as I climbed up those steep stairs! But still I
felt the die was cast, and that I must go on. I can
speak Italian easily; so that I soon explained my
business, and asked to be received into the Church.
The good old Canon hesitated: "he had only once
received an Anglican before;" "he was not sure I was
prepared;" "he did not know the form of abjuration
exactly;" and "he must first ask the consent of the
Archbishop," &c. To these objections I answered that
I had for years been preparing myself for this step;
that I had no doubts or difficulties of any sort; that I
had long been leading the life of a Catholic as far as I
could; that I had only delayed my reception on account
of my children; and that I would copy out the form of

adjuration for him in Latin that evening, and send it to him, if he would only see the Archbishop about it.

He consented to this, though I do not think he was very encouraging at first. And now, when I see the difficulties and fuss some people make about their reception and the way in which everything has to be done for them, I am inclined to laugh at the recollection of the manner I forced myself into the Church, as it were, in spite of anything and everybody! However, the next morning, the Canon wrote to me very kindly, saying that he had seen the Archbishop, who had given him leave to receive me, and fixing the eve of the Epiphany for that purpose in his own private chapel. I had already explained to him the imperative necessity of secrecy in the matter, at any rate for the present; so that he added that there would be no one there but himself. On the vigil of that Feast, therefore, I again walked to the Canon's house; made my abjuration in Latin and my general confession in Italian; and answered at my first real Mass. There was no one, as he had promised, but himself and me—and God!

Then I returned home to my children as if nothing had happened, and we went that afternoon to see the Cathedral. I never shall forget the exultation of heart with which I entered it and felt: "All this is *mine*, now and for evermore!" Before, I had felt like an impostor in Catholic churches; *now*, mine were the promises, mine the consolations, mine the joys for evermore!

A few weeks later, the Superior of the Sisters of Charity, whom I had let into my secret, dressed me in white threw a white veil over my head, and took me to the Archbishop's, where I was confirmed in his private chapel. No one was present but the superior (who was my godmother) and one of her sisters, the old Canon who had received me into the Church, and a very holy missionary priest whose prayers I had specially begged for on the occasion. It was a solemn and beautiful service, and when the venerable old Archbishop began making me a little allocution, as I knelt before him, he suddenly broke down and burst out crying, exclaiming : "It is a fore-taste of Paradise! " (*E un squarcio di Paradiso !*) and the Canon had to continue the address in his place. Afterwards he gave me Holy Communion, and then we breakfasted with the kind old man, after which I went back to the Sisters, who gave me a beautiful Benediction service in their chapel. I hung up my white wreath on the altar of Our Lady, whom long since I had learned to love.

And so I came home at last !

STEPS TO THE CHURCH.

1. Reason compels us to believe in the existence of a Creator. To deny this, is to assert that this wonderful world, and we ourselves, with our faculties of intellect, of memory, and of will, are the results of blind chance. The law and order that we see in the Universe speak to us no less clearly of an Intelligence directing it. Even if we say that things came to be what they are by the action of some 'law'—whether it be evolution or selection, or what you will—there must have been some Intelligence which so ordered the nature of things from the beginning.

2. Conscience (or the moral sense) likewise testifies to Him; for how otherwise are we to account for our knowledge of right and wrong, good and evil, and our ideas of sympathy, charity, duty, justice, mercy? Every time we use the word "ought," we imply that there is some law, beyond and above our own desires and wills, which obliges and commands our voluntary choice. That law is what we call the Holy Will of God.

3. If the existence of a God Who cares for us be granted, it follows that He must be knowable in some way, and that it is surely our duty, as His creatures, to seek Him. If He wills our good, He cannot be supposed to have left us without the necessary knowledge of Himself and access to Him. Since we owe Him everything, we are bound to acknowledge this dependence by rendering Him love, service and devotion.

4. How are we to render Him this tribute, unless He reveal Himself in some way to us?

5. We Catholics claim that the Catholic Faith is this revelation, offering to us as it does a perfectly reasonable and sufficient knowledge of the Eternal God,

(82)

and of man's relation to Him.   The Catholic Religion
is also the only one that enables us to *worship* God in a
way worthy of Him and pleasing to Him.

6.   The Catholic Faith teaches us that God has made
Himself knowable to mankind, especially by assuming
the nature of man in the person of Jesus Christ, and not
knowable only, but lovable and adorable also.   Jesus
Christ is truly the " Light of the World."

7.   Catholic theologians teach that from all eternity
it had been the purpose of God to become man.   It is
to the mystery of the Incarnation that they point as the
only key to the problem of the Universe (the why and
the wherefore thereof).   It was the very reason for all
creation.

8.   Almighty God foresaw the fall of man that would
ensue from the abuse of free will.   In His mercy, therefore, He provided that through the Incarnation He
would Himself make the atonement due to His infinite
Justice for our sins, and would Himself pay the price of
our Redemption.   All that He demands is that we
should rightly accept Him as our Saviour, and love,
serve, obey and worship Him.

9,   History itself testifies that Jesus Christ, Whom
we believe to be true God and true Man, lived and died,
preached the Gospel, and founded a Church.   We
believe this Church to be the custodian, and the only
authoritative exponent of His Gospel ; to be the means
of perpetuating the good news concerning Himself to
the end of time, and of conveying it to the ends of the
earth.

10.   He promised this Church (the One, Holy,
Catholic, and Apostolic Church) the special assistance
of His Holy Spirit.   He declared that He would be
with it always, even to the end of the world.   This gift
of the Holy Spirit was bestowed on the day of Pentecost.
In consequence of this divine assistance, the Church is
of necessity infallible, and cannot err in any decision
concerning faith or morals.

11.   Now as the Holy Spirit is to be with the Church
till the consummation of the world, He must be with it
at the present moment.   Consequently those who call

themselves Christians, yet resist against the dictate of conscience the claims of the Catholic Church, resist also the Holy Spirit of God, Who guides and governs it. They are in heresy or schism. The Catholic Church acknowledges as her own, all those men and women who, desiring to please God, are living good lives and acting up to their conscience, and who are only outside the visible unity of the One Faith through invincible ignorance of the Church's authority.

12. The Catholic Church, then, we believe to be the only authorized guardian, exponent, and interpreter of the Gospel; and the ordinary channel by which the graces and help which were promised by our Lord are ministered to men.

13. It bids us offer supreme worship to God alone, and in a secondary way (but in a secondary way only) it charges us to render honour to the Blessed Virgin Mary as His Mother, and to the Saints as His chosen servants, and to seek their intercession.

14. The Catholic Church tells us that God has not only made Himself knowable, lovable, and adorable in His Incarnation, but also lovable, adorable, and *accessible* in many ways, and above all, in the Blessed Sacrament of the Altar, and that in this way He is truly Emmanuel or "God with us."

15. Jesus Christ had in view this institution of the Blessed Eucharist, this Real Presence of Himself amongst us, when in that wonderful discourse recorded in the 6th chapter of St. John's Gospel, He repeatedly invited us to communion with Him, saying: "I am the Living Bread which came down from heaven. If any man eat this Bread he shall live for ever: and the Bread that I will give is My Flesh for the life of the world" (verses 51-52); again, when He said: "Except you eat the Flesh of the Son of Man, and drink His Blood, you shall not have life in you" (verse 54); and yet again: "He that eateth My Flesh and drinketh My Blood abideth in Me and I in him" (verse 57).

The first Protestants were those of whom it is recorded that after hearing this, "many of His disciples went back and walked no more with Him" (verse 67).

Is not the question of the Jews, when they heard these words from our Lord's Divine lips, still the question of the Protestant and infidel world of to-day? "How can this Man give us His flesh to eat?"

16. This Presence of God on our altars is the reason for all the ritual (the incense, the music, the vestments, the bending of the knee), that strangers observe in our services. We offer Him the best we have, realizing all the while that nothing is good enough for Him.

17. In Holy Mass the Catholic believes there is daily renewed amongst us the great Sacrifice made on Calvary, that Jesus Christ is there at the altar both as Priest and Victim, making propitiation for the sins of the world; and that in Holy Mass is fulfilled the prophecy made by the last of the prophets (Malachi, i. 11): "From the rising of the sun to the going down, My Name is great among the Gentiles, *and in every place there is sacrifice,* and there is offered to My Name a clean oblation."

18. This was the great act of worship offered up on innumerable altars throughout this land, till in the sixteenth century the people of England were robbed of their religion by the lust and greed of Henry VIII., aided by the servility and rapacity of his courtiers, and by the malice of wicked men; and this in spite of the protest of such great Englishmen as the Blessed Martyr, Sir Thomas More, and of many other true-hearted men and women, who were faithful even unto death.

May God in His mercy help all earnest inquirers, and bring them into His Church, the Church of our Catholic forefathers, which is the one fold of the one Shepherd. So will they receive consolation in this world, and eternal happiness in the next.

CATHOLIC TRUTH SOCIETY, 18 West Square, London, S.E.
[1s. per 100.]

AN APPEAL TO ANGLICANS.

THE wonderful revival of the Catholic Church in this country after three centuries of persecution and repression, and her claim to be the old Church of England, God's one true Church, are now forcing many Anglicans to consider their own position and her claim.

To help such as these to come to a right conclusion, I would, in the cause of truth, venture to recommend the consideration of the description, given in Holy Scripture, of the Church which our Blessed Lord came on earth to found, and advise them to ask themselves whether the Established Church, of which they are members, accords with that description.

Take, for instance, what is said in Holy Scripture about the Church as a visible body invested with authority to teach. We read that, just before His Ascension, our Lord said to His Apostles "All power is given to Me in heaven and in earth; going, therefore, teach ye all nations" (St. Matt. xxviii. 18, 19); and He also said: "I send the promise of My Father upon you: but stay you in the city, till you be endued with power from on high" (St. Luke xxiv. 49). In St. John's Gospel He tells them what this promise is. He says: "But the Paraclete, the Holy Ghost, Whom the Father will send in My Name, He will teach you all things, and bring all things to your mind, whatsoever I shall have said to you" (St. John xiv. 26); and: "When He, the Spirit of truth, is come, He will teach you all truth" (St. John xvi. 13). On the Feast of Pentecost, the "Spirit of

(83)

truth" came down on the Apostles to abide with them, and with those who, in after ages, should be called to be rulers in the Church of Christ, and to teach them all truth.

The Church, having received such a commission, and being under such guidance, is indeed, as St. Paul says: "the Church of the living God, the pillar and ground of the truth," * in a word, is infallible. It would be impossible for such a Church to err, to vary her teaching, to declare through her authorized teachers a doctrine false which she had previously declared to be true, or a doctrine true which she had previously declared to be false.

Now, is this oneness of faith, this infallible, this unvarying and uniform teaching, to be found in the Established Church? If we study the history of that Church, I think that what will strike us most will be its contradictory teaching about many of the essential doctrines of the Christian religion. We shall find a doctrine taught as true at one period, and denounced as erroneous at another and we shall find the teaching dependent on the ascendency of this or that religious party.

Look, for instance, at the teaching in the Established Church at the time of the Reformation, or in the last century, or, I may say, fifty years ago, and compare it with that which prevails in it now-a-days. The doctrines now taught in the Established Church not only differ from those which went before them, but directly contradict them It is the same also with the

* 1 Tim iii. 15.

religious practices which are the outcome of that teaching. Take one doctrine only, viz., that connected with what in the Anglican Prayer Book is called the "Lord's Supper." Until recently the general teaching on this subject was that it was not the Mass, but only a Communion Service; not a sacrifice, only a commemoration of a Sacrifice; that, as the thirty-first Article says: "the Sacrifices of Masses" were "blasphemous fables and dangerous deceits;" that in that ordinance Christ's Presence was owing, not to the words of Consecration, but to the faith of the recipient; that "the mean whereby the Body of Christ is received and eaten in the Supper is faith;"† and that therefore no adoration ought to be paid to Christ under the outward appearance of bread or wine. And all the surroundings of this ordinance, the practices of minister and people, were in accord with this teaching. The High Church party, which is now an influential one in the Established Church, has changed all this. They teach that the Lord's Supper is a Sacrifice, which is offered for the living and the dead; they lay great stress on their clergy being Priests; the word Mass is no longer a word to be hated, but to be used; it is their belief that Christ is really and truly present in the "consecrated elements," and is to be therein adored: and their ceremonial and practices, and private devotions are made to agree with this altered teaching. Such is the present compared with the past.

And now let us look around us and see what is going on in our own day in the Established Church. Is it not

† Art. xxviii.

a well-known fact that the religious teaching in each
parish is dependent on the views of the Rector, or
Vicar, who may be High, or Low, or Broad, and that
even the same pulpit may in the course of a few weeks
be occupied by a representative of each of the three
Anglican parties ?   Can it be denied, that every Sunday
Anglicans are receiving most contradictory teaching on
such essential doctrines as the Incarnation and its
effects, the Atonement, Baptism, the "Lord's Supper,"
and Confession ?

  To those whose rule of faith is "the Bible and the
Bible only," this contradictory teaching of their Church
is a matter of no great importance, but to High Churchmen, to those who have been taught to feel the need of
a teaching Church, such as they know our Blessed Lord
came on earth to found, it must be a trouble and a
perplexity.   In the minds of the latter, if they allow
themselves to think, doubts must arise about the Established Church.

  Since the Reformation, the Established Church has
been, more or less, the Church of the nation, and they
must be led to ask themselves how it is that, if it has
Christ's commission, is guided by the Spirit of truth, is
the "pillar and ground of the truth," it has allowed its
members for centuries to live in ignorance of those
doctrines, which they themselves believe to be essential,
or, still worse, has taught them that these doctrines
are erroneous and should be rejected :—how it is that the
teaching of their clergy in the present day is so uncertain, so contradictory.

  If, dear reader, you are one of these perplexed Anglicans, I would earnestly advise you to study the history of

her who alone proclaims herself to be God's one true Church. If you do so, you will find that she has always, from her first beginning to the present day, answered the description given us in Holy Scripture of Christ's Church as an infallible teacher. One of her marks has ever been unity of faith. You may search diligently throughout all the centuries that have elapsed, and you will not find a single instance of her having, through her authorized teachers, contradicted any defined doctrine. And in the present day you may go into any Catholic Church in England, or any part of the world, and you will, as regards doctrines which are of faith, hear the same teaching—there will be no contradiction.

You have, no doubt, heard it said that the Church's teaching does vary; that she imposes on her people new doctrines : and you may have been reminded of the dogma of the Pope's infallibility. Certainly, this doctrine was for the first time explicitly defined as an article of faith at the Vatican Council, but it was no new doctrine. At the Nicene Council, held in 325, the doctrine of the Divinity of the Son of God was first explicitly defined as an article of faith, but one would not say that that was then a new doctrine. An old doctrine may have been misunderstood, or imperfectly understood, by the faithful ; controversies may have arisen about it, and it may have been necessary that it should be explicitly defined, by the Church ; when so defined, it becomes a dogma, which it would be heresy to deny.

The Pope's infallibility is no new doctrine. We find it in the Bible. It was taught by our Blessed Lord, when He said: "Thou art Peter ; and upon this rock I

will build My Church, and the gates of hell shall not
prevail against it. And I will give to thee the keys of
the kingdom of heaven ; and whatsoever thou shalt
bind upon earth, it shall be bound also in heaven ; and
whatsoever thou shalt loose on earth, it shall be loosed
also in heaven" (St. Matt. xvi. 18, 19). And: "Simon,
Simon, behold Satan hath desired to have *you*, that he
may sift *you* as wheat. But I have prayed for *thee*, that
thy faith fail not: and thou being once converted, confirm thy brethren" (St. Luke xxii. 31, 32). And also
when, just before His Ascension, He said to the same
Apostle: "Feed my lambs," "Feed my sheep" (St.
John xxi. 16, 17).

This doctrine was not unknown in the 2nd century,
for Tertullian says : "Was anything hidden from Peter,
who was called the rock on which the Church was to
be built, and who obtained the keys of the kingdom of
heaven, and the power of loosing and binding in heaven
and on earth?" (*Liber de Præscript. Hæres. Cap. xxii.
Migne*).

And St. Cyprian, who lived in the 3rd century, says :
"Peter, to whom the Lord entrusts His sheep to be
fed and guarded, on whom He placed and founded His
Church." (*De Habitu Virg., edit. Oxon*, p. 70.) And
St. Jerome, who lived in the 4th century, addressing
Pope Damasus, says : "I speak with the successor of the
Fisherman ;" and: "Following none as the first but
Christ, I am associated in communion with your Bles-
sedness, that is, with the chair of Peter; on that rock I
know that the Church was built. Whosoever eateth the
lamb out of this house is profane. If anyone is not in

the ark of Noe, he will perish when the flood prevails"
(*Epist. xv. ad Damasum Papam.*)

At the General Council of Chalcedon, held in 451,
after the reading of an Epistle of Pope Leo, the Bishops
exclaimed: "That is the faith of the Fathers: that is
the faith of the Apostles. So we all believe. So the
orthodox believe. Anathema to him who does not thus
believe. Peter has spoken these things through Leo"
(*Act. ii. Labbe*, p. 368).

At the General Council of Florence, held in 1439, it
was declared that "the Holy Apostolic See and Roman
Pontiff holds the primacy over all the world; that the
Roman Pontiff is the successor of Peter, prince of the
Apostles; that he is the true Vicar of Christ, the head
of the whole Church, the father and teacher of all
Christians, and that to him in Blessed Peter full power
has been committed by our Lord Jesus Christ of feeding,
ruling, and governing the Universal Church" (*Sessio
xxv. Binius, tom. iv.* p. 476).

Innumerable instances might be quoted, but these are,
I think, sufficient to prove that the dogma of the infallibility of the Pope, which is so often referred to as
an argument against the unchangeable teaching of the
Catholic Church, is really no new doctrine.

Of course, in a short paper one cannot treat a subject
of this kind as fully as one could wish, but, I hope that
what I have said may cause you to persevere in your
endeavour to arrive at the truth.

Unfortunately, there is a risk of your religious advisers
trying to deter you from thinking out this matter. But,
would this be reasonable? You are a member of a

Church whose clergy claim for themselves the greatest freedom of thought. They claim for themselves the right to criticise the Bible, to retain some parts of it as inspired, and to reject other parts as mythical, to decide when our Blessed Lord spoke as an infallible Teacher, and when as a fallible one, to select their own doctrines and their own rites and ceremonies. Is it then reasonable, that these same clergy should check you in your search after God's one true Church ? Situated as you are, it would be wrong for you to allow yourself to be thus deterred ; it is your duty to give this matter your prayerful consideration.

H. M.

THE CATHOLIC TRUTH SOCIETY, 18 West Square, London, S.E.
Price 2s. per 100.

A HOUSE DIVIDED AGAINST ITSELF.

IS the Established Church of England the true Church, or any part of the true Church, of Christ?

This is the question which is agitating the minds of many at the present time.

Let the following, from the Visitation Charge of one of her Bishops, delivered at Liverpool, in November, 1893, speak for itself.

Dr. Ryle, the Protestant Bishop of Liverpool, says:

"I do not forget that myriads of unthinking people suppose that the present divisions of Churchmen are entirely about trifles and petty matters of ritual detail. 'A little more or less music! A few more or less flowers! A few more vestures, and gestures, and turnings, and postures!' This is all the difference they can see between one clergyman and another.— 'Why should they be divided? Why not work harmoniously together, if they are both earnest men?'— Superficial judgments like this are the great misfortune of our times. An immense number of laymen cannot or will not see that our 'unhappy divisions' arise almost entirely from discordant opinions about the Lord's Supper. But, surely, the importance of that blessed Sacrament can hardly be overstated. It is the very ordinance about which, history tells us, our Martyred Reformers laid down their lives at the stake. If the clergy of this generation are entirely divided about the Lord's Supper, the laity may not understand it, but they may be sure **our Church is in very evil plight.**

*   *   *   *   *   *

"**It is useless to shut our eyes to plain facts,** when the ship is really in danger, and there are breakers ahead. Are we really much divided? Are our differences very serious? Let us see. I shall not shrink

(84)

from naming some notorious points which appear to me to demand attention, and supply sorrowful proof that **our divisions are real.**

"(*a*) One section of our clergy, and probably the majority, maintains that the Lord's Supper is a **sacrifice.** Another, and probably the minority, maintains, with equal firmness, that it is not, and should only be called a **sacrament.**

"(*b*) One maintains that the Communion table is an **altar,** and should be always treated as such. Another maintains that it is only the **Holy Table.**

"(*c*) One maintains that the minister at the Lord's Supper is a **sacrificing priest.** Another maintains that he is only an **officiating presbyter,** though called a priest, and that there is no authority for sacerdotalism in the New Testament or the Prayer-book.

"(*d*) One maintains that the Lord's Supper does good, more or less, **to all who receive it,** and that as a general rule all persons should be urged to become communicants. The other maintains that it only does good **to believing and worthy** communicants, and to those who are destitute of lively faith does no good at all— but rather harm.

"(*e*) One maintains that the Lord's Supper should always be received **fasting,** and after **confession** to a clergyman. The other regards both these additions to the Sacrament with deep aversion, as **not warranted** by Scripture or the Prayer-book.

"(*f*) One maintains that there is a **real objective presence** of Christ's body and blood under the forms of the consecrated bread and wine. The other maintains that there is **no real presence** whatever, except ' in the hearts of believing communicants.

"Now, I shall not for a moment attempt to argue these disputed points, or to say, on this occasion, who is right and who is wrong, whatever my own private opinions may be. I only place before you plain facts which nobody can deny, and ask you to observe what an immense cause of weakness these divisions must be, and are, to the Church of England. When a clergyman

on one side of a street or road administers the Lord's
Supper in one way, and his neighbour a few hundred
yards off in another way, there is a **terrible lack of
unity.**

" Here is a great problem, and I know not how it is to
be solved. I only ask you to ponder the solemn words
of our Lord Jesus Christ, '**Every kingdom divided
against itself is brought to desolation, and a
house divided against itself shall not stand.**'
(St. Matt. xii. 25.)

" One thing is very certain, if we cannot lessen our
unhappy divisions, there is only one conclusion before
us. That conclusion is **the disruption and complete
break-up of the Established Church of England.**"
Thus far Dr. Ryle.

How can any reasonable person say, in the face of
this, that the Established Church has any part with
that Church which Christ

1. **Commanded to teach all nations** (St. Matt.
xxviii. 19).

Surely a Church which cannot teach two parishes
the same doctrine, is unfit to be the teacher of nations.

2. **Gave the Spirit of Truth to guide it in all
Truth** (St. John xvi. 13).

Can the Spirit of Truth be guiding at the same
time the High Church party, who teach that Christ is
really present in the Sacrament, and the Low Church
party, who hold that He is really absent from the
Sacrament?

3. **Commanded all men to hear under pain of
damnation** (St. Mark xvi. 16).

Which are we to hear under so dreadful a penalty—
the High Church party or the Low Church party?

4. **Prayed might be one, even as He and His
Father are one** (St. John xvii. 11).

What has been the answer to this prayer if the Established Church is the Church of Christ?

5. Declared that the gates of hell shall not prevail against (St. Matt. xvi. 18).

What has become of this promise if it was given with regard to the Established Church?

Reader! God is not mocked: He is a God of Truth, not of falsehood: a God of Unity, not of disruption.

There is one Lord, one Faith, one Baptism (St. Paul, Ephes. iv. 5).

Where are these alone to be found?

In the **Catholic and Roman Church,** which has taught all nations, since the Day of Pentecost, and will teach to the end of time, **one doctrine;** which **alone** manifests the guiding power of the Spirit of Truth; and in which **alone** have the prayer and promise of Jesus Christ been answered and fulfilled.

Reader! For the sake of the Saviour Who died for you upon the Cross—for the sake of your own immortal soul—inquire into the claims of the Catholic Church upon your conscience.

As surely as there is a God in Heaven above so surely is the Catholic and Roman Church that Church of whose teaching Christ has said:

"He that believeth and is baptized shall be saved, and he that believeth not shall be condemned' (St. Mark xvi. 16).

THE CATHOLIC TRUTH SOCIETY, 18 West Square, London, S.E.

[1s. per 100.]

"THE CHURCH DEFENCE INSTITUTION"

AND

THE EARLY ENGLISH CHURCH.

————— — — ————

SOME of the readers of this leaflet may be aware of the existence of a Society called "The Church Defence Institution," one of the principal objects of which is to maintain the right of the Established Church to the position of her endowments. In furtherance of this object, itinerant lecturers are employed, who traverse the country, and in their addresses endeavour to persuade their hearers of the identity of the present Church of England with that of St. Augustine and St. Anselm. One of these lecturers is the Rev. C. A. Lane, author of "Illustrated Notes of English Church History." An Anglican periodical states that, during the season 1888–9, 133 lectures, in 22 English dioceses, were delivered by this gentleman to immense audiences in the largest halls of our populous towns. The aggregate number of persons attending them exceeded, it is stated, 83,000.

Now, what are the qualifications of this reverend lecturer for imparting to his auditors correct views of English Ecclesiastical History? An answer to this question will, perhaps, be best obtained by the perusal of the letter which is subjoined. The letter was written by a Catholic, and it was forwarded to the Rev. C. A. Lane by the friend to whom it was addressed—a clergyman of

(68)

the Church of England, who was desirous of obtaining an answer, if an answer could be given, to the charge contained therein. It is perhaps scarcely necessary to add, that, although nearly a year has elapsed since the letter was sent, no answer has been attempted.

It will be seen how baseless is the statement made in the "Illustrated Notes of English Church History;" and the reader will be able to judge what reliance can be placed on any future assertions of the Rev. C. A. Lane.

The letter ran as follows :—

"My dear Nephew,

"During my recent stay with you, I came across a book entitled, I believe, 'Illustrated Notes on English Church History,' by the Rev. C. A. Lane, published by the S. P. C. K. At page 147, I met with the following astounding statement: 'Before the Conquest the Spiritual and Temporal Supremacy of the Popes in England were alike denied.' Now this assertion (an assertion worthy of the *Church Times* itself) fairly takes away one's breath, seeing that every Archbishop from the time of St. Augustine till the Conquest, and indeed, for nearly a thousand years, till the time of Cranmer, recognized the Spiritual Supremacy of the Pope by waiting to receive the Pallium before exercising any archiepiscopal jurisdiction. The Archbishop might be chosen by the King or Witan, but he could not act as Metropolitan—that is, summon the Bishops of his province in Synod, or sit on his throne— till he had received from the Pope the badge by which metropolitan authority was conveyed. Thus, in A.D. 958, Elsey was chosen as the successor of Odo, but he never sat on the Archiepiscopal throne, because he died before the Pallium was received. In the same manner, Eanbald of York was chosen in 796, but it was not till a year later that he received the Pallium, when he was solemnly confirmed as Archbishop. The method of conferring the Pallium rested entirely with the Popes. At one time its transmission by special envoy was allowed. At another time it was obligatory on the Archbishop to repair to Rome, and to petition for it in person. Can there be clearer evidence of the claim to authority on one side, and of submission to it on the other?

"The very creation of the Metropolitan Sees was the work of the Popes. By Gregory the Great it had been decreed that there should be two—one in London, and the other at York—each with twelve suffragans. The expulsion of Mellitus from London and of Paulinus from York frustrated this arrangement. In 657, Pope Vitalian granted metropolitan rights over all England to Canterbury, and limited the number of Anglo-Saxon bishops to twelve. In 735, Egbert of York, resting his pretensions on the original scheme of Gregory the Great, applied to the reigning Pontiff to grant to his See Archiepiscopal dignity; and by a decree of Gregory the Third the Bishops north of the Humber were removed from the jurisdiction of Canterbury, and were subjected to that of the bishop of York, to whom the Pallium was sent. Encouraged by the success of Egbert, Offa of Mercia, by representations sent to Rome, succeeded in obtaining from Pope Adrian a decree making Lichfield an Archiepiscopal See, and rendering the Mercian bishops subject to it. Leo, the successor of Adrian, revoked the grant, however, on the ground that it had been obtained from his predecessor by false representations, and restored to Canterbury the jurisdiction over all the southern bishops which it has ever since retained. The right to sit in judgment on the bishop of Lincoln, now claimed by Dr. Benson, rests, indeed, on a pre-eminence given by Popes thirteen hundred years ago to the See of Canterbury.

"Enough, I think, has been said to show that the statement before referred to, to have been correct, should have read: 'Before the Conquest, and for several centuries later, till the time of Henry VIII., the spiritual supremacy of the Popes in England was never denied.' Nor can this be considered surprising, when we remember that, nearly two centuries before the mission of St. Augustine of Canterbury, a greater Saint, Augustine of Hippo, had asked, 'Who is ignorant that

the most Blessed Peter was the chief of the Apostles?'
And St. Chrysostom calls him 'that leader of the
Choir, that head of the Brotherhood, that one set over
the entire universe, that foundation of the Church.'
St. Jerome had said, 'For this reason is one chosen
out of the twelve, that a head being appointed,
the occasion of schism might be removed;' and St.
Ambrose had declared 'where Peter is, there is the
Church, and where the Church is, death is not but life
eternal.'

" Believe me,

" Yours, etc.,

"_____

" P.S.—I ought perhaps to have added that, besides
the prerogative believed to be inherent in the Pope by
Divine right, there were certain other prerogatives which
were, in the Middle Ages, ascribed to him in many
countries of Europe. These, being merely of human
origin, were liable to great modifications and were
frequently the subjects of treaties and arrangements."

:

THE CATHOLIC TRUTH SOCIETY, 18 West Square, London, S.E.
[1s. per 100.]

ARCHBISHOP BENSON

AND

"THE NEW ITALIAN MISSION."*

Archbishop Benson has lately spoken of the Catholic Church in this country as "The New Italian Mission."

Now it is undoubtedly true that we hold our jurisdiction by our communion with the Apostolic See of Rome. In common with the rest of the Catholic Church, we are subject to it, and stand to it in the relation of "members to a head." (The expression is not ours. It was used by the Fathers of the Council of Chalcedon in 451, addressing Pope Leo, and submitting to him their decrees "for confirmation and assent.")

It is also true that Rome is in Italy. If these two conditions suffice to constitute an "Italian Mission," they are abundantly verified. But in that case, "Italian Missions" are about as old as Christianity. It is a fairly long time since Irenæus in the second century singled out the Apostolic See as the centre with which "all churches must agree." It is longer still since Rome began to be in Italy.

Perhaps the most noteworthy instance of an "Italian Mission" in this sense, was that of St. Augustine and his fellow monks who came here from Rome and founded the English Church and the Primatial See of Canterbury. That was an Italian Mission *par excellence*.

In every other sense, the Archbishop's epithet is all that is illogical. Our union with the Apostolic See connects us with the *See* of Rome. It does not connect us with *Italy*, any more than it connects us with Spain or Portugal. According to the practice of Christian antiquity Sees are named from cities, not from tracts of country. Bishoprics which are styled "Southern Europe," or "Ohio," strike a jarring note of modernity and incongruity in the ears of all students of Church history. Thence, we are Roman—not Italian. We are "Roman" in the sense that we have the Bishop of the Roman See for our spiritual head. But we are no more Italian than we are French or German. Italy is the name of a

* Reprinted from *The Tablet*, Jan. 10, 1891.

nation. We are Catholics. Our Church is the mother of the nations, but she wears the badge of none. As Catholic, she is the Church of "*all* nations" and in her beloved fold, all frontiers of nationhood disappear. The Spouse of Christ cannot be draped in the Italian tricolor any more than she could be rolled up in the Union Jack.

The Archbishop claims that the "Ancient Church of England is with him." To us the whole history of the Ancient Church of England says just the reverse. The Church history of this land is with us, and proves to us with overwhelming and irresistible evidence that from the very foundation of the English Church Papal jurisdiction was both exercised and recognised in this country.

Here are ten main facts:

1. Foundation.—St. Augustine and his fellow monks, who laid the earliest foundations of the English Church, were sent and commissioned from Rome, and the Pope gave them "authority" to found the Sees of Canterbury and York and the neighbouring bishoprics. The English Church was thus born in an act of Papal jurisdiction.

2. The Pallium.—St. Augustine and his successors in the See of Canterbury for nearly a thousand years went, or sent, to Rome for the Pallium, an investiture that conveyed with it "vicarial powers" *(vices agere)* from the Apostolic See.*

3. Theodore.—The great Archbishop Theodore, who finally organised the English Church into its existing framework, was chosen, constituted, and consecrated Primate of England by the Pope in 668. Before the Council of Hertford he declared himself "appointed by the Apostolic See." †

4. Wilfrid.—St. Wilfrid, when deprived of the See of York, appealed three times to the Holy See, and in deference to its award was finally received with honour, and had given to him the See of Ripon and Hexham. "This is the will of the King and of his princes that to the commands of the Apostolic See, and to the directions of King Alfrid, we should all render obedience." Such was the manifesto of the King's representative in the final council in the affairs of Wilfrid.‡

---

* Bede, H. E. i. 29, Labbe. ix. 643.   † Bede, iv. 5.
‡ Eddius, Gale 86.

5. **The Liturgy.**—The Liturgy of the English Church was the Roman rite, and for a thousand years the Pope was prayed for in the Canon of the Mass. The Church music and services were faithfully modelled upon those of Rome, and books and vestments, and even choir masters were brought from Rome for the purpose.*

6. **Peter's Pence.**—Peter's pence was commanded by law to be collected and sent to Rome.†

7. **Archbishop-making.** — Under King Offa, Lichfield was raised to the rank of an Archdiocese, and its Bishop, with a number of suffragan bishops, was exempted from the control of the see of Canterbury. In 802 both Lichfield and its suffragan sees were restored to their original condition. Both the elevation and the deposition, the exemption and the re-submission were effected by the authority of the Apostolic See, to whom both Bishops and Kings applied for the purpose.‡

8. **Obedience.**—In 791 King Kenulf, in the name of himself and all his nobles and bishops, wrote to Pope Leo, asking the Pope to signify his commands, and promising to love him as a father, and to "embrace him with all the strength of obedience."

9. **Monasteries**—When King Offa founded the Abbey of St. Albans he went himself to Rome to procure for it the Papal sanction and privileges, and the Pope promised to adopt the Abbey as a "special daughter of the Church of Rome."§

10. **Westminster Abbey** was built by Edward the Confessor in obedience to a decision of the Pope "in virtue of holy obedience" in commutation for the fulfilment of a vow. (Wilkins i. 316.)

Here are ten others :

1. William the Conqueror was crowned by Papal Legates, and was himself a suitor at the Court of Rome.

2. Papal Legates carried out the reorganisation of the English Church in a number of Councils presided over by them, and summoned by authority of the Roman See.‖

3. Lanfranc caused two English Bishops (one an Archbishop of York) to go to Rome and surrender their pastoral staffs into the hands of the Pope.**

* Bede, iv. 17-18. † Laws of Edmund Thorpe, 1244. ‡ Letter of Leo XIII. Wilkins, i, 165. § Monasticon Anglicanum, St. Albans. ‖ Wilkins, i. 316. ¶ Wilkins, i. 323. ** Eadmer, *Hist. Novell.* 6-7.

4.   The transfer of Sees, as in the case of Lincoln and Exeter, were made by the authority of the Pope.*

5.   Disputed elections and *causae majores* were decided by the Court of Rome. Bishop Stubbs admits that between 1215 and 1264 there were no less than 30 of them.†

6.   The Archbishops and Bishops of England took publicly a solemn oath of allegiance to the Pope. " I will be faithful to Blessed Peter, and to the Holy Roman Church and to our Lord the Pope. . . . . . The Roman Papacy I will be their helper to maintain against all men. . . . . . The commands of the Holy See I will observe with my whole strength and cause them to be observed by others.   So help me God and these holy Gospels." ‡

7.   The Constitutions drawn up by the Papal Legates, Otho and Othobon, formed part of the Canon Law pleaded in the Ecclesiastical Courts of England.§

8.   By the Canon Law of England a whole class of sins and censures were reserved to the Holy See, and could only be absolved by the Pope.‖

9.   In 1246 the English Bishops declared to the Pope that England had been "ever specially devoted to the Roman Church," while the English Abbots and Priors protested that the " English Church has many glories, and has ever been a special limb (*membrum*) of the Holy Church of Rome."   In the same year, the nobles and Parliament of England assured the Pope " Our Mother, the Church of Rome, we love with all our hearts, as our duty is . . . . . to whom we ought always to fly for refuge."¶

10.   For nearly two centuries before the Reformation the vast majority of Bishops were appointed by Papal provision, namely, by the direct authority of the Pope, and by Papal Bulls issued to that effect.**

It would be easier for Dr. Benson to lift Great Britain out of the ocean than to remove these facts from the structure and fibre of English history, or to give to these facts any other direction or significance than their plain historical meaning—that the ancient Church of England was one that held, and not one that denied, that "the Pope hath jurisdiction over this realm of England."

* Charter of Lincoln Cathedral.   Preface of Leofric's Missal.
† Vol. iii. 315. *Const. Hist.*   ‡ Rymer, xiii. 256.   § Lynwood's *Provinciale, Constitutiones Legat.*   ‖ Lynwood's *Provinciale.* 314.
¶ Matthew Paris, 928.   ** Le Neve's *Fasti.*

DOES AN ANGLICAN "FORSAKE THE CHURCH OF HIS BAPTISM"

BY BECOMING
A ROMAN CATHOLIC?

Answer:—No, he does not. Even according to Anglican doctrine he still *remains in* "the Church of his baptism." And by Roman Catholic doctrine, he *returns to* "the Church of his baptism."

Proof of this. (1.) By his baptism, the Anglican is told that he enters "the congregation of Christ's flock," that he is "grafted into the Body of Christ's Church." (Book of Common Prayer.)

(2.) This expression must imply not any one National Church but the entire Catholic Church of Christ. If it means the Anglican Church only, it will be necessary to suppose either (*a*) that the Anglican Church is the whole "congregation of Christ's flock," or (*b*) that each of the various churches or sects—supposed to comprise the whole Church of Christ—has its own distinctive Baptism; so that by receiving "Anglican Baptism" an infant becomes a member of the Anglican Church, by "Wesleyan Baptism" a member of Wesleyan Methodism, and so forth.

But the former alternative (*a*) is not even an Anglican doctrine. And the latter (*b*) is equally contrary to Anglican teaching, since it is inconsistent with the confession of "*One Baptism* for the remission of sins;" and it also contradicts Anglican practice, seeing that no baptized person seceding to Anglicanism from any other body of Christians is ever re-baptized.

(3.) Therefore, all baptized infants—wheresoever and by whomsoever baptized, provided that proper matter and form be used in the Sacrament—are by virtue of their baptism members of the Catholic Church of Christ. And this is generally admitted by all Anglican writers.

(4.) Therefore, in order to "forsake the Church of his baptism," a man must needs forsake the Catholic Church.

(5.) But no one pretends that the convert to Roman Catholicism has ceased to be a Catholic.

(66)

(6.) Therefore the convert to Roman Catholicism has not "forsaken the Church of his baptism."

(7.) On admitted Anglican principles, then, he still *remains in* the Church of his baptism, namely, the Catholic Church of Christ.

(8.) But further, the reason of such a man's conversion is his conviction that Anglicanism, as an external and visible society, is neither the Catholic Church nor any part of it.

(9.) And this is equally the teaching of the Roman Catholic Church.

(10.) Hence, according to the belief of the convert himself and of the Holy Roman Catholic Church, he has, by becoming a Roman Catholic, neither *forsaken* nor *remained in* "the Church of his baptism," but has *returned to* that Holy Church of Christ into which he was admitted by his baptism as an infant, and from whose communion he has since been estranged by the misfortune of his education in Protestantism and (possibly) by his own culpable ignorance or wilful persistence in a state of heresy and schism.

Note. (i.) There is not one word in the Anglican Book of Common Prayer or Articles supporting or suggesting the narrow and absurd notion that the Church into which a child is admitted by baptism is exclusively and specially the so-called Church of England. Such a theory would, moreover, fall under the condemnation pronounced by St. Paul on the Corinthian sectaries, when he wrote,—"*Is Christ divided?* . . . *Were ye baptized into the name of Paul?*"

(ii.) One may suppose fairly that Anglicans agree with Roman Catholics that there still exists now, as at all other times in the history of Christendom, only *one* "Holy, Catholic and Apostolic Church," and *many* separated bodies of Christians in a state of schism. It cannot then be disputed that whatever and wherever this one—and only one—True Church of Jesus Christ may be, all duly baptized infants—made by their baptism the "members of Christ"—do in God's eyes belong to that One Church and nothing else.

Hence arises the teaching of Roman Catholicism that *all baptized infants* are Roman Catholics, and not in any sense whatever schismatics.

THE CATHOLIC TRUTH SOCIETY, 18 West Square, London, S.E.

[Price 6*d.* per 100.]

ARE THEY PRIESTS?

T HIS is certainly an age of claimants. We have
had a claimant to the honours and birth-right of
the Tichborne family. We have had a claimant to the
title and estates of Derwentwater. Scarcely a year
passes in which claimants do not come forward to prove
before the House of Peers their right to assume the
inheritance of family honours of the past. Not to be
behind the age, a certain number of Anglican clergy
have of late come forward as claimants to the honours
of the Catholic priesthood, and have asked to be
recognized as true priests, who have succeeded to the
inheritance by an unbroken Apostolic Succession.
They assume the dress and bearing of a Catholic priest.
They give out to the world at large that they are what
they profess to be. They present themselves even to
some of the Catholic poor and tell them that there is
nothing to choose between their own pastor and his
Anglican copy, as there is no real difference, &c., &c.
When taken to task by the learned, and confronted with
the many stern facts which stand in the way of any such
conclusion, they answer: "We are satisfied that our
Orders are valid." That may be; still it is well to
remind these persons that the satisfaction of those most
concerned in the issue goes for very little in such a
question. A man, for instance, may personally be quite
satisfied of his right to a peerage, and a seat in the
House of Lords. Does this private conviction confer
the right upon him and justify him in using it? By no
means. He must prove his claim to be valid to the
satisfaction of those amongst whom he aspires to rank,
and until he does this he is compelled to act as a
commoner. If every one, who would be a lord, is to be
acknowledged as such because *he* is satisfied that he is

one, what would become of the peerage? The English people may well be thankful that there is a tribunal to adjudicate upon all such pretentious claims, and that no amount of satisfaction on the part of individuals can supply the defect if it refuses its recognition. It tends to keep nobodies of all classes in their place.

The same is true of the priesthood. The fact that the old Catholic rite for administering the Sacrament of Orders was deliberately, and for doctrinal purposes, almost destroyed by the Reformers, throws upon those who stand by the new Anglican one the *onus probandi* of showing that this mutilation has not invalidated the sacrament. At times for the last three hundred years they have been trying to prove this, and have not succeeded in doing so to the satisfaction of any one besides themselves.

The practical rejection of their claim by the combined voice of those Christians in the East and West, who are acknowledged by all to have retained a valid priesthood, is a fact which ought to have some weight even with Anglicans. Sufficient weight indeed to suggest a doubt as to the existence of those spiritual powers which are so universally questioned; a doubt serious enough to render any attempt to use them unlawful, and this, for the obvious reason that the reverence due to the Christian ministry does not permit us even to risk its profanation by the assumption of priestly powers whose validity is at all doubtful. For when dealing with the sacraments, we cannot, in a case like this, lawfully act even upon a probable opinion, but are bound to choose the safer side.

The historical facts necessary even on the Anglican theory of valid Orders are highly questionable. They never have been proved, and cannot be. Until they are, Anglican Orders must be held as historically doubtful, and for all practical purposes dealt with as if they had no existence.

Shall we ever satisfy our Anglican friends that to attempt to confer sacraments, and to send souls into eternity only in the probability or improbability, as the case may be, of their being valid priests, is the very refinement of trifling with God?

The historical facts, which must ever be an insuperable difficulty in their way, are the following :

1. Queen Elizabeth, having no right whatever to do so, deposed all the Catholic Bishops, except Kitchin, who had conformed, and resolved to re-place them by Protestants. Then came the difficulty, how to get such men consecrated. Of the lawful English bishops, not one would have hand or part in any such transaction. Even Kitchen refused. The Queen therefore was compelled to look elsewhere, and called in a man named Barlow to carry out her will. He was Bishop elect beyond a doubt, but was he ever *consecrated ?* * We have no documentary evidence to show the day, the place, or the fact of his consecration ; and (this makes the clause *elect* more significant) the more we learn of him, the stronger is the case against the supposition that he was a consecrated Bishop. He openly held that election was all that was requisite. Cranmer, his Primate, whose business it was to see that he was consecrated, has laid down for us the following principle as Christian and true, upon which doubtless he would be prepared to act when a suitable opportunity presented itself. "In the New Testament he that is *appointed* to be a bishop or priest needeth no consecration by the Scripture, for *election* or *appointing* thereto is sufficient." † We know that Lancaster, another Reformer, conferred Orders on the strength of his election without consecration, and that they were not questioned, although his conduct was blamed as being irregular.

In April, 1536, Barlow was *elected* bishop of St. David's. On the 21st of the same month his election was confirmed by Cranmer. On the 26th he received the grant of temporalities, after which he was called and acted as "Bishop of St. David's." On the 27th he was summoned to the House of Peers as Bishop, and on May the 1st was enthroned in his see. All this without having been consecrated. For the grant of temporalities to Barlow is quite incompatible with the fact of his consecration, being such as was sometimes made to a Bishop *elect* before his consecration, but never

* See 'Was Barlow a Bishop?' C.T.S., 1d.
† Collier, vol. ii. App. p. 51.

to a consecrated Bishop.   Moreover, when Barlow took
his seat in the House of Peers, June 30th, the Bishop of
Norwich, who was consecrated on June the 11th, took
precedence.   That Barlow was not consecrated before
the 12th of June is further proved by the fact that he is
styled Bishop *elect* of St. David's on the 12th of June,
in an official document by Cromwell, the King's vicar-
general, who must have known the facts of the case.   A
consecrated Bishop in possession of his see, as Barlow
was, was never styled Bishop *elect*.   Haddan, Barlow's
defender, fixes the 11th of June, 1536, as the latest date
on which his consecration could have taken place.   In
Cranmer's Register is found the entry of Barlow's
confirmation by Cranmer with a blank space left for the
entry of his consecration.   This blank space has never
been filled up.   What reason can be assigned for the
omission to make the entry except that the consecration
never took place?   Besides, the fact that the present
official entry in the Lambeth Register states that Parker
had four consecrators instead of being consecrated by
Barlow alone, the other three being assistants, as
is stated in the copy of the previous entry found
amongst Foxe's MSS. in the British Museum, proves
that the official wire-pullers were anxious for appearance sake to dispense with Barlow as the connecting
link in the Anglican succession.   Again, what reason
can there be for this, except to cover the fact,
that Barlow was acting as consecrator without having
been consecrated himself?   This is the only case
in which documentary evidence is not forthcoming. *

---

* See Stubbs, *Registrum Sacrum Anglicanum*, who has been
able to supply *documentary* evidence in every case, including
Bonner's, except' Barlow's.   All he can do for him is to refer to
" Haddan on Bramhall," who assumes, quite gratuitously, that
Barlow must have been consecrated on June the 11th, along with
the Bishop of Norwich, and have had the same consecrators,
because they took their seats together in the House of Lords, June
30, Barlow, however, taking the lower place, which would not
have been the case had they been consecrated together, as his was
the senior appointment.   Cromwell's warrant, however, to the
Garter King-at-Arms, dated June 12th, in which Barlow is
described as still " *elect* of St. David's," has since been discovered,
and it clearly proves that he had not been consecrated on the 11th,
and that Haddan's assumption is quite baseless.

As Barlow consecrated Parker, the first Anglican Archbishop of Canterbury, the Anglican claim hangs by him, and until the fact of his consecration can be cleared of the doubts that hang over it, and fully established beyond all question, the Anglican claim to a certainly valid Priesthood must undoubtedly be disallowed.*

2. The great laxity of teaching and practice regarding Baptism in the Church of England is another insuperable difficulty. The denial of regeneration in Baptism has always been allowed and practically acted upon within her pale. As a necessary consequence there have been generations of her children who have never received valid Baptism. Some clergymen have administered the rite without water; some with a damp finger; others by sprinkling the child's clothes; or in some other way invalidating the sacrament. Hence in a given case, unless there is direct evidence to the contrary, we cannot take for granted the existence of valid Baptism. There is a very strong presumption then, that, where our Lord has not left a certain rule as to Baptism, He has not left a valid priesthood. A man who is not, formally speaking, even a Christian, cannot be a Christian priest or Bishop, and as long as there is a question about Anglican Baptism in the past, a certainly valid priesthood is out of the question. There is grave reason to doubt the valid Baptism of the following Anglican archbishops: Tait, Longley, Sumner, Thompson, Musgrave, Vernon Harcourt, Markham, Drummond, Howley, Sutton, Moore, Cornwallis, Herring, Tillotson, and Secker—because of the laxity in practice *common* at the time of their Baptism.† Not one of these men would now be admitted even into lay communion in the Catholic Church, or even in the schismatic Greek Churches, without receiving at least conditional Baptism; and as the Anglican succession has passed through their hands,‡ the grave doubt that attaches to the validity of their Baptisms must attach

* See p. 12.
† Dr. Tait, *e.g.*, was baptized only as a Presbyterian, and the general practice in Scotland amongst the better class of Anglicans is to baptize all such converts conditionally.
‡ See Hutton's *Anglican Ministry*, p. 543, where the Anglican Succession from Barlow to Tait is given.

also to the validity of their Orders, even if the Anglican
succession had otherwise been continuous and all the
requisites for valid ordination had been otherwise complied with, which is by no means the case.

3.   The instruments, or emblems, of office were not
delivered to the candidate in the case of Parker and
others.   We know that in the case of a Catholic candidate this omission, when accidental, necessitates the
repetition of the ordination conditionally.   In the case of
Anglicans, this omission was intentional, and for a
doctrinal purpose, and is much more serious.   For, in
accordance with a principle we shall have to discuss
later, he who purposely mutilates a sacramental rite
must be taken not to intend to do that which the Church
does when she uses that rite, and hence the sacrament
is not conferred.   Such are a few of the historical
difficulties which render the recognition of certainly
valid Anglican Orders impossible.

II.

The theological difficulties are even greater than the
historical ones.   As far back as A.D. 398, the Fourth
Council of Carthage, Canon 11, decreed as follows:
"When a bishop is ordained let two bishops place and
hold the copy of the Gospels over his head and neck;
and while one is saying over him the Benediction, let
all the other bishops touch his head with their hands."
This rite here described was at this early date fully
established throughout the West.   This Benediction,
given in all the Liturgies of the West, begins *Propitiare
Domine* and continues *Deus honor omnium,* as it is found
in the Roman Pontifical of the present day.   And to
mark its importance it is styled, together with the
accompanying imposition of hands, the *Consecration.*
This portion of the rite is so essentially a part of the
matter and form of the sacrament that even its *accidental* omission in the case of a Catholic bishop would,
as the Sacred Congregation of Rites has decided,* neces-

* *Vide* Benedict XIV., *de Syn.* l. 8. c. 10. no. 13.

sitate his being consecrated over again conditionally. Much more so, then, if the omission was sacrilegious, of set purpose and on doctrinal grounds. Now, Cranmer devised a new ordinal in accordance with his Calvinistic ideas about Orders, in which he swept away the whole of this rite, prescribed by all the Western liturgies, and by which alone up to about the fourteenth century, all the bishops of the Church of England had been consecrated. The Anglican Bishop of Worcester, in a charge published June 1883, says of Cranmer's ordinal: "There is, perhaps, no formulary or document which marks more clearly the *essential difference* between the office of ministers of the Church of Rome and the functions of ministers of the Church of England." He proceeds to point out the mutilations which the old rite for consecrating the bishops of the Church of England underwent in order to reduce it to the level of a Calvinistic ordinance, and concludes that the powers conferred by these rites which were made to differ essentially and intentionally must be essentially different. This argument is perfectly sound. It is that of St. Thomas, who teaches that where there is a question of the sacraments, if a man of set purpose alters the form which the Church uses, when she confers her sacraments, he must be taken not to mean to do that which the Church does when she uses that form, and hence that the sacrament is not conferred.* It is also that of Cardinal Newman, who says of the Church's rite: "It is a concrete whole, one, and indivisible, and acts *per modum unius*, and having been established by the Church, and being in possession, it cannot be cut up into bits, be docked and twisted into essentials and non-essentials, genus and species, matter and form, at the heretical will of a Cranmer or Ridley, or turned into a fancy ordinal by a royal commission of divines without a sacrilege perilous to its validity."†

The old Catholic writer Sancta Clara, who has been claimed as a believer in Anglican Orders, thus states the

* *Summa*, p. 3 q. 60 a. 7 ad 3.

† Essays Crit. and Hist., vol. ii of the *Church of England*, p. 82.

same theological principle: "Since they have changed
the Church's forms *de industria* and declare that they do
not what the Church intends . . . and have solemnly
decreed against the power of sacrificing and consecrating,
that is, in the sense of the old and present Catholic
Church, of changing the elements of bread and wine into
the Body and Blood of Christ our Lord, as appears in
the twenty-eighth and twenty-first articles, it evidently
concludes that they never did or could validly ordain
priests, and consequently bishops; having, as I said,
expressed clearly the deprivation of their intentions in
order to the first and principal part of ordination, which
consisteth in the power *super corpus Christi verum* of
consecrating and sacrificing His true Body, by them
professedly denied, and the sacrifice declared a *pernicious
imposture.*" *

This ordinal of Cranmer was used up to 1662, when
it was altered to meet the view of those who thought it
insufficient—a distinct admission that the use of the said
ordinal cast doubt on the validity of Anglican orders in
many minds. †

Again, by the fourth Canon of the first General
Council of Nice, which was the universal law of the
whole Christian Church, for a lawful consecration, three
bishops were required who were bishops of the province,
and whose consecrations were unquestionable. Now, at
the consecration of Parker, the first Anglican Archbishop of Canterbury, this custom was not complied with.
No three English bishops would have anything to do
with it. Barlow, the consecrator, as far as we know,
was only a bishop elect. Scory and Coverdale had
never been consecrated by the rite of the Church of
England but only by Cranmer's ordinal—the very one

---

* *Vide* Estcourt's *Anglican Ordinations*, p. 239.
† Burnet says "they agreed on a form of ordaining Deacons,
Priests, and Bishops which is the same we yet use, except in some
few words, that have been added since in the ordination of a Priest
or Bishop. *For there was then no express mention made in the
words of ordaining them that it was for the one or other office.* In
both it was said, 'Receive thou the Holy Ghost, in the name of
the Father,' &c. . . . *But that having been since made use of to
prove both functions the same,* it was of late years altered, as it is
now," &c. (*Hist. of Ref.* ii. b. i. p. 252, ed. Pocock).

whose sufficiency is in question, and Hodgskins was present only as assistant. So that there was but one certainly consecrated bishop present on the occasion, and he was not the consecrator. In fact, up to the time of the Tractarian movement Anglicans themselves strenuously maintain that—since the altars of the old Church of England, together with its Priesthood and Christian Sacrifice, in which Christ was offered for the living and the dead were swept away in the sixteenth century, and replaced by tables, ministers, a communion service, and articles which denounce the offering of Christ for the living and the dead, as a "blasphemous fable and dangerous deceit"—they had no real Priesthood amongst them in the old Catholic sense of the word, but only in the sense of elders or ministers. Mason is careful to explain that ministers are called priests *only by way of allusion,** and he denies emphatically the existence of a real Christian Priesthood. And Hooker writes in the same sense: "Seeing that *Sacrifice is now no part of the Church ministry*, how should the name of priesthood be thereunto rightly applied? Surely even as St. Paul applieth the name of flesh unto that very substance of fishes, which hath a proportionable correspondence to flesh, *although it be in nature another thing*."† Even Waterland, following Mede, contends that Anglicans have only a "material sacrifice, the sacrifice of bread and wine, analogous to the *Mincha* of the old Law,"‡ but this was two hundred years after Hooker's time.

Such, in short, are some of the reasons why in Mary's reign we find those consecrated by the Anglican ordinal put on one side, one after the other, by *reason of the nullity of their consecration*,§ and why the validity of Anglican Orders has ever since been regarded by the

---

* *Consecration of Bishops in the Church of England*, bk. v. ch. i., &c.

† *Eccl. Polity*, bk. v. ch. lxxviii. (vol. ii. p. 471, ed. Keble).

‡ Waterland's Works, vol. vii. p. 341, &c., ed. Oxford, 1823.

§ *E.g.*, Taylor, Hooper, and Harley, who had been consecrated by Cranmer's ordinal, were deprived expressly *ob nullitatem consecrationis*—because their consecration was invalid (See *Cant. Reg.*).

Catholic world as a phantom. "Show me," says
Cardinal Newman, "if you can, any religious communion of present or past time which has eventually on all
hands been acknowledged to be a portion of the Catholic
Church on the strength of its Catholic Orders, which,
nevertheless, has been for three whole centuries un-
animously ignored by East and West, which for three
centuries has employed the pens of its occasional and
self-constituted defenders in laboriously clearing away,
with but poor success, the aboriginal suspicions which
have clung to it, on the part of so many, of the invalidity
of those Orders; which, as if unthankful for such
defence, has for three centuries persistently suffered the
Apostolicity of those Orders, and the necessity and
grace of such Apostolicity, to be slighted or denied by
its Bishops, priests and people, with utter impunity;
which has for three centuries been careless to make sure
that its consecrating Bishops, and the Bishops who
ordained the priests who were to be consecrated, and
those priests themselves, had been validly baptized;
which has for three centuries neglected to protect its
Eucharist from the profanations, not only of ignorance
and unbelief, but of open sacrilege; show me such a
case, such a long sustained anomaly, and such ultimate
recognition, and then I will allow that the recognition
of Anglicanism on the part of the Holy See is not
beyond the limits of reasonable expectation." *

III.

It is replied that in Cranmer's ordinal the words,
"Receive the Holy Ghost," &c., were retained, and
that these with the accompanying imposition of hands
is all the form that is essential. This is not true.
These words and the accompanying imposition of hands
were introduced into the ritual only about the fourteenth
century to make it more explicit. "None of the
English Pontificals, except the Exeter, contain this

* *The Month*, October, 1868, p. 425.

form." *   When Archbishop Chichele was consecrated
by Pope Gregory XII. at Sienna, in 1408, its use was
considered so unusual, that a record was made of the
fact in the register of the event.   So that it is impossible
to hold the doctrine that this part of the rite constitutes the essential matter and form of the sacrament,
by which the grace of the high Priesthood is conferred,
for if so, Orders must have long since disappeared
•altogether throughout the Church, owing to the absence
of the essential matter and form in handing them on.
And if it were further insisted that the words, *Accipe
Spiritum Sanctum*, are a valid substitute for the *Propitiare, Domine*, and what follows, because the former
words are certainly an invocation of the Holy Spirit,
and some form of invocation seems all that is
required, we reply that the words in question are not an
invocation and therefore not equivalent to the suppressed
prayers.   But even if they could be considered in any
sense an invocation, it is quite certain that the studied
suppression of prayers which so explicitly mention the
priestly grace and the dignity of the high priesthood,
is an evidence of heretical intent.   The form is left
ambiguous; the change is made with intent to alter the
Church's form; and it is, therefore, on principles
already laid down, an invalid administration of the
sacrament.

Again it is replied that, even if Barlow were not a
bishop, the Lambeth Register says that Parker had
four consecrators and not one.   The entry is, however, such a forgery on the face of it that it cannot
seriously be appealed to.   Its history is well known.
When Bonner challenged the fact that his Anglican
rival, Horne, was a bishop even such as the law
required, because Cranmer's ordinal, which was used,
was not legal, the bench held that the plea was good in
law and that Horne's right must be looked into.   The
Crown lawyers drew up a defence which was so
weak that they dared not come into court with it.   The
document, however, still exists, and proves that the
present official entry in the Lambeth Register has been

* Monument. Rit. 2nd ed. v. ii. p. 274, Maskell.

amended in accordance with it.* The copy of the previous entry, amongst Foxe's MSS. in the British Museum,
states explicitly that the ordinal of Cranmer, called
Edward VI.'s, which prescribes that the consecrator *alone*
should pronounce the words of consecration, was used,
and that Barlow was the consecrator. That he was, is
clear even from the Lambeth Register. Besides, the
present entry in the Lambeth Register refutes itself. It
says that Parker was consecrated according to the form
of a book published by the authority of Parliament, and
then goes on to state that Parker had four consecrators,
and to describe an extraordinary and unprecedented
ceremony not according to the form of any book
ever published by the authority of Parliament. For the
old English rituals as well as the ordinal of Edward VI.,
prescribe that the words of consecration be said by the
consecrator *alone*. It matters little, however, whether
Parker had four or four hundred consecrators, as
Cranmer's ordinal, which was undoubtedly used, was
absolutely invalid, as has been already pointed out.

J. D. Breen, O.S.B.

* The record of Parker's consecration amongst Foxe's MSS.
contains an abstract of the Register of Bonner's consecration,
followed by an account of Parker's, evidently inserted as a *tu
quoque* against Bonner's plea that Parker's consecration was
illegal, on the ground that his own consecration was not
legal, having been performed by three bishops instead of four,
as required by Henry VIII.'s Act of 1534. Hence it would follow
that the entry in its present form did not exist till after the
Bonner-Horne incident, *i.e.*, till after 1563. The entry in the
Lambeth Register, in its present form, which embodies the official
corrections found in the copy in the Record Office, is also an after-
thought, drawn up to meet the charge that Parker's consecration
was invalid, because Barlow, his consecrator, was no bishop. Its
statement that Parker had four consecrators, which is contradicted
by the copy amongst Foxe's MSS., and which is at variance with
the rubric of the ordinal of Edward VI., which was used on the
occasion, was not made without a reason.

The Catholic Truth Society, 18, West Square, London, S.E.
[Price ½d. ; 3s. 6d. per 100.]

The Branch Theory.

—

—

IF there is one point which the members of the High
Church party in the Anglican Communion bring forward
more than another, it is the statement that they are
members of the One Holy Catholic Church. When asked
how can this be, seeing that they are cut off from unity,
that unity which alone comes from the Chair of Peter, the
reply at once is "there are three great branches, Roman,
Greek and Anglican, and these three form the Catholic
Church." It is the branch theory, as it has been called,
which I propose to try and refute upon its own ground.

If the branch theory is founded upon truth, it ought
to hold together when looked at from all points; and
conversely, if when thus looked at it does not hold
together, we may fairly conclude it to be in error.

Anglicans who advance this theory believe in an
historical Catholic Church with an Apostolic Ministry,
which Church they hold to be the keeper and expounder
of the Truth and administrator of the Sacraments. They
believe further that, if the Catholic Church is called together in General Council, the decrees passed by such a
Council are true and cannot err.

Consequently from this we have a Church founded by
Our Blessed Lord with a regular ministry, etc., which
under certain circumstances is infallible, but which under
certain other circumstances is not so. As an instance
we take the Church of the first three centuries. This,
on the above argument, was an infallible Church, because
it could and did hold General Councils from time to time

(35)

as necessity required; while in the same way there cannot be an infallible Church now, as the holding of a General Council would be impossible.

Then comes the question: A General Council being impossible, what is the standard of orthodoxy for this divided Church by which each branch shall judge itself, and to which it must refer all its doctrines? If we say, as the formularies of Anglicanism do, the Holy Scriptures, these require an interpreter; but we agreed at starting that the whole Church was the interpreter, and that Church is unable to speak now, on account of her divisions; consequently we are forced to the conclusion that this cannot be the standard. If again we say, with the Greek Church, the decrees of the first seven or eight Councils, the same objection as in the former case holds; for only the Church can interpret her own decrees. Since, then, both these standards prove false, there is only one other to fall back upon, viz., an infallible head of the Church on earth; either this must be true or else there is no longer any standard of orthodoxy.

If we accept this latter conclusion that there is no longer any living standard of orthodoxy, or that the living standard is at the present time dormant, and if a dead standard such as the Holy Scriptures and decrees of Councils is useless—itself requiring an interpreter which we have concluded does not exist—we must then admit that for centuries the Voice of the Holy Spirit, speaking through the Church, has been silent, and that the authoritative interpretation of the Holy Scriptures has ceased. Then for all practical purposes, at least as far as we are concerned, the Church has ceased to be the expounder of Holy Scripture, and in a sense also has ceased to be its guardian. But this was one of its offices as stated at the beginning of our argument. Consequently, on the branch theory, the Church has ceased to perform the first of its functions; the Holy Ghost, Who was to abide for ever and lead the Church into all truth, has been silenced; and man, by his divisions, has succeeded in depriving the Church of God, against which the gates of hell were not to prevail, of one of its chief functions.   What is the result of this deprivation of the speaking voice?

1.   Heresy cannot be expelled.

For if the heresy be a new one, there is no authority which can decide whether it really be heresy or not, as the speaking voice has been silenced.

Again, if an old heresy rise up again, even this cannot be condemned except by the private judgment of individuals, or of individual " Churches," for, as before stated, the Church as a whole is silent.

2.   The three "branches" in consequence cannot tell whether they are in heresy themselves or not, and as a further consequence have opposed and do oppose each other upon certain important points.   Take, for instance, the Roman and Anglican "branches" upon the Real Presence, or the Roman and Greek upon the *Filioque*.

But how can branches of the same Church, which was to have the Holy Spirit for ever with it leading it into all truth, remain branches, and at the same time teach different doctrines about the same point?

The Greeks assert that their doctrine alone is the true one, the Romans do the same, and condemn anyone who denies it.   And the Anglicans, while more mild because holding less positive truth, say the Church of Rome has erred in matters of Truth, and by accepting only four General Councils—by implication at least— condemns the Greeks.   Then either these "three branches," each to a greater or lesser extent condemning each other as teaching error, are to be held as in some miraculous way all teaching the same undivided truth, which from the nature of the case is impossible, or else one is right and the others are wrong.

All three "branches" admit that the Catholic Church cannot fail in the end, but only one of them declares itself and itself only to be the Catholic Church, and this is the Roman Church.

She says that she only is the Catholic Church, that in her the Holy Spirit speaks and has never ceased to speak, that in her all the promises concerning the Church's infallibility have been fulfilled, and that all who are out of her communion are out of the Catholic Church.

Can she, then, be a "branch," and deny that the branch theory exists? If she is a "branch" and has put forth doctrines which unless she were, as she claims to be, the whole Church, must be untrue, has she not, by the fact of having put forth those doctrines, ceased to be a "branch"? Either she has ceased to be a "branch," or else the very widest divergence of doctrine is possible within the Church.

If, then, divergences of this kind are allowed, what is heresy? And how is it that branches can excommunicate those whom they call heretics from their own communion while the whole Church is powerless to do so?

The branch theory has left us with a lifeless Church which has no living standard of orthodoxy, no power to excommunicate heretics; which is at war with itself, branch differing from branch, as to the truth upon certain vital points. And we are asked to believe that this is the fulfilment of the promise given by our Blessed Lord of His Church that the gates of hell should not prevail against it and that the Holy Spirit should abide with it for ever leading it into all truth! If the branch theory be false, there is only one other and it must be the true one: that of the Holy Roman Church. She is the One Holy Catholic Church, the Pope, the successor of St. Peter, remains ever the living standard of orthodoxy, keeping the whole body united in one. In her the promise is fulfilled, and against her the gates of hell have not prevailed and never will prevail.

THE CATHOLIC TRUTH SOCIETY, 18 West Square, London, S.E.
[1s. per 100.]

TWELVE FACTS

PROVING THAT THE ENGLISH CHURCH BEFORE THE REFORMATION WAS ROMAN CATHOLIC.

"ROMAN Catholic" means, first, any person or body of persons who receive all the articles of faith which the Catholic Church in communion with the See of Rome proposes to his or their belief.

That is the doctrinal test.

Before the Reformation the Church in England was absolutely one with the Church of Rome and with the whole Catholic Church then in communion with the Apostolic See, in all matters of faith and doctrine. I am not aware that this truth has even been called in question.

Secondly, "Roman Catholic" means any person or body of persons who are recognised as fellow-Catholics by the whole Catholic Church in communion with the See of Rome.

This is the organic test.

Before the Reformation, the English Church was absolutely one in communion with the Roman See and with all the other Churches in communion with Rome. In those days, when an Archbishop of Canterbury went to Rome or journeyed on the Continent, he was received by the Pope and by every Catholic bishop on the route with the same cordiality and fraternity of faith as that with which Cardinal

(77)

Manning or Archbishop Walsh would be welcomed at the present day.* Every English priest and Catholic layman received precisely the same recognition throughout Catholic Christendom as any Roman Catholic priest or layman would receive at the present time. The organic union was as close and as complete as the doctrinal one.

Thirdly, " Roman Catholic" means a person or body of persons who recognise the Pope as possessing supreme spiritual jurisdiction in all parts of the Catholic Church.

This final test is both doctrinal and organic, and it is upon it that the whole proof may be said to chiefly depend.

Thus the entire question—Was the Church in this country before the Reformation Roman Catholic?—narrows itself down to one single obvious issue: Did or did not the English Church before the Reformation recognise the supreme spiritual jurisdiction of the Pope? That it did I take to be one of the plainest facts in English history.

I now give a summary of the main facts which establish the recognition of Roman authority by the pre-Reformation Church in England.

Fact 1.—The Archbishops of Canterbury or Primates of the English Church were not enthroned or recognised until their appointment had been confirmed by the Pope.

Fact 2.—The Primates of the English Church went or sent to Rome for the pallium, and were solemnly invested with it. The pallium was a

* Witness the journey of Archbishop Lanfranc and the Archbishop of York and the bishop of Lincoln in 1070—Eadmer, Hist. Novell. pp. 6 and 7; of Archbishop Peckham in 1279; of Archbishop Chicheley in 1414.

Y-shaped stole, of white wool, given by the Popes to Primates in various countries as a symbol of jurisdiction, and was worn on public occasions to show that the wearer had given to him special powers to act as the delegate or vicar of the Roman See. (The words used in the Brief of the Pope granting the pallium to Dunstan, Archbishop of Canterbury, in 959 are :—"Thy primacy, in which it belongs to you to act as a Vicar of the Apostolic See—*vices Apostolicæ Sedis exercere*—after the manner of thy predecessors, We confirm to thee as fully as St. Augustine and his successors, the bishops of the said Church, are known to have possessed it."—Mansi, *Collect. Concil.*, vol. xviii., p. 449.) Such was the importance attached by the Primates of the English See to this investiture with the Roman pallium that, as Bishop Stubbs says, before receiving it they hardly ever ventured to exercise any archiepiscopal function, and Archbishop Arundel, in 1382, although actually present at the consecration of the Bishops of London and Durham, refused to lay on hands, because his pallium had not yet arrived from Rome. (*Constitutional History*, vol. iii., p. 305.)

Fact 3.—For centuries before the Reformation, the Archbishops of Canterbury at their consecration, and at their investiture with the pallium, took publicly before the representatives of the Church and the nation and of the Papal Commissioners a solemn oath of obedience and allegiance to the Pope. In this oath they swore to "defend the Roman Papacy against all men," and to obey the commands of the Apostolic See "with their whole strength" and to "cause them to be obeyed by others." (The copy of the oath is in Rymer's *Fœdera*, vol. vi., p. 80. Edit. 1741.)

Fact 4.—In public documents and letters, the Primates of the English Church constantly declared themselves to be the "Legates of the Apostolic See." They avowed that their precedence over York and their Primatial jurisdiction over suffragans was founded on decrees and grants of the Roman Pontiffs.*

Fact 5.—The Primates and bishops of the English Church in their letters to the Pope constantly begin by making a declaration of "reverence" and "subjection" and "obedience." "Most blessed Father, only supreme and indubitable Pontiff, Vicar of Jesus Christ on earth, kissing most devoutly your blessed feet with all promptitude of service and obedience" is the fairly explicit formula used by Archbishop Chicheley to Pope Martin V. in 1426.†

Fact 6.—In the pre-Reformation Church no English bishop was consecrated or recognised until his appointment was confirmed by the Pope, either indirectly through the Archbishop, who was himself the delegate and confirmee of the Pope, or directly by receiving his appointment by Bulls of Provision from the Holy See. For centuries before the Reformation the vast majority of English bishops were appointed directly by the Pope, and such provisions, embodying as they did the highest exercise of Papal authority ("*ex plenitudine Apostolicæ potestatis*," they were styled in the Royal writs), far from being practically opposed by the English Church or nation, were, on the contrary, eagerly solicited both by the English Kings, the Privy Council,

* See Letter of Lancfranc, Archbishop of Canterbury in 1070, in Wilkins's *Concilia*, vol. i., 326.

† Wilkins's *Concilia*, iii., p. 476.

and by the bishops themselves. Thus the Statute of Provisors * supposed to exclude this direct confirmation was so utterly disregarded by the English Crown and the English Church that the number of appointments made by direct Papal provision was vastly greater after the passing of the Statute than before it.

Fact 7.—For centuries before the Reformation, English bishops at their consecration took a solemn and public oath of allegiance and obedience to the Pope, according to the tenour of that taken by the Primate.

Fact 8.—In the government of the English Church, all important cases of trial—*causæ majores*—were referred by the Archbishop and bishops to the judgment of the Pope as the Supreme Court of Appeal. "Between 1215 and 1264, there were not fewer than thirty disputed elections carried to Rome for decision." † Not less than seven appeals as to elections went to Rome from the chapters of the diocese of Lichfield and Coventry. Hugh Oldham, Bishop of Exeter in 1505, well known to Manchester as the founder of its Grammar School, joined in more than one appeal to the "Holy Apostolic See," which is described in his *Register* as the "sole refuge of the oppressed." ‡

Fact 9.—Throughout all England, in every cathedral, collegiate, and parish church, the Mass was said and the sacraments administered according to the Latin and Roman rite,

---

* When the statute was confirmed in 1391, the two Archbishops caused to be entered on the rolls of parliament their public protest against it as an infringement of the Papal Prerogative. This protest may be seen in the Rolls of Parliament, vol. iii. p. 264.

† Bishop Stubbs's *Constit. Hist.*, vol. iii., p. 315.

‡ Oldham's *Register*, fol. 44.

adapted to the local uses, such as Sarum,
York, Hereford, and Bangor. In the canon of
every Mass (which is verbally the same as that
which is said at the present day in all Roman
Catholic Churches) there was a prayer for "our
Pope." Moreover, on every Sunday and feast
day, in the parish churches throughout the land,
the people prayed for the Pope in the "Bidding
Prayer." ("Ye shal praye for the state of al
holy churche and for oure holy fader the Pope,
with all his college of cardinals."—See preface
to *Exeter Cathedral*.

The same was the public practice of the Eng-
lish nation in Anglo-Saxon times. ("Witan we
gebiddan for urne Papan on Rome, for urne
Cyning, for ne Arceb., for ne ealdon man," &c.
In Codex of the Gospel Book preserved at York
Cathedral.)

Fact 10.—The jurisdiction of the Pope and
the relation of the English Church to the See of
Rome, was clearly and officially recognised by
the English Church itself. Thus, in the solemn
Declaration of Faith drawn up by Archbishop
Arundel in 1413, with the approval of the English bishops and the English clergy in convocation assembled, to be used as a test against the
Lollards, we find the following clear statement
of what the English Church believed concerning
the Pope:—"Christ ordeyned Saint Petir the
Apostell to be His Vicar here on erthe: whos
See is the Church of Rome, ordeyning and
graunting the same power that He gaf to Peter,
shoulde succeede to all Peter's successours, the
which we now callyn Popes of Rome, by whos
power in churches particular special be ordeyned
prelates, as archbysshopes, bysshopes, curates,
and other degrees, to whom all Cristen men

ought to obey after the lawes of the Church of Rome." *

Fact 11.—The English Church and the English nation repeatedly and cordially declared their devotion and allegiance to the Church of Rome. In 1245, owing to the monetary exactions of the Roman Curia, the relations between England and the Pope were strained to the uttermost. Yet in the very worst of the crisis the English Primate and the bishops assembled at Westminster declared to Pope Innocent that "the said kingdom [of England] was specially devoted to the Most Holy Roman Church." The clergy of England on the same occasion wrote to the Pope affirming the "English Church" to be "a special member of the Most Holy Church of Rome," and declaring themselves to be "faithful and devoted sons of the Most Holy Roman Church." The nobles of England had already in 1245 sent an address of remonstrance to the Pope, which begins with the protestation, "Our Mother, the Roman Church, we love and cherish with all our hearts as our duty it is, and we seek her honour, increase, and welfare with all the affection of which we are capable." They speak of the English King as "the most dear son of the Roman Church." † I take it that the above is the language of Roman Catholics. If these English kings, bishops and clergy themselves affirm that they are "faithful sons" and "special members of the Church of Rome," must I believe certain Anglican lecturers when they say that they were not?

---

* This test-declaration may be seen in the record of Convocation in Wilkins's *Concilia*, vol. iii., p. 355.

† Mathew Paris, 902 and 930, edit. 1571.

8

Fact 12.—Peter's Pence, or "Rome-fee," a contribution from the English people to the Pope, was paid by this country even from Anglo-Saxon times.*

The above are twelve main facts very plainly stamped on the face of English history, and irremovably interwoven in the fibre of the national life of England in pre-Reformation times. They are twelve facts which every student of English Church history may be rightly supposed to have at his fingers' ends. A Church whose doctrine was absolutely one with the Church of Rome's, whose Primates wore the pallium or insignia of Roman vicars, and styled themselves Legates of the Roman See, whose bishops and Primates held their Sees by appointment from the Pope; who swore oaths of allegiance and obedience to the Pope, whose clergy and people prayed in every Mass for the Pope (even before the King), who protested even in the most trying moment that they were "faithful and devoted sons of the Holy Roman Church;" and, finally, a Church which is declared by its own bishops to be "a special member of the Church of Rome," and which paid generous tribute for centuries to the Roman See, appears to us to be just nothing at all if not Roman Catholic. No amount of special pleading can drown the voice of History.

J. MOYES.

* "Tithe we enjoin to every Christian man and Rome Fee."—"Laws of Eadmund." Thorpe, vol. i., 244. "And let God's dues be willingly paid every year, Rome Fee at St. Peter's Mass "—"Laws of Canute." Kemble, vol. ii., p. 547.

THE CATHOLIC TRUTH SOCIETY, 18 West Square, London, S.E.
[Price 2s. per 100.]

Continuity Reconsidered.*

BY J. HOBSON MATTHEWS,

Hon. Sec. St. Teilo's Catholic Historical Society.

The last fifty years have witnessed discoveries of the highest importance to the country in which we live, but we have to deal to-night with an English invention which, for the splendid audacity of its conception, and its wholesale subversion of previous ideas, eclipses all the other discoveries of this nineteenth century. I allude to what is known as the Continuity Theory, popularly summarised in the now familiar formula : "The Church of England of to-day is one and the same with that which existed before the Reformation."

If anyone had informed our great-great-grand-parents of the impending discovery that the Church of England, the bulwark of pure religion and the terror of Popery, had really been Catholic all the time it was supposed to be Protestant, and that its ministers, instead of being simple preachers of the Word, as they styled themselves, had been all along (without knowing or intending it) massing priests—I say, if our not very remote ancestors had been told this, their incredulity would have altogether merged in their indignant rejection of such an absurd and revolting prophecy.

The Anglican idea, prior to the diffusion of the Continuity Theory, was that Roman Catholicism, or "Popery," lay like a hideous nightmare over the face of our land, until it pleased God to raise up a series of

---

* A lecture delivered at Cardiff and Brecon in 1894.

deliverers in the persons of King Henry the Eighth, and his children Edward and Elizabeth, who freed England from the long tyranny of the "Roman Antichrist," gave the English Bible to the people, and so conferred upon them the blessings of a pure, scriptural, spiritual religion for the first time in the national history. Thus the 2nd Homily "Against Peril of Idolatry" (one of those thrilling polemical treatises of which modern Anglicans are very much ashamed, but which the thirty-fifth Article guarantees to contain a "'godly and wholesome doctrine") comfortably declares "that laity and clergy, learned and unlearned, all ages, sects, and degrees of men, women, and children of whole Christendom—a horrible and dreadful thing to think—have been at once drowned in abominable idolatry ; of all other vices most detested of God, and most damnable to man ; and that by the space of eight hundred years and more."

Such a terrible national apostasy certainly called for a potent remedy. Eight centuries is a long time; but, better late than never, and at the end of that dismal period, behold true Christianity once more established.

This happy consummation is forcibly if ruggedly pictured by an inscription still to be seen over the entrance to the church of St. Andrew, at Norwich:—

"This church was builded of timber, stone and bricks,
In the year of our Lord fifteen hundred and six,
And lately translated from extreme idolatry,
A thousand, five hundred and seven and forty.
And in the first year of our noble King Edward,
The Gospel in Parliament was mightily set forward.
Thanks be to God.   Anno Domini 1547, December.

As the good King Josiah, being tender of age,
Purged the realm of all idolatry,
Even so our noble Queen, and Council sage,
Set up the Gospel, and banished Popery,
At twenty-four years she began her reign,
And about forty-four did it maintain.
Glory be given to God."

I once asked an Anglican Church Defence lecturer a question with reference to the Homily "Against Peril of Idolatry." His answer was characteristic. He said "Who reads the Homilies? I have never seen them in my life." One can easily understand that the Homilies are unpleasant reading to Anglicans of the new school, and it was no doubt quite true that this gentleman had never seen them. But I *have* seen and read them; and the Reformers, who compiled them, read them to their flocks, until the Elizabethan State religion was saturated with the spirit of the Homilies. It is therefore useless for latter-day Anglicans to ignore these formal expositions of doctrine, which have been so authoritatively approved by their Church.

We have lately been favoured with some more of the lectures of the Church Defence Institution. These are all so very much alike, that they can be seen to have been formed on one model. The good point about this is that it enables you conveniently to summarise the arguments of our High Church opponents, and to answer all their lectures at once.

So I propose to take what I call the typical Church Defence lecture, and to criticise it in its principal component parts, shewing you why I cannot agree with it.

The primary object in the typical lecture is, as I said before, to prove that, notwithstanding the Reformation, the body which is now termed the Church of England is one and the same, or in direct "continuity" with the ancient Church of England of pre-Reformation ages.

Being at the very outset confronted with the un-questionable fact that the Reformers altered at least the religious headship of the old Church, by casting off the jurisdiction of the Pope, our typical lecturer explains that the ecclesiastical jurisdiction of the Bishop of Rome in this land was no part of the system of the ancient Church of England, but the result of a gradual encroachment on the part of the Roman Pontiffs, which the Church of this country always steadily resisted and at length happily put an end to. I think this is a fair statement of Anglican belief on this point.

Now, what are the supposed proofs most commonly brought forward by the typical lecturer in support of this theory as to Papal jurisdiction?   Well, here I must admit that the various Church Defence authorities do not maintain their customary unanimity.   In the year 1885, when the question of Disestablishment was very much to the fore, and when, in consequence, the continuity theory was first thoroughly popularised, I had some controversy in the columns of the *Nottingham Guardian*, and it turned on the question: When was Papalism first imposed upon the English Church?   It so happened that four clergymen gave expression to their opinions on this point in the same paper.   One reverend gentleman said that undoubtedly the first English Roman Catholics were called into existence in 1850, when our hierarchy was constituted in its present form; another gave it as 1572, when the Pope forbade attendance at the parish churches. (It did not seem to strike this gentleman as odd that people who up to that time had not been Papists should all at once obey a Papal brief.)   The third clergyman said there could be no question that the Saxon Church was free and independent, and that it was the Norman Conquest which imposed the Papal yoke upon us.   The fourth held it quite undeniable that the ancient British Church was pure and primitive, and that Popery was first introduced by St. Augustine of Canterbury.

Of these three gentlemen, I hold that the last was least wrong.   I cannot say he was right, because there is abundant evidence that the Ancient Britons themselves were hopelessly Romanist : and indeed it would have been strange had they not acknowledged the jurisdiction of the Roman Pontiffs, seeing that their country was a part of the Roman Empire for no less than four hundred years, and that they during that period became thoroughly imbued with the Roman civilisation, and everything else that was Roman.   That the Britons, as might have been expected, derived their Christianity also from the imperial city, is evident from the mere fact that their liturgy, their form of worship, was distinctly Roman. Their Mass was said in the Roman, that is to say the Latin, language, and was in fact the very Mass-ritual which was arranged by Pope St. Gelasius.*

It is also worth while to note that those who say the British Church was not Roman Catholic have against them the overwhelming testimony of the national traditions of the Welsh people, as well as their oldest extant records. So decisive is Welsh tradition in asserting the Roman origin of British Christianity, that it even definitely names the Roman missionaries who first brought the Faith to Britain, and of the Pope who sent them.† I know that our Protestant friends do not attach much value to traditions, when these tell in favour of Rome; but there is the solid and significant fact that Welsh antiquity knew no origin of British Christianity save a Roman and Papal origin.

But we are told the Britons refused to submit to "the imperious Italian prelate, Augustine," when he wanted to impose the Papal yoke upon the Britons. What are the facts? St. Augustine desired the Britons to join with him in preaching the Gospel to the heathen English. Now, does anybody seriously suppose that an "imperious Italian prelate," the Pope's special envoy, would wish to engage the missionary services of a set of schismatics, not to say heretics, to help him in converting Pagans? Can we imagine Cardinal Vaughan holding a conference with "Father Ignatius," Dr. Lewis, and Canon Thompson, under an oak at Llanthony, with a view to enlisting them as Catholic missionaries to the Welsh Methodists? The cases would be very similar. Surely, the overtures made by St. Augustine to the British Bishops are an incontrovertible proof that Rome held the British Church

* *The Liturgy and Ritual of the Celtic Church.* By F. E. Warren, Oxford, 1881.

† *The Myvyrian Archaiology of Wales.* 2nd ed. Denbigh, 1870. Triads and Bruts, passim.

to be doctrinally orthodox, and in communion with the
Roman See.

Here I am reminded of the fact that many Anglican
controversialists frankly admit that the British Church,
as well as the Saxon, Norman and later mediæval English
Church, was "Catholic and in communion with Rome."
But this means Roman Catholic, if words have any mean-
ings at all.   What am I, what is our chairman Father
Cormack, what are Bishop Hedley and his flock, but
"Catholics in communion with Rome?"   Those who
make this admission seem to me to give away their whole
case, so I must pass on to other Anglican arguments.

We hear a great deal about religious differences between the Britons and the followers of St. Augustine; but
my experience is that very few people who talk and write
about these separate British customs have any lucid idea
as to what they really were.   It is not asserted that
there was any doctrinal difference; in fact, the Protestant Archbishop of Canterbury, in his sermon before
the Cardiff Church Congress in 1889, distinctly admitted
that there was none.   What, then, were the differences
of ecclesiastical usage or discipline between the Britons and St. Augustine?

In the first and most important place, the Britons
did not celebrate the festival of Easter at the same time
as it was kept at Rome.   That was admittedly the foremost difference; the only other which St. Augustine
deemed important related to the mode of administering
Baptism; the rest were peculiar customs of less significance than those which at the present day differentiate the
Roman Catholics of this country from the local Church
of the diocese of Rome.   And as the difference in regard
to Baptism consisted merely in the fact that the Britons
immersed the neophyte once, while the Romans dipped
him thrice, * I think I may confine myself to the question
of the British Easter.

St. Augustine required the British Bishops to celebrate
Easter on the same day of each year as at Rome.   The

* *Lit. and Rit. of Celt. Ch.*

Britons kept the festival according to an erroneous calendar, and they shewed themselves extremely averse to altering their mode of calculating the date of the Easter celebration.

But there is one important fact which the typical Church Defence lecturer does not bring out; and that is, that the erroneous mode of calculating Easter, to which the Britons were so much attached, was itself a Roman mode, though an obsolete one. It was, in fact, the mode which the Britons had learned from Rome long before the time of St. Augustine.* As astronomical knowledge progressed, the learned men of Rome and Alexandria amended the ecclesiastical calendar from time to time. And so long as the Britons and Irish were able to keep up communication with Rome, they kept posted up in these improvements of the almanack, and shifted the dates of their moveable feasts accordingly. Our typical lecturer never tells us, for instance, that in the year 453 the Britons altered their Easter cycle for no other reason than that the Pope so ordained. The *Annales Cambriae*, that earliest and most reliable of Welsh chronicles, under the date 453 tells us that this year "Easter is changed to Sunday with Pope Leo, the Bishop of Rome." This was 143 years before St. Augustine set foot in Britain. I think these are facts which Church Defence lecturers ought not to withhold from you, because they have a very important bearing upon the question whether the Britons were Roman Catholics or not. In the Law Courts, if the legal adviser of one of the contending parties withholds from the jury any material fact, he is liable to have some very unpleasant remarks addressed to him by the learned judge.

You will perhaps say that even when St. Augustine acquainted the Britons with the alteration in the date of Easter, they refused to comply with it. It is undoubtedly true that the Britons utterly declined to recognise St. Augustine as their Archbishop, or to have

* *Lit. and Rit. of Celt. Ch.*; Haddan and Stubbs' *Councils.*

any dealing with him. Why? Our Anglican friends insist on cherishing the belief that it was because they rejected the jurisdiction of the Bishops of Rome. But this ingenious theory, which, by the bye, was never heard of before the Reformation, does not agree with the plain facts of history, which show that the Britons had recognised the Pope's jurisdiction long before the coming of St. Augustine, and that they recognised it in the times which followed. You must observe, too, that the Pope had not as yet given St. Augustine jurisdiction over the Bishops of Britain, at the time of his first conference with them.

Before the coming of St. Augustine, the three British Bishops, St. David, St. Teilo and St. Oudoceus, had gone on pilgrimage to Rome—the latter several times.* There is even good reason to believe, from an examination of the old Welsh writings, that St. David and St. Teilo received their episcopal consecration at Rome.†

Now if we turn to the period following after St. Augustine's conference with the Celtic Bishops, we find that, notwithstanding the Britons' prejudice in favour of the older Easter, they again complied with the requirements of Rome in 768.‡

It will be well to inquire what *was* the reason of the British Bishop's refusal to unite with St. Augustine. I reply unhesitatingly and without any fear of being controverted, it was because St. Augustine came before them as the friend and Archbishop of their hated foes, the English, who had driven the poor Britons into the far west of their own country and had harassed them cruelly for generations. The Britons recognized the Bishop of Rome, but they would have nothing to do with an Archbishop of Canterbury; and this attitude of opposition to the English, even in religious matters, the Welsh people maintained for centuries after the time of

* *Liber Landavensis*, Welsh MSS. Society, Oxford, 1893.

† Ib. *Iolo, MSS*, and *Cambro-British Saints*, Welsh MSS. Society.

‡ Haddan and Stubbs.

St. Augustine, all the while being peculiarly devoted to Rome.

There is in existence a certain manuscript which to historical students possesses the great interest of being the most ancient piece of consecutive writing in the Welsh language. It dates from about the year 1150, but is a transcript from an original hundreds of years older. This fragment is specially suited to my purpose, so I will read it to you and will then translate it :—

" Llyma cyfraith a braint Eglwys Teilo o Landâf, a roddes y brenhinoedd hyn a thywysogion Cymru yn dragywyddol i Eglwys Teilo ac i'r esgobion oll wedi ef, ymgadarnedig o awdurdod Pabau Rhufain."

(This is the law and privilege of the Church of Teilo of Llandaf, which these kings and princes of Wales gave in perpetuity to the Church of Teilo and to all the bishops after him, confirmed by the authority of the Popes of Rome.)*

The British Church is the forlorn hope of our typical friend. Show him the essentially Popish character of the mediæval Church of England, and he will say : Yes, but the Saxon Church was independent of Rome. Prove to demonstration that the Saxons were thorough-paced Romanists, and he urges that the British Church, at least, cared nothing for the Pope. However, I leave it to you to say whether or no I have demonstrated the erroneousness of the supposition that the Church of the Britons was less Romanist than the Church of any of the succeeding periods of our history.

This brings me to a point on which I would ask your careful attention. I want you to particularly notice the astonishing lack of consistency and logic which permits Church Defence lecturers to appeal to the British Church in support of their theory of Anglican continuity. In the first instance, to show the Britons' supposed independence of the Pope, they take great pains to impress upon us that the British Church would have nothing to do with St. Augustine of Canterbury, the head of the English Church ; and then they claim that the English

* *Liber Landavensis.*

*

Church is in direct continuity with the British Church!
Could worse reasoning be employed in a wrong cause?
Surely our friends must stick to one statement or the
other.   If the British Church refused to have anything
to do with the English Church, how can the latter be
in continuity with the former?   And if the Britons'
opposition to St. Augustine, amounted to a rejection
of Papal jurisdiction, is not this admitting that St.
Augustine, the first Archbishop of Canterbury, the
first hierarchical head of the Church of England,
was neither more nor less than a Papal emissary?
But then, what becomes of the independent national
character claimed for the Church of England, if it
was so Popish at its very birth?   And above all, what
becomes of the last new nickname for the English
Catholics of to-day, "the Italian Mission?"   Surely,
unless universally acknowledged statements of history
are totally false, the Church in this country, as it must
of necessity be in true continuity with the Church of
St. Augustine, must therefore also necessarily be in a
very real sense an Italian Mission, if it is to be Catholic
at all.

It is quite remarkable how our typical lecturer takes
up St. Augustine and drops him again, just as suits his
purpose at the moment.   If he is speaking about Dr.
Benson, he describes him as "occupying the chair
of St. Augustine," or as "the worthy successor of St.
Augustine."   But when he is dealing with the differences
between St. Augustine and the British Bishops, the great
first Archbishop of Canterbury all at once becomes an
"imperious Italian"—a phrase employed by Dr. Benson
himself at Cardiff—or "the haughty Roman prelate,"
and so on.   To show continuity with the early Saxon
Church, St. Augustine is indeed exalted to the skies;
but for the purpose of continuity with ancient Britons,
he is humbled into the dust.

The first Anglican Reformers were quite above trying
to tack on the new Anglicanism to the Benedictine
gown of St. Augustine of Canterbury.   Thus John Bale,
one of their foremost writers, tells us that "Augustine

the Roman was sent by Gregory the First to convert the English Saxons to the Papistical faith," and that " King Ethelbert at length received Popery with all its superstitions."*   It never occurred to honest John Bale that the church of which he was so prominent an ornament was in direct continuity with that which he so energetically denounced.

One fact is admitted on all hands, namely that St. Augustine, the Italian missionary monk, was sent to England by the Pope to found and organise the Church of England.   You see, the old Church of the Britons, so far as England proper was concerned, had been swept away by Pagans, and a new "Italian mission" had to reconstruct it; just as had to be done by a long subsequent act of "Papal aggression" under very similar circumstances.†   But here our typical lecturer finds comfort in the reflection (an erroneous reflection, though) that "the mission of Augustine was a comparative failure."   Previously he had derived consolation from the fact that the Britons refused to preach Christianity to the English ; and now he says we need not worry about the Romish character of the first Archbishop of Canterbury, as his mission was a comparative failure.   It is surprising what dismal circumstances afford satisfaction to our typical friend.

He says St. Augustine's mission was a comparative failure, because its permanent result was chiefly confined to the Kingdom of Kent.   But here comes a question. Since it is admitted that St. Augustine converted the people of Kent, are not the Roman Catholics who now live in Kent strictly and exclusively in continuity with their Roman Catholic apostle?   And, as a corollary, are not the Anglicans in that county, including Dr. Benson of Canterbury, obvious schismatics?   I believe High Churchmen hold that the Roman Catholics are schismatics in those countries of which Anglican bishops were the first to take missionary possession.   Apply this argu-

---

* *Cent.*, vol. 5.
† The restoration of the English hierarchy, in 1850.

ment to Kent, confessedly evangelised by a Roman Catholic missionary bishop, and it seems to me that, in that county at least, the Roman Catholic, and not the Anglican body, are the real old Church.

But is it a fact that little beyond the kingdom of Kent was christianised by Roman missionaries in the Anglo-Saxon period ? Bede's *Ecclesiastical History* is the prime authority on the subject, and it tells us that St. Paulinus converted the county of which York was the capital, St. Birinus, the kingdom of Wessex, St. Felix, East Anglia, and St. Wilfrid, Sussex. These apostles were all either Romans or commissioned by the Pope. They all followed Roman usages as closely as they could; and one of them, St. Wilfrid, is well known for his strong opposition to the Celtic customs. Therefore it seems to me that the same causes which, if my argument is sound, make Roman Catholicism the true and original religion of Kent, make it equally the one true Church of the greater part of England.

And to maintain this involves no slight upon the memory and reputation of the holy and zealous Scottish missionaries who converted to the Faith of Christ so extensive a portion of northern England. Our typical lecturer regards the Celtic missions of the North as so many set-offs against the Roman missions of the South of England, as though both were not in complete doctrinal accord and communion. The Celtic ecclesiastical discipline certainly differed in many particulars from that of Rome and the rest of Christendom ; but Roman authority, though it strongly discountenanced the obsolete calculation of Easter, never even on that account pronounced the Celtic Church schismatic. Far from that, Rome has always paid high honour to the memory of the British and Irish missionary saints, and accounted them saints of the universal calendar. Our Anglican friends are pleased to exalt such Celtic missionary monks as St. Aidan and St. Colman of Lindisfarn at the expense of men like St. Wilfrid of York— quite oblivious of the fact that in so doing they are belittling the heroes of the Church which they themselves claim to belong to. Yet, St. Aidan has his special office in the Benedictine Breviary, along with St. Wilfrid (neither of them figures in the *Book of Common Prayer*) because the Roman Church does not and never has considered the Northern missioners as having been separated from her communion. Indeed, if anyone wishes to cherish the idea that the monks of Iona and Lindisfarn were a kind of early Protestants, or High Church Anglicans of a primitive type, he had better not read such works as St. Adamnan's Life of his abbot St. Columba, which would show him that every doctrine condemned by the Thirty-nine Articles as Romish and corrupt was held by those zealous and saintly Gaelic missionaries of the North, who are paraded by our typical lecturer as rivals to the pretensions of the Roman Church.

As for the question of their views with regard to Roman supremacy, let me once and for all say that I challenge anybody to refer me to an instance of a denial of the Pope's spiritual jurisdiction by the Church in this country, prior to the movement called the Reformation.

The next great point in our typical lecture is the dispute between St. Wilfrid and Archbishop Theodore of Canterbury concerning the deposition of St. Chad. Theodore had deposed St. Chad from the See of York, because it belonged canonically to St. Wilfrid. But, a few years later, Theodore thrust a prelate into Wilfrid's bishopric during the latter's absence, who thereupon appealed to Rome. The Pope restored Wilfrid to his See; but the king imprisoned him on a charge of having bought the Papal decree, and Theodore connived at this injustice. This is a brief outline of the principal facts of the case. But on this slender basis of fact our typical lecturer builds up an imposing edifice of fiction. He tells his audience that "Theodore simply ignored the Pope and his decree," and "resisted absolutely the supremacy of Rome." Please bear those statements in mind while I place a few more facts before you. In the first place when deposing Chad in favour of Wilfrid, Theodore was styled and styled himself

"Envoy of the Apostolic See." That is to say, he exercised the power of deposition on the strength of a Papal commission. So that you see he did not at that time "resist absolutely the supremacy of Rome." Secondly you must know that, when Wilfrid appealed to Rome, so far was Theodore from considering this an unjustifiable proceeding, that he himself, with what speed he might, despatched a messenger to forestall Wilfrid with the Pope. Observe also that nobody alleged the Pope had no authority to decide the matter. What Wilfrid's opponents did, was to accuse him of having obtained the Pope's decree by underhand means. In fact the king offered to release him from prison if he would say the Papal instrument was forged.* It is also important to notice that, years later, when Theodore felt his end approaching, he made what amends he could, and "obeyed the Pontifical decrees," as it is expressed in a contemporary document cited by Haddan and Stubbs.† So that he did not *then* "absolutely resist the supremacy of Rome," nor "ignore the Pope and his decree." This is just an instance of the reckless manner in which our typical friend, like a sort of controversial rocket, throws off his dazzling showers of "continuity" sparks, very pretty to look at, and greatly admired by High Church friends who stand by in the dark, anxious to think the pyrotechnic display all genuine and true : until, for want of the substance of historic truth, down comes the blackened and discredited stick, and all our opponents can do is to light up another and go through the process again.

Up soars the next rocket, with a prodigious hiss and a brilliant blaze of light, displaying the motto : " Magna Charta : The Church of England shall be free ! " What do you think of that, you Romans, you Italian Missioners ? Observe, not "the Church of Rome," but "the Church of England shall be free, and hold her rights and liberties inviolate."

---

* Gale, *Rer. Angl. Script.*, tom. iii, cap. 35., p. 70. *Vita S Wilfr.*, Oxon., 1691.

† pp. 171, 262.

I never yet heard of a Continuity lecture where this rocket was not let off amid great applause from the delighted spectators. But really, when you come to think, is it not marvellous that learned clergymen, men of light and leading, can find satisfaction in the childish argument that the Great Charter does not speak of the " Roman Church" in its text, but of the "English Church "—*Ecclesia Anglicana.* Our typical lecturer quite takes it for granted that, because the present established Church is commonly termed, even by Roman Catholics, "the Church of England," that this same Established Church of England is necessarily the one referred to in Magna Charta. But this is a wholesale begging of the question that we ought not to expect from an intelligent man. It ignores the fact that the term "Church of England" is simply one of courtesy, when applied to the State Church by Roman Catholics. We Catholics do not acknowledge that the Anglicans of to-day are the Church of England. We think that they usurp a title to which they have no real right.

What our typical lecturer has to do is to show that the *Anglicana Ecclesia* of the Great Charter is in very deed and in fact one and the same as the religious community which is popularly termed the Church of England at the present day. Supposing some person arose to-morrow to claim the title of Duke of Norfolk. What should we think of his logic or his sense of propriety if he pointed to some ancient deed which contained mention of a Duke of Norfolk and said, "there you are, there is the Duke of Norfolk distinctly named; what further proof do you want that I am his descendant and representative ?"

The question is, not whether the pre-Reformation Church in this country was known as the "Church of England," or "English Church," but whether that Church of England was or was not Roman Catholic. Our friends would not say that there was anything more incongruous or essentially absurd in the idea of an English Church that was Roman Catholic, than in the idea of an Italian, a Spanish or an Austrian Church that is Roman Catholic.

In addressing briefs to the Bishops of Spain, the Pope constantly refers to them and their flocks as "*Ecclesia Hispaniola* "*—the Church of Spain—not "the Church of Rome." But is not the Spanish Church Roman Catholic? If so, it doesn't evidently appear why the English Church named in Magna Charta was not Roman Catholic also. And yet our typical lecturer points out in the Great Charter the words "Church of England," and asks triumphantly what more proof is needed that *that* Church of England was independent of the Pope!

But our friend hastens to add, the great Charter declares that "the English Church shall be free." Free, yes. But from what? Free from Papal authority? That is what the typical lecturer likes his audience to suppose; but it is not what Magna Charta says. The Great Charter of our country's liberties lays down that "the Church of England shall be free" from the tyranny and greed of English Sovereigns like King John and Henry the Eighth—free to maintain unimpeded her ancient intercourse with her mother and mistress the Church of the City of Rome. Our typical friend does not tell us that; but it is true. The freedom claimed for the Church of England by Magna Charta was the freedom to elect her Bishops without royal interference, as secured to her by the Pope of Rome. To show you I am stating a simple fact I will read you the translation of the clause in question :—

"The Church of England shall be free and enjoy all her rights in their integrity and her liberties untouched. And that We will so to be observed appears from the fact that We of Our mere and free will, before the outbreak of the dissensions between Us and Our barons, granted, confirmed, and procured to be confirmed by Pope Innocent the Third, the freedom of elections which is considered most important and necessary to the English Church." †

* In the Brief of the Beatification of the English Martyrs the term "Ecclesia Anglicana" was used by Leo XIII.

† Transl. by W. B. Saunders, Assistant-Keeper of H. M. Records.

The Charter, you will observe, is expressed to be granted by the advice, among others, of "Stephen, Archbishop of Canterbury and Cardinal of the Holy Roman Church," and "Pandulph, the Pope's Sub-deacon and Familiar." Cardinal Langton and Monsignor Pandolfo—likely men to set the English Church free from Papal jurisdiction!

But is it not true, I may be asked, that a number of Acts of Parliament were passed from time to time, long before the Reformation, to withstand Papal encroachment? Undoubtedly, I answer, many Statutes were passed curtailing certain powers claimed by the Popes in this realm. But my point is, that they were all directed against such of the Pope's claims as were declared in those Acts to be in respect of matters temporal; and that none of them, strain their meaning as you may, purport to oppose his spiritual jurisdiction. And after all, unless these anti-papal Acts of Parliament can be shewn to have disallowed the spiritual jurisdiction of the Bishops of Rome, they cannot support the theories of my friend the typical Anglican lecturer. On the contrary, the more vehemently these Statutes oppose the Pope's claims to authority in temporal or secular concerns, the more conclusively does their silence with regard to his spiritual jurisdiction prove that the latter was deemed unquestionable.

Let me illustrate this. One of the strongest of the anti-papal Statutes of pre-Reformation times is the Statute of Provisors of Benefices, 25th of Edward the Third, 1350. This complains in strong terms of the custom of granting English benefices to aliens and others, "as if he (the Pope) had been patron or advowee of the said benefices, as he was not of right by the Law of England." Well, undoubtedly, the Pope was neither patron nor advowee of those benefices, either by the Law of England or the Canon Law; and it may be that Parliament was not exceeding its legitimate powers by restraining the abuse. But observe, the Act only professes to check the Pope's claim to seignioral rights over the temporalities of English benefices, and to vindicate the King's right to prevent to livings in his own gift. No doubt this Statute, and others, were meant to stretch at the Royal pleasure; but it is equally true that they do not profess to touch the spiritual jurisdiction of the Roman Bishop over the Church of England.

Only 28 years later, in 1378, Statute 2 of Richard the Second was passed, chapter 6 of which forbade anyone to slander the Pope, (Urban), who, it says, "having been duly chosen Pope, ought to be accepted and obeyed."

Another Act of Parliament of which the typical lecturer and his audiences are passionately fond, is Statute 16 of Richard the Second, Chapter 5, 1392. This I think is quite the strongest of the Statutes of this anti-papal class. It recites that the Pope had laid censures of excommunication on divers English Bishops, for carrying out the Civil Law with regard to English benefices, and had also translated prelates out of the realm, and from one diocese to another, without the King's assent, "and so the Crown of England, which hath been so free at all times, that it hath been in no earthly subjection, but immediately subject to God in all things touching the Regalty of the same Crown, and to none other, should be submitted to the Pope, and the Laws and Statutes of the Realm be by him defeated and avoided at his will;" and it proceeds to enact that no one shall "purchase, in the Court of Rome or elsewhere, by any such translations, processes and sentences of excommunications, bulls, instruments or any other things whatsoever which touch the King."

There can be no doubt that this Statute comes dangerously near to a royal encroachment upon the spiritual power of the Papacy, in saying that the Pope was not to translate Bishops without the King's consent. But my Anglican friends know as well as I do that there is not a Roman Catholic State in Christendom which has not at times endeavoured to encroach upon the Papal prerogatives. This has been done in every country in Europe; the same thing is going on at the present day in France, Italy, Austria, Spain and Portugal, to an extent which we cannot find equalled in the Statutes of the pre-Reformation period in England. But will anybody say that, because of this unceasing conflict between Church and State, the Church of Portugal, or of Spain, or Austria, France, or, Italy is not Roman Catholic. Catholics cannot fail to be struck with the extreme care with which even this strong Statute is so worded as not, professedly at least, to interfere with the Popes spiritual supremacy and jurisdiction :—" In all things touching the Regalty of the said Crown," and " in any other things whatsoever which touch the King." These words are surely definite enough to show that this Act, like the others, professes to limit itself strictly to the Popes alleged encroachments on the King's temporal sovereignty and secular rights.

Now I have cited the two most strongly anti-papal Acts of Parliament in the whole Statute Book, previous to the Reformation ; and I hope I have made it clear that even they are very far from supporting Anglican theories. In fact, however perilously Erastian in tone some of the pre-reformation Statutes are, they all certainly fall very far short of anything like a denial of the Pope's spiritual jurisdiction. On the contrary, it is precisely the most aggressive of them which display the most elaborate care in defining, or attempting to define, the boundary between the time-honoured, sacred and unassailable spiritual province of the Papacy, and the temporal jurisdiction of the Sovereign. True, the King was always endeavouring to shift the landmarks on the debateable ground between these two separate regions, and to confine the spiritual province within ever-narrowing limits ; but the principle that the Bishop of Rome ought to have, and had, jurisdiction in this realm in all matters touching the spirituality, was a principle which neither King nor Parliament ever dreamed of calling in question.

When we come to select illustrations of the devotion and loyalty of the ancient Catholic Church of England to the Holy See, we are embarrassed by the inexhaustible mine of testimony which lies ready to hand.

Robert Grostete, Bishop of Lincoln, resisted the Pope when the latter wished to appoint a nominee whom Grostete could not accept. This was a bold attitude for a Bishop to assume, and it is for this reason that the typical lecturer trots out Grostete as a champion of independent Anglicanism in the 13th century—a kind of early primose of the Protestant Spring. He does not tell us that it was precisely in his resistance to the Papal provision that Robert Grostete protested the deepest submission to Papal authority, when he wrote that " to the Most Apostolic See all power has been entrusted for edification, not destruction, by the Holy of Holies, our Lord Jesus Christ," and again, that " to the Holy Roman Church is due from every son of the Church the most devoted obedience, the most reverential veneration, the most fervent love, the most submissive fear."* With all his boldness, I do not think Robert Grostete would have been equal to signing the Thirty-nine Articles.

I very much wish time permitted me to give you many more such illustrations of the obstinate Popishness of the old Church of England, but it would spin this lecture out to a length beyond that of your admirable patience. I must therefore be content with just one more instance, briefly recounted.

In Wilkins' *Concilia* you will find the test declaration of Archbishop Arundel, approved by Convocation in 1413. Part of it runs as follows :—

"Christ ordained Saint Peter the Apostle to be His Vicar here on earth, whose See is the Church of Rome; ordaining and granting the same power that he gave to Peter should succeed to all Peter's successors, the which we callen now Popes of Rome ; by whose power in Churches particular special be ordained prelates, as Archbishops, Bishops, Curates and other degrees, whom all Christian men ought to obey after the laws of the Church of Rome."

* Letter 127, p. 390, Rolls Series.

In the Statutes we had the State legislating in temporal affairs; but in the document I have just quoted, you have the Church dogmatising on spiritual concerns. It is to statements of this latter class that we ought to look for information as to the belief of the ancient Church of England concerning the Pope.

When now we come to the Statutes of the Reformation epoch, we find ourselves confronted by an entirely different state of things. Unlike those of earlier times the schismatical and Protestant Statutes are at no pains at all to discriminate between the Pope's spiritual and the King's temporal jurisdictions, but boldly declare their intention of placing all power, both secular and religious, in the hands of the monarch.

The first of the schismatical statutes is the one passed in the 24th year of Henry VIII., 1533. Chapter 3 provides "for the restraint of appeals" to Rome. It begins with a bold, straightforward series of parliamentary lies, and is the composition of the King himself (worse composition, by the way, it would be impossible to imagine). The Statute is too long for me to quote, and to quote a part would only spoil the effect of the beautiful whole. Suffice it to say that it plunges boldly into schism, with no more apology or preface than a deliberately false summary of the Statutes of earlier times. I say deliberately false, because it was quite within the knowledge of Henry and his advisers, as it is known to all of us, that in ancient times the English Church had not always been, as the Act says, reputed sufficient of itself to determine all questions " in any cause of the Law Divine." Nobody knew better than the framer of the Act, that the Pope had always been considered the supreme authority in questions of doctrine, and that his decision had been the final sentence in questions of ecclesiastical discipline, as well as in causes matrimonial, testamentary, &c. Indeed these fraudulent recitals are contradicted in the operative part of the Act itself, which distinctly admits a " a custom, use, or sufferance " of abiding by the Pope's arbitrament in such cases.

It is the habit of the typical Continuity lecturer to
point to the recitals in the Reformation Acts of Parliament, as if the statements made in those recitals were
so many proofs of the Anglican theory.   The absurdity
of this is surely self-evident.   King Henry VIII. was
hardly likely to label his measures " brand-new," to
guarantee them as so many original inventions ;   on the
contrary, he might naturally have been expected to do
just what he did, namely, to endeavour, so far as auda-
cious misstatement could, a false atmosphere of pre-
cedent, of antiquity even, around his revolutionary
enactments.   To bring forward the bare recitals of
Statutes, as if they were evidence of the matters alleged
by those statutes, is as curious a method of argument
as could well be devised, even by such an ingenious
thinker as our typical lecturer.

Now that we are arrived at that epoch of wholesale
destruction, which the early Protestants styled "the
Reformation," it is time to notice another strong point,
as he considers it, of our friend.   If, he says, our
Church of England was established at the Reformation,
be good enough to tell me in what year, and by what
Act of Parliament it was established.   Hereupon, his
audience cheers him vociferously.   The point looks
plausible, at first sight ; but, like a good .many other
plausibilities of Anglicanism, there's not much in it
when you come to examine it.   It involves the fallacy
that nothing is done unless it be done at one given
point of time.   My friend the Continuityist would think
I was very foolish if I said to him : You say that Rome
was built ; but pray tell me, on what day was it built ?
Was it Sunday, Monday, Tuesday, or Wednesday ? and
so on.   Of course the fact is, Rome was not built
in a day ; nor was the Protestant Church of England
established by the King's signing one particular Act of
Parliament.   But a series of Acts of Parliament first
abolished the real old Catholic Church of England, so
far as its governmental framework was concerned, and
then built up, brick by brick, or established, the State
religious corporation which at the present day claims to
be the Church of England.

If, however, our Anglican friends still press for a precise date for the establishing of the Protestant Church of England, I can satisfy them on no less an authority than that of the erstwhile head of the establishment, "the high and mighty Prince James." At the Hampton Court Conference, held in 1604, at which it was endeavoured to bring about a union between English Prelacy and Scottish Presbyterianism, his sapient Majesty made a valuable pronouncement on the subject, which you will find *verbatim* in Cobbett's "State Trials." Speaking of the apostolic age, the King said : " Great the difference between those times and ours. Then, a Church not fully established; now, ours *long established*. How long will such brethren be weak ? [He is referring to the sign of the cross in Baptism, at which the Puritans were scandalised.] Are not *forty-five years* sufficient for them to grow strong in ? " His Majesty, you see, in 1604, speaks of his Church as " long established," and then credits it with an antiquity of 45 years. Well, of course that was a respectable age for a reformed communion ; and it fixes 1559 as the date of the actual establishment of Anglicanism.

There is another highly popular argument which never fails to parade for duty at typical lectures, nor to elicit hearty applause from the large class of Anglicans who don't take the trouble to think. They are told that the very word " Reformation " is evidence of Continuity. If, says the lecturer, an institution has been reformed—re-formed—that implies that it remains the identical institution it was before. To this argument from the word "reform" I should reply that it depends how you take it. There are reforms which entirely destroy the identity of the thing reformed. For instance, take the case of a Protestant goldsmith in the reign of Edward the Sixth, who melts down a gold chalice, and with the same material makes a butter-dish. He has taken the mass of metal which was a chalice, and has re-formed it ; and now it is no longer what it was, but something else. That is the sort of re-formation that I hold the sixteenth century religious changes to have been.   My Protestant hearers think I am wrong, but I merely give this illustration for the purpose of showing that they cannot make much capital out of the significance of the word " Reformation."

We are all familiar with the typical lecturer's other famous illustration of the Continuity Theory.   He says : " If that dirty, drunken fellow, Bill Sikes, is taken to a reformatory, has his face washed, sobers down, and becomes a respectable member of society, isn't he still the same Bill Sikes ? "   This is certainly very complimentary to the ancient Church of our forefathers, with which it is the Anglican's great ambition to prove himself in continuity !   But if the Reformation had been a change from Catholicism to Presbyterianism in this country, as in Scotland, or to Calvinism as in Holland, the very same argument might have been used with equal force by Presbyterian or Calvinist.   He would say, just as Anglicans say, that *his* Reformation was nothing but a purifying of the national religion from the errors of Popery.   You Anglicans would say he was wrong ; but I merely want to show that your argument is untenable.

To move on a point, I accept for the moment, for the sake of argument, the Anglican position that the Reformation involved no change of religion.   Now I ask : Supposing that in point of fact the Reformers *had* intended to change the national religion from Catholicism to an absolutely non-Catholic religion, what more could they possibly have done than they did ?

There can be no disputing the fact that they did change the religion of the country in respect of its *headship*, because Parliament professedly transferred to the Sovereign the supremacy which, rightly or wrongly, had, as a matter of fact, been exercised by the Pope.

Neither will anyone deny that the *government* of the English Church was changed, when Elizabeth imprisoned and expatriated the entire hierarchy, and by her mere authority put new " Parliament Bishops " into the sees.

I do not think, either, that I shall be contradicted when I say that the country's religion was changed as to *doctrine*, since so many vitally important articles of belief which had previously been held and cherished by the Catholics of England, in common with their brethren throughout Christendom, were at the Reformation proclaimed to be soul-destroying errors.

Nor will it, I am sure, be denied that the ancient *discipline* and practices of the national religion were abolished and proscribed, and an entirely new discipline substituted. That is quite too notorious for discussion.

As to the *liturgy* and form of public worship, could any change have been more complete than was effected by the Rerformers? The Roman rites and ceremonies, even the liturgical Roman language, which had prevailed since England was first christianised, were forbidden under the direst penalties, and the service-books were destroyed by the new bishops themselves. The very altar, the centre and focus of the old religion, was ignominiously destroyed by authority; and the celebration of Mass, which from the beginning had been the most solemn act of Christian worship, was made a crime punishable by an atrocious death.

Now I want to know, since the Reformation involved a change of the headship, government, doctrine, discipline and form of worship of the national religion, how can our Continuityist lecturer say that there was no change of the national religion as a whole? If you change first one blade, then another, and finally the handle, of your pocket-knife, how can you say it is still the same dear old English knife? *

I must confess it is flagrantly irregular for a lecturer to question his audience; but a question is often the directest way of conveying an affirmative idea, and there is just one more question that I beg leave to put to my Anglican hearers: You will admit, I suppose, that at

* How indeed? The Anglican steel is indelibly stamped "made in Germany."

the beginning of the sixteenth century the Church of
Spain was Roman Catholic.   Now, what was there
about the Church of Spain which made that Church
Roman Catholic, but which was absent in the case of
the Church of England ?

  I think I anticipate your answer.   You reply, the
Church of England *was* at that time in communion with
Rome, and had long tacitly and wrongfully allowed the
Pope's usurped jurisdiction over her.

  To this I say again, if, as you admit, the Church of
England was Catholic and in communion with Rome,
she was Roman Catholic, neither more nor less, just
like the Church of Spain.   And since a Church which
is Roman Catholic, and a Church which is not Roman
Catholic, are two perfectly distinct and different
Churches, it must follow that the Reformation effected
a complete alteration, and that the community which is
to-day styled "the Church of England," is not identical
with the pre-Reformation Church.

  Fortunately, there is abundant testimony as to the
real character of the Reformation, from the Reformers
themselves, who must be allowed to know what their own
movements were intended to be, better than typical
lecturers of 1894.   Bishop Jewel, in a letter to the
foreign Puritan, Peter Martyr, written in 1562, assumes
that the reformed Church of England was practically
Zuinglian, for he says : " As for matters of devotion,
we have pared away everything to the very quick, and
do not differ from your doctrine by a nail's breadth."
This Parliament Bishop, the great apologist of Anglicanism, does not attempt to minimise the effect of the
Reformation, for in the same letter he goes on to say:
" We have lately published an apology for the change
of religion among us, and our departure from the
Church of Rome."   I am afraid Bishop Jewel wouldn't
have done for a Church Defence lecturer.   If, indeed,
the Church of England is a branch of the Catholic
Church, then of necessity, Jewel was a Catholic Bishop,
although at the same time a Protestant of the most
uncompromising type.   How there can be Protestant

Bishops of the Catholic Church, I must leave the typical lecturer to explain next time he visits us.

From the year 1560 right down to about 1760, in the eyes of our fellow-countrymen of the Established Church, a Catholic priest was a creature scarcely human—part malevolent fiend, part grotesque bogey; if a man at all, a man whom it was the duty of Society to shun, and of the State to hunt down, to subject to a mock trial for high treason, then to half hang and cut open alive, and finally to blacken in the eyes of posterity. In the year of grace 1894, ministers of the same Established Church aspire to be considered—of all things in the world—Catholic priests. No doubt this religious right-about-face is an encouraging sign of an incipient return to ancient truths on the part of our Anglican friends; but we Roman Catholics of to-day have a serious · objection to make. It is that clergymen of the Church of England did not discover they were massing priests at the time when to be so meant ignominy, torture and death, but only when priest-hunting had passed out of fashion, and priests had been readmitted to the ordinary privileges of civilised society. Just as in those penal days the Established Church endeavoured to rob our forefathers of their holy Faith, so now it is trying to steal our glorious name of Catholic. We have every confidence that this last attempt will be as signally unsuccessful as the first. We do not believe that the time will ever come when a letter addressed "to the Catholic Bishop" of this district will be conveyed by the simple-minded postman to Llandaff instead of to Llanishen. Or, if that happens, it will be because our ancient hierarchy is reinstated in its former dignities.

One more quotation, and I conclude this lecture. It is from the *History of the Church of England*, written by an Anglican Bishop, the late Dr. Short, of St. Asaph. At page 593, he says: "The Church of England first ceased to be a member of the Church of Rome during the reign of Henry VIII., but it could hardly be called Protestant till that of Edward VI. . . . . During the

short reign of Edward VI. it became entirely Protestant, and, in point of doctrine, assumed its present form."
There is the deliberate opinion of a learned Anglican
Bishop, delivered, it is true, in 1847, before the Continuity Theory had been fairly broached—but perhaps
all the more likely to be a calm and unprejudiced view
of the facts.

I have got to the end of my lecture at last, and thank
you for the patience with which you have listened to
what I had to say. You have doubtless observed that I
have not attempted to do more than answer the assertions which form the stock-in-trade of every Continuityist
lecturer. I have advanced none of the innumerable and
overwhelming proofs of the exclusive right of my own
Church to the dignity of Continuity with the Church of
pre-Reformation days, except the few which come into
immediate conflict with the Anglican fallacies. I
venture to hope I have at least shewn my High Church
hearers that the Theory of Continuity is not so simple
and satisfactory as the typical Church Defence lecturer
would have them suppose. We have at all events
reconsidered Continuity, the rest is left to their further
study and reflection. And if only they will really think
for themselves, and not accept the Continuity Theory
simply because their favourite clergyman believes it to
be all right, I have no fear for the result.

www.ingramcontent.com/pod-product-compliance
Lightning Source LLC
Chambersburg PA
CBHW030316270326
41926CB00010B/1393